POVERTY
and the
WORKHOUSE
in
VICTORIAN
BRITAIN

POVERTY
and the
WORKHOUSE
in
VICTORIAN
BRITAIN

PETER WOOD

ALAN SUTTON

First published in the United Kingdom in 1991 by
Alan Sutton Publishing Limited · Phoenix Mill · Far Thrupp ·
Stroud · Gloucestershire

First published in the United States of America in 1991 by
Alan Sutton Publishing Inc. · Wolfeboro Falls · NH 03896–0848

British Library Cataloguing in Publication Data

Wood, Peter *1929* –
Poverty and the workhouse in Victorian Britain.
1. Great Britain. Welfare services, history
I. Title
361.941

ISBN 0–86299–701–1

Library of Congress Cataloging in Publication Data
applied for

Jacket: 'Awaiting Admission to the Casual Ward', *by Sir Luke Fildes,
in Royal Holloway & Bedford New College, Surrey. Photograph: The
Bridgeman Art Library.*

Typeset in Garamond 11/12.
Typesetting and origination by
Alan Sutton Publishing Limited.
Printed in Great Britain by
The Bath Press, Bath.

CONTENTS

ACKNOWLEDGEMENTS

Over the years I have been conscious of a number of influences which have inspired and assisted me in the production of this book. My initial debt is to the late Professor W.L. Burn, who first interested me in the possibilities of nineteenth-century administrative records and to my student friend, and later mentor in Poor Law matters, Professor Norman McCord. I have also received much encouragement from my colleagues at the Huddersfield Polytechnic and I owe a very considerable debt to Dr Keith Laybourn, who has always found time to give advice and who has saved me from a number of errors. I am also grateful to over two decades of students at the Sunderland and Huddersfield Polytechnics who have helped to shape my priorities.

I have also received welcome assistance from a number of archivists and library staffs and in particular I should like to thank the Public Records staff at Ashridge and the staff of the Manchester Central Reference Library who provided aid with the official records. I am also grateful to the staff of the Huddersfield Polytechnic Library for access to the G.H. Wood collection, which was so useful for the section on poverty.

Finally, I must thank the forbearance of my family and especially my wife, Joan, who can certainly claim to have suffered as a result of the New Poor Law.

Author's Note

Poverty largely ignored the internal boundaries of a rapidly industrializing Victorian Britain. Thus, although the materials I have used in discussing its nature are largely based on English sources, the issues raised are of general significance. More likely to cause concern is the fact that my consideration of the role of the State in the relief of poverty is limited to the operation of the Poor Laws in England and Wales. The Scottish system, although having some similarities, had very significant differences – especially in the relief of the able-bodied. However, it was the experimental dogma of the New Poor Law of 1834 and its subsequent administration which has tended to dominate both discussion of the State's provision of social welfare in Victorian Britain and estimations of the extent to which Victorian policy has influenced later developments.

INTRODUCTION

There is a considerable division of opinion on the significance of Victorian ideas and institutions. For some they represent values whose passing has been to our national disadvantage, while for others they are the cause of many of our twentieth-century problems.[1] Historians have put forward widely differing interpretations of the impact of Victorian developments on the social services of the twentieth century. This division is particularly marked when considering the treatment of poverty. For those inclined to optimism, there is evidence that the Victorians were responsible for laying the foundation on which the post-Second World War welfare state was established. For some the nineteenth century provided the administrative base from which twentieth-century improvement was to be launched. Others have seen the origins of national insurance, which lies at the core of twentieth-century development, in the Victorian spirit of self-help, while perhaps even more ambitious is the claim that the National Health Service originated in the medical activities of the New Poor Law before 1871.[2] Such views run counter to long-held opinion that the development of the social services in this century arose as a reaction to the inadequacies of nineteenth-century provision and in particular to the cruelty of the New Poor Law. For supporters of the traditional view the workhouse normally appears in the role of chief supporting villain.[3]

This work commences with a survey of the extent and nature of Victorian poverty and a review of the agencies which sought to provide some measure of relief. In seeking to assess the extent of poverty there are major problems relating to changes in the definition over time and the defective nature of much of the evidence. The best, although by no means perfect, information is provided later on in the period by the social surveys, and it makes for grim reading. When examining the larger part of the Victorian period it is necessary to consider the views of contemporary statisticians in the light of the findings of historians on such issues as the progress of wages in real terms, the rise in occupational status, and improved life expectancy. In considering the causes of poverty Chapter One makes use of the conclusions of late nineteenth- and early twentieth-century social surveys to introduce discussion of the role of environmental and personal factors and to relate the latter group of causes to the Victorian concept of respectability. It is against this background that the nineteenth-century views on the relief of poverty can be understood. Respectability found its partner in the notion of individual responsibility, which showed itself both in widely held opinions on the proper role of government and in the hierarchy of relief organizations with their emphasis on deserving and undeserving poor.

The remainder of the work is devoted to the Victorian, or New Poor Law. Theoretically the New Poor Law was not expected to concern itself directly with the poor, but rather was aimed at the special treatment of the pauper. This group was originally regarded as a separate category, a feckless underclass, who relied on public money for their support. It was the duty of the Poor Law to provide only for the genuinely destitute while at the same time acting as a deterrent to the scrounger and serving a general warning to the poor about the dangers of becoming dependent on the Poor Rate.

Administrative records often show institutions advancing haphazardly from problem to problem. The New Poor Law with its doctrinaire principles and the creation of a supervisory central authority might have been expected to have had a clearer sense of direction. Modern research has increasingly suggested that this was unlikely to have been the reality. It has been usual to arrange the history of the New Poor Law according to the periods of control by the successive central authorities. However, the relegation of the central authority to a more subordinate position has prompted the decision to arrange the chapters according to the main trends in activity. Hence, after a chapter examining the origins of the new regime, the material is subsequently divided in the mid-1860s and the mid-1890s. These divisions not only have the support of modern research but also reflect the best of the statistical evidence.[4]

In seeking the origins of the new regime, Chapter Two examines some of the main characteristics of the Old Poor Law paying particular attention to the emergence of experiments and criticisms which culminated in the recommendations of the Royal Commission of 1832.

The resulting New Poor Law was intended to introduce uniformity by means of a reformed administration and the issue of clear principles governing relief. Chapter Three is concerned initially with the administrative problems involved in establishing a revolution in central and local government relations. In this context it was the limitations of the system in practice which overshadowed the guiding principles. Progress is considered first in the areas of staffing and workhouse provision and later in the consideration of the relief provided for the various categories of pauper. Here particular attention is paid to the respective roles of the workhouse and the provision made for outdoor relief. Here also, as with the provision of an effective administration, for better or for worse, principles were often at variance with practice.

Chapter Four considers the New Poor Law at its most robust stage. Improvement in local authority finance in the 1860s had removed a major constraint. It is in this period that developments in the care of the sick and of children begin to give the New Poor Law its most attractive image, while at the same time the growing demand for a wider use of the workhouse test proceeded to turn the nightmare of many into a reality.

By the mid-1890s all was again a matter for debate. Chapter Five commences with doubts on both the principles and practice of poor law policy. Demands for better treatment of such deserving groups as children and the sick were being expanded to include the aged and some of the unemployed. Others resented the cost of what appeared to many, of a wide range of political persuasions, as a most inefficient service. The chapter concludes with the evidence of progress made and division on the future presented by the Royal Commission of 1905–9, at which nineteenth- and twentieth-century values met in a confused, and, at the time, irrelevant confrontation.

This book can make little claim to present the fruits of original research, but is rather concerned to provide the student and the general reader with a synthesis of what appears to be emerging as the current orthodoxy. As such it seeks to fill a niche between the many textbook introductions to wider coverage of social policy and the excellent specialist monographs on both Victorian poverty and aspects of the New Poor Law, the debt to which it is hoped has been fully recognized in both the notes and the Bibliography.

NOTES

1. See J. Walvin, *Victorian Values*, (1987), especially ch. 1 and its references.
2. For examples see respectively: D. Roberts, *Victorian Origins of the British Welfare State*, (1960); B.B. Gilbert, *The Evolution of National Insurance in Great Britain*, (1966), 290; R.G. Hodgkinson, *The Origins of the National Health Service*, (1967). Generally on this issue see D. Fraser, 'The English Poor Law and the Origins of the British Welfare State', in W.J. Mommsen (ed.), *The Emergence of the Welfare State in Britain and Germany*, (1981).
3. For a recent example see N. Longmate, *The Workhouse*, (1972).
4. On the Poor Law see M.E. Rose, 'The Crisis of Poor Relief in England, 1860–1890', in W.J. Mommsen (ed.), *op. cit.* For contemporary opinion see E.P. Hennock, 'Poverty and social theory in England: the experience of the eighteen-eighties', *Social History*, vol. 1, (1976). Statistical evidence is introduced in ch. 3, 4 and 5 below.

CHAPTER ONE

PROGRESS, LIVELIHOOD AND POVERTY

In making any judgement on poverty or patterns of poor relief in the Victorian era, it is necessary to recognize that there were major differences in the general view taken in the nineteenth century from that which is broadly accepted in this century. There appear to be three areas of divergence that are worthy of special consideration. In the twentieth century rising living standards have been accompanied by the recognition that poverty is a problem. Discussions on methods of relieving and, if possible, reducing this problem have initially involved attempts at measurement and analysis as a preparation for examining the effectiveness of existing methods of relief. Measurement to a large extent is dependent on definition. For much of this century poverty has been regarded as the failure to reach a minimum acceptable standard of living, usually defined as the poverty line. In the context of rising living standards the level of the poverty line has shown a tendency to rise and, in the period of greater affluence since the ending of the Second World War, even the traditional concept of a poverty line has been challenged by those who see poverty as relative to the prosperity of society as a whole.[1]

For much of the nineteenth century poverty was not regarded as a problem but was seen as a fact of life for a considerable portion of the population. Consequently, discussion was less concerned with its measurement than with defining the more limited area regarded as suitable for social concern. Thus, although the historian concerned with the relief of poverty in either century will make use of both quantitive and qualitative evidence, there is a difference of emphasis in the two centuries. In this century there is a greater dependence on the evidence of such enquiries as social surveys, whereas the studies of developments in the nineteenth century rely more on qualitative evidence and much of this is gleaned from enquiries only indirectly concerned with poverty.

The nature of the evidence contributes to a second important difference concerning the analysis of poverty in the two centuries. In the twentieth century there has been a growing tendency to see the most significant causes of poverty as arising from the social and economic environment of the poor. In the nineteenth century, although impersonal causes were accepted, and in some cases calculated, there was a tendency to place a much greater emphasis on the character of the individual lifestyle as exposed by the greater volume of more impressionistic qualitative evidence.

This differing view of fundamental causation plays an important role in explaining the third major difference between the two centuries. In this century the stress on the environment of the poor as the principal cause of poverty has produced successful demands for increasing and expensive intervention by the State. In the nineteenth century the more restricted view of the problem, combined with the belief that the individual was to a considerable extent responsible for his situation, produced a greater emphasis on the role of less expensive, voluntary activity and a tendency to judge all forms of administrative activity in this area by their reformative possibilities.

Before considering the nature and extent of nineteenth-century poverty it is revealing to consider contemporary definitions at the beginning and end of the century. In the first decade of the century, Patrick Colquhoun, a prominent supporter of Poor Law reform, defined poverty as, 'the state of everyone who must labour for subsistence'. With such an all-embracing definition there was little need for systematic measurement and the acceptable degree of social concern was inevitably pitched at a very low level. Colquhoun saw relief as necessary only for the 'indigent'. This group he defined as, 'the state of anyone who is destitute of the means of subsistence, and is unable to procure it to the extent nature requires'. It was this level of destitution which was to be accepted by the Royal Commission on the Poor Laws in 1834 as the basis for the New Poor Law.[2]

By the close of the nineteenth century poverty was beginning to be recognized as a problem. This growing awareness was accompanied and strengthened by the appearance of the first social surveys designed to measure and analyse the problem.[3] The definition of poverty accepted by these surveys was the minimum level of earnings calculated as necessary to maintain mere physical efficiency. In a deservedly much quoted passage B.S. Rowntree defined what this meant in practice:

> And let us understand what 'merely physical efficiency' means. A family living on the scale allowed for in this estimate must never spend a penny on railway fare or omnibus. They must never go into the country unless they walk. They must never purchase a halfpenny newspaper or spend a penny to buy a ticket for a popular concert. They must write no letters to absent children, for they cannot afford to pay the postage. They must never contribute anything to church or chapel, or give any help to a neighbour which costs them money. They cannot save, nor can they join a sickness club or Trade Union, because they cannot pay the necessary subscriptions. The children must have no pocket money for dolls, marbles, or sweets. The father must smoke no tobacco, and drink no beer. The mother must never buy any pretty clothes for herself and her children, the character of the family wardrobe as for the family diet being governed by the regulation. 'Nothing must be bought but that which is absolutely necessary for the maintenance of physical health, and what is bought must be of the plainest and most economical description'. Should a child fall ill, it must be attended by the parish doctor; should it die, it must be buried by the parish. Finally, the wage-earner must never be absent from his work for a single day. If any of these conditions are broken the extra expenditure is met, *and can only be met,* by limiting the diet; or in other words by sacrificing physical efficiency.[4]

Although both definitions suggest an area of concern pitched close to the level of basic survival, in practice the definition of the early social surveys was more generous in that they extended their coverage beyond the minimum to consider those subsisting precariously just above the poverty line. In Charles Booth's original surveys of London, commenced around a decade before Rowntree, the majority of those below the poverty line had been termed 'very poor' and those above it, 'poor'. Rowntree was to provide the terminology of the twentieth century, describing these groups as being in 'primary' and 'secondary' poverty respectively. Thus greater prosperity had by the close of the nineteenth century produced an apparent widening of the area of social concern. Since it was the object of the New Poor Law not only to relieve the destitute but to influence the lifestyle of those likely to become applicants for relief, it is the wider definition of poverty which governs the sections which follow.

The Extent of Poverty

Unfortunately, the only serious attempts at measuring the extent of nineteenth-century poverty occur with the poverty surveys in its later years and in the years before the outbreak of the First World War. The variations in methods and the differences in both the areas covered and the times at which the surveys were taken, have tended to cast doubts on their individual conclusions.[5] For Booth it was always alleged, with some justice, that London was not typical. There are doubts on his use of school visitors as assistants on the grounds that this resulted in the over-representation of families, thus increasing the estimate of the numbers in poverty. His instructions to his assistants and his calculation of the poverty line are both regarded as hazy. Although Rowntree is regarded as more scientific in his approach, York was also not regarded as typical. His more sophisticated poverty line was based on a calorific intake for men of 3,500 calories. This has produced some debate, although many would regard as more serious the vagueness of his concept of secondary poverty, much of which appears to be based on impressionistic evidence. In the case of both surveys the high level of statistical accuracy presented in the analysis of the constituent groups appears to be suspect. There seems to be less cause for complaint when considering the work of Bowley and Hurst. On the eve of the First World War, Bowley, the leading statistician of the day, used random sampling to measure poverty in four industrial communities and then proceeded to compare his results with those found by Rowntree in York. The degree of difference which this survey showed between the communities should perhaps deter historians from generalization, yet the extent to which the surveys confirm one another in the overall calculation of poverty has resulted in their measurement of extent being widely accepted. Broadly, the situation presented is that between one-quarter and one-third of the urban population of late-Victorian and Edwardian England existed in a state of poverty, with approximately one-tenth subsisting in primary poverty, i.e., below the poverty line. Moreover, consideration of the rural worker was to suggest that his position was certainly no better.[6]

A further contribution from Rowntree to the measurement of poverty was his analysis of the poverty cycle. This is a concept which is now universally accepted. Rowntree showed that poverty struck most strongly in a child's early years when it presented a financial burden to its family. On reaching working age and during the early years of marriage, with possibly two incomes, the individual described passed through a period of comparative prosperity, only to return to poverty when the burden of children arrived. Later the rise of the children into the working-age group raised the family above the poverty line again, but with these additional workers leaving home, and old age reducing earning power, poverty would again return to the parents. Thus Rowntree concluded that as a result of this cycle, the number in poverty at some stage in their lives would be, 'much greater and the injurious effects of such a condition . . . much more widespread than would appear from a consideration of the number who can be shown to be below the poverty line at any given moment.'[7]

In considering the extent of poverty earlier in the century historians have to depend on less reliable evidence. To the statisticians during the late-Victorian period, who sought to measure the progress of the working class there had been a remarkable rise in living standards. They based their conclusions on the fact that real wages, i.e., wages related to prices, had risen considerably; that the consumption of items such as meat had greatly increased; that there had been a large-scale movement from low paid, unskilled occupations into better paid positions and that the death rate had declined.

Robert Giffen, head of the statistical department at the Board of Trade, writing in 1887 on the occasion of Queen Victoria's Golden Jubilee contended, 'The general conclusion from all facts is, that what has happened to the working classes in the last fifty years is not so much what can be called an improvement, as a revolution of the most remarkable description.' For Giffen, millions had been raised from 'the brink of starvation' and 'untold privations'.

Giffen's case for improvement was based primarily on the movement of real wages. He believed that while the prices of the main items of working-class consumption had either fallen or remained constant, money wages had risen between 50 and 100 per cent. At the same time the number of low paid agricultural workers had decreased from one-third to one-eighth of the total work-force. As additional support to his argument that improvements had been made he advanced the increased consumption of many basic items of diet, the increase in working-class savings, the extension of popular education and the decline in the levels of crime and pauperism. Finally he cited the novelists and Bluebooks produced around the start of Victoria's reign as providing an illustration of the deplorable conditions under which the working classes lived at that time.[8]

Had Giffen's been the only optimistic voice his views could be dismissed as an over-enthusiastic celebration of the royal jubilee. However, such views were commonly held during this period. Writing in 1902, and using more sophisticated statistics, G.H. Wood suggested an overall improvement during the second half of the century of 80 per cent in the standard of working-class comfort. Fifty per cent of the increase was the result of the rise in wages and a reduction in the cost of living while a further 30 per cent was the result of the movement from ill-paid occupations to more remunerative positions. Wood supported his argument with statistics showing an increase in the per capita consumption of the main articles of domestic use.[9] Clearly if these conclusions are to be accepted the level of poverty exposed by the social surveys represented a considerable improvement on earlier conditions.

For the historian the answer has proved less simple, even the general trend of living standards for over half of the century produces considerable debate. Statistical evidence often appears to present more problems than solutions and this is especially the case in the important matter of real wages. Evidence on wages by industry is patchy and fragmented over time, with the emphasis being on wage rates rather than actual earnings. The coverage of prices is even less satisfactory. Wholesale prices are better known than retail prices, and even where the latter are available, it is often London figures which are accepted as national. In the case of both wages and prices local variations appear to have been very significant and the fact that these variations may have diminished over time merely adds to the confusion.[10]

The limitations of the evidence on wages and prices have resulted in historians following the path of the contemporary statisticians in seeking the corroboration of other statistical material. Unfortunately, this evidence also presents serious problems. Customs and excise returns are of limited value in tracing the pattern of working-class consumption and this is particularly the case in considering the significant areas of food and drink. Some progress has been made in the analysis of family budgets, although these present some difficulties and are strongest in the latter part of the period. Census material has been examined for information on occupational structure and housing, and pioneering work has been done on the use of census enumerators' books for details of internal migration, family composition and urban segregation. Here much remains to be discovered, and, as with other statistical material, the census improved over time. The annual reports of the registrar general and of medical officers of health have been used to deepen our knowledge of trends in the death rate. In this area more sophisticated analysis has suggested the variety of factors which could have caused improvement and the wide range of local experience. In the following section health, diet and housing will be treated together because of their interconnection with the problem of poverty. Of the other statistics cited by Giffen much has been found wanting, and unfortunately this is the case with the mass of statistics produced by the Poor Law.[11]

The weakness of the statistical evidence has meant that some historians have placed considerable weight on qualitative material. Although such evidence is comparatively plentiful it also has serious limitations. Evidence is strongest at times of crisis and is somewhat coloured by this fact. There is a general tendency for reformers in any period to exaggerate problems by selecting the worst examples, although in the case of public health and housing the sheer volume of material is overpowering. Comment was strongest where conscience was aroused, where law and order were threatened or where there were thought to be serious threats to public health or morals. These threats became more obvious in an urban context and consequently towns and cities were given increasing attention as the century progressed. Evidence on problem groups such as the handloom weavers, factory children, Irish immigrants, vagrants and prostitutes is stronger than that relating to the mass of the poor. Work has not been assisted by the fact that the historians of the working class have displayed greater interest in the more plentiful evidence relating to political and trade union activities. To some

11

extent qualitative impressions can be supplemented by the local material being uncovered by research into the Poor Law. However, this material has the ovious defect of being more concerned with the development of administration than with the recipients of relief.[12]

Of other sources of information, the work of journalists and novelists has proved to be of limited value. Despite the exceptional work of those such as Mayhew, in general evidence in this area was often selected with a view to capturing a wider readership. Thus there was an undue concern with the sensational, with a particular emphasis on moral failings. Finally there has been a growing interest in the writings, and, late in the period, the oral testimony of the working class themselves. Such evidence is extremely uneven in its coverage of both occupations and regions. It certainly increases as the twentieth century progresses, but in no case can the claim be made that the provider of the information is typical of any particular group. Nevertheless, such evidence does often provide valuable supportive insights into working-class values, which are often neglected by other enquirers.[13]

From this collection of disparate material it is impossible to produce any realistic measurement of the extent of poverty, but it is hoped to draw some conclusions on its general trend. Much consideration has been given to the living standards of the working class as a whole. The first half of the nineteenth century produced considerable debate concerning the movement of real wages and the pattern of consumption, reflecting in part the limitations of the evidence. Initially, despite the vigour of the debate, conclusions tended to be cautious. Thus in the early 1960s R.M. Hartwell, a leading supporter of the optimistic case, nevertheless concluded that, 'to say that the standard living of most workers was rising, is not to say that it was high, nor is it to affirm that it was improving fast, nor that there was no dire poverty, and cyclical fluctuations and technological unemployment of a most disturbing character.'[14]

The position is now clearer with regard to the overall trend in real wages and the pattern of consumption for the working groups generally. G.N. von Tunzelmann has recently summed up the current optimistic position:

> Roughly speaking, the period from around 1790 to 1850 can be divided into two parts, with real wages fairly constant for the working class as a whole between 1790 and 1820, then rising in a sustained fashion after

about 1820. There are minor disagreements over the dating of the turning point(s) and rather more significant ones over the scale of improvement between 1820 and 1850, but the general story holds good. Moreover, the result accords in both degree and timing with what has emerged from the alternative 'macro' approach, attempting to derive average per capita consumption from national income data.[15]

The debate on living standards has been so concerned with assessing the initial impact of industrialization upon the working class that the latter part of the century has suffered from some measure of neglect. There is a long-held view that the second half of the century witnessed a considerable improvement in living standards if measured by either real wages or consumption. There are doubts on exactly when the improvement started, and of its extent in the third quarter of the century, but fairly general agreement on a more rapid rise in the final quarter. In the period 1850–75 the case for improvement rests upon wages rising faster than prices. Unfortunately there are major deficiencies in the wage evidence, hence the difficulty in deciding a starting date, although most accept somewhere in the 1860s. The agreement on a better performance in the final quarter rests on the fact that at this time prices were falling faster than wages and, not unreasonably, it is felt that this would have had a wider impact. In this period the evidence for higher consumption lends support to the general view of improvement. The overall conclusion is that in the period 1830 – 1900 real wages for the working class improved considerably with the most rapid advance occurring in the period 1860–1900.[16] Table One below summarizes the present position.

The general trend in real wages presented in Table One provides only a notional guide to the realities of the situation. In the first place local and occupational studies show a wide range of variations from the norm.[17] Secondly, as they are based on wage rates they do not indicate real earnings. Indeed, as Rowntree's poverty cycle indicates, what is needed are family rather than individual earnings. It follows that ideally there are a number of additions and subtractions to be made to general indices. Items such as overtime, payments in kind, family income, including payment by lodgers, must be added, while, perhaps more significantly, there is a need to subtract loss of earnings resulting from unemployment, short time and sickness. Adjustments would also be needed for dependents and limitations to earnings resulting from the age of the worker. There

Table One
(a) Real Wages 1780–1850
(% increase per annum)

	Deane & Cole	Phelps-Brown & Hopkins	Lindert & Williamson	Crafts*
1780–1820	0.71	– 0.03	0.28	0.71
1820–1850	1.19	0.92	1.92	0.94

* Crafts' dates are 1780–1821 and 1821–50.
Source: N.F.R. Crafts, *British Economic Growth During the Industrial Revolution,* (1985) Table 5.5, p. 103.

(b) Real Wage Index 1850–1900
(1850 = 100)

1850	1855	1860	1866	1871	1874	1880	1886	1891	1896	1900
100	94	105	117	125	136	132	142	166	177	184

Source: P. Deane and W.A. Cole, *British Economic Growth 1688–1959,* (1964), p. 25.

are also regional variations in diet and, more significantly, in rents which affect the construction of a cost of living index. These difficulties can be clearly illustrated in considering the progress of the poor.

Even nominal wage evidence relating to such occupations as outworkers and many in casual employment is negligible and there are general problems in estimating the earnings of women and children. The reference group for the low paid is often taken as the male agricultural worker,[18] but even with this group regional variations appear to be substantial. Further problems relate to the assessment of non-monetary payments, family earnings and the extent of underemployment and seasonal unemployment. The poor were generally to be found in occupations of easy entry and they may therefore be assumed to have suffered loss of income from under-employment and unemployment to a greater degree than the working class as a whole. There has long been a recognition of the connection between poverty and ill-health and it is likely that loss of income through sickness would also be higher. Against such losses there would be a need to add any income from charity and the Poor Law, although the losses would normally considerably outweigh the gains.

The impact of the poverty cycle meant that any group repre-senting the poor would contain a larger number of workers with dependents and a greater proportion of aged, which would obviously affect family earnings and could also mean that the pattern of purchases might differ somewhat from the standard basket of goods on which cost of living indices are based. The limited budgetary evidence available suggests that cereals, bread and potatoes require a greater weighting, and there is the additional complexity that rents for the poor in many urban communities took a higher proportion of the family income than for the working class in general. A further complication arises from the fact that the poor appear to have purchased groceries in very small quantities and often on credit, paying more for these privileges. [19]

In considering change over time it seems certain that during the French Wars and the subsequent depression the living standards of the poor would have worsened. Rapid inflation of food prices was accompanied by an increase in the rate of growth of the population which more than counterbalanced improved employment prospects. For the period 1820–50 much depends on the level of statistical improvement accepted. Although this was a period of falling prices, the price of wheat remained comparatively stable, and to some extent the periods of greatest price fall were also the years of greatest unemployment, in effect cancelling out much of the advantage. A great deal depended on occupation and region. Although the most optimistic assessment of this period suggests a considerable rise in the living standards of the agricultural labourer, it also shows that this group did significantly less well than other groups of workers. For the agricultural labourer in the south, denied the competition of industry for his labour, research reveals periods of extreme distress and low earnings generally. Serious concern over the plight of this group dominated the discussions on the reform of the Poor Law. The earnings of those in industry were generally significantly better, but not all benefited equally. Much related to employment prospects. Unemployment showed itself in a declining trade such as the handloom weavers or in Mayhew's description of those struggling to survive on the thin pickings at the margin of the London labour market.[20] It can also be seen in the graphic descriptions of want during the downturns of the economy. Joseph Adshead described the plight of the unemployed in Manchester in the early 1840s citing among other evidence the experience of a Mr Bradshaw, a missionary to the poor, in 1840:

> The visiting of the abodes of distress and poverty was no novelty to me; but I must confirm that in no period like that which was devoted to this inquiry have I ever seen a tithe of the suffering and misery which was then brought under observation. I cannot attempt to sketch even the outlines of that frightfully distressing picture: nothing short of the evidence of the senses can afford an adequate description of the length and breadth of its deformity. We found vast numbers either totally unemployed, or having work only at short and uncertain intervals. It was no uncommon thing to hear men and women say one after another, we have had no work for several weeks and sometimes months. Indeed, it was a rare thing among the numerous families we visited to find one that it could be strictly said was fully employed. As to domestic artefacts – alas! in very many cases there were none. Of clothing and bedding we found large numbers quite destitute. Several families were almost in a state of absolute nudity. A few shavings, or, a little straw not infrequently on the floor, or bare flags with scarcely a bit of covering, constituted the hard pillow on which some half-dozen of a family were compelled to rest their weary heads. In these homes we find that the best and most necessary articles were at the pawn shop . . . . Indeed in a great number of cases we found that all the most useful articles of bedding and wearing apparel had been pawned.[21]

For the urban poor a further handicap was the rising cost of house rents. The most obvious consequence was shown in the incredible levels of overcrowding in the urban slums revealed in the public health enquiries of the 1840s.[22]

Further evidence of the low level at which many were surviving around mid-century has been provided by historians who have produced calculations on the level of primary poverty based on the standards adopted by the late nineteenth- and early twentieth-century social surveys. John Foster has suggested that in 1849 15 per cent of the population of Oldham, 28 per cent in

Northampton and 23 per cent in South Shields were living in primary poverty and, using a slightly different method of calculation, Michael Anderson found 20 per cent of his Preston families living in this distressed condition.[23]

The improvement in the third quarter of the century is largely regarded as resulting from wage rises and there must be some doubts as to the extent to which the poor benefited. The limited work of local historians on the problem of living standards in this period confirms the existence of serious levels of poverty. Nevertheless, the evidence of wage improvement from the 1860s is widespread. Moreover, although this was an inflationary period, analysis of price movements suggests that the rise was mainly on raw materials with the most significant food prices rising at below average rates or even falling. On balance therefore and allowing for local differences, such as the degree of pressure on housing and the impact of unemployment, the statistics for real wages seem sufficient to suggest that improvement in this period would have reached some of the poor.[24]

The evidence of lower food prices provides the main case for claiming improvement in the final quarter of the century. Wages, although showing some overall rise, have falls in the second half of the 1870s and in the depression of the mid-1880s. Unemployment appears a significant factor in local studies of this period and variations in both earnings and rent remain a problem. Despite these negative influences most commentators see the lower price of many basic food imports, assisted by improved methods of processing and distribution, as more than countering any losses for the vast majority. For all but the very poorest there appears to have been some move away from the cheap carbohydrate fillers to more expensive protein such as meat. Nevertheless, even in this, the most promising period, there remains room for debate as to the extent to which the poor profited.[25]

Although the statistics for real wages and increased consumption support some improvement in the position of the poor in the second half of the nineteenth century, the improvement started from a very low base and compared with the working class as a whole they appear to have done less well. A.L. Bowley supports such a conclusion, basing his calculations on the wage census material of 1886 and 1906. Excluding mining and agriculture, Bowley found that the earnings for a week for the lowest quartile showed a 16 per cent increase, whereas the median group showed an increase of

21 per cent and the upper quartile had an increase of 26 per cent.[26] Thus, although the lot of the poor improved, the sense of relative poverty probably increased.

In view of the doubts concerning earnings and prices the historian has been forced to imitate the action of the contemporary statistician in seeking evidence of amelioration in other areas. The widespread conviction of a 'shifting up' of occupations appears to have considerable potential. Although it is difficult to measure the earnings of an agricultural labourer there is widespread agreement that he remained close to the bottom of the male earnings league throughout the century. It is difficult to gauge his numbers before the 1851 census, but the 1811 census stated that agriculture employed one-third of all families, showing this worker's relative importance and justifying the degree of contemporary concern with his problems. By 1851 agriculture was employing over 20 per cent of all male workers, and although a declining percentage of the labour force, the group remained the largest male occupation, and, in terms of absolute numbers, agriculture probably employed more labour than ever before. However, between 1851 and 1911 the number of agriculture labourers almost halved.[27]

Although Giffen was correct in pointing to the movement of the agricultural labourer he probably overestimated the benefits. While the migration may have prevented a further deterioration in the living standards of those who remained upon the land the immediate impact of the labourers who left was often to swell the ranks of the urban unskilled. This group are almost impossible to enumerate in the early part of the century. The 1851 census gave a total of 367,000 unclassified labourers. They were the third largest group of male employees and were in many cases associated with the second largest group, the building workers. However, unskilled labourers could be found also in all varieties of transport undertaking and in an increasingly wide range of manufacturing and service occupations. As the century progressed problems of classification became more difficult. Among the better paid labourers there was a tendency to specialize, as for example the handlers of tea cargoes on the London docks, the 'holders-up' who assisted the highly paid platers in the steel shipbuilding industry, and the concrete labourers in the building industry. These workers merged with the semi-skilled occupational groups as regards to income. They could expect to obtain not only higher wage rates, but also more regular employment, so long as they retained their physical strength. The route downwards through the hierarchy of the unskilled was through varying degrees of irregularity of employment ending with the casual general labourer.[28]

Geoffrey Best gives some support to G.H. Wood's conclusions. He believes that, on balance, in the two decades following 1851, the numbers of skilled workers increased and prospered as a group. However, he adds the important proviso that this 'thickening' of the middle and upper layers of working-class occupations did not mean 'an absolute shrinkage in the number of the unskilled'. He point out that, 'still so abundant was the supply of men ready for any coarse and/or casual labour that it was not yet a management concern to find labour saving means to replace it'. His overall conclusion is therefore that, 'the style and proportions of labour, skilled and unskilled alike, must therefore be judged to have changed little before the eighties'.[29]

This view has some support. Stedman Jones in a comparison of London occupations in the 1861 census with that of 1891 shows that the numbers in his unskilled category had increased by 60 per cent, forming just over one-fifth of the labour force on both occasions. The London experience appears different only in the higher percentage of unskilled workers. J.A. Banks' analysis of the census material by occupational group shows a rise in the unskilled category for males aged over twenty from 14.2 per cent in 1851 to 18.4 per cent in 1881, the increase being largely at the expense of the partly skilled. The two groups together totalled 57.4 per cent in 1851 and 54.7 per cent in 1881. Thus it would appear that any significant improvement in occupational status occurred rather late in the century.[30]

The census of 1911 reported that 11 per cent of the male work-force was unskilled, suggesting that the group in secondary poverty contained many semi-skilled. However, the census definition of unskilled was rather restricted and a clearer guide which is closer to the descriptions given by the social surveys is provided by Table Two.

The table has a more generous definition of unskilled than the classification adopted by the 1911 census. However, in other respects they are supportive, notably in the widening of the unskilled group suggested for 1880. Both suggest an upgrading of the labour force was taking place, although the size of the unskilled

19

Table Two

	1860	1880	1914
Lowest decile	Average agricultural labourer	Top agricultural labourer	Bottom unskilled
Lower quartile	Bottom unskilled	Average unskilled	Top unskilled
Median	Top unskilled	Average unskilled	Top semi-skilled
Upper quartile	Ordinary semi-skilled	Top semi-skilled	Skilled

Source: A.L. Bowley, *Wages and Income Since 1860*, (1937), p. 46.

group throughout is sufficient to cast doubts on the optimistic assertions of Giffen and Wood.

Contemporary opinion in early-Victorian England had no difficulty in seeing poverty as connected to disease. However, as it was sufficiently commonplace and widely regarded as self-inflicted little effort was made to measure or analyse the problem. However, the fall in the death rate became significant after 1850 and even more obvious in the final quarter of the century. The death rate had risen from 21.4 per thousand in 1841–5 to 23.3 in 1846–50. It then fell to 22.0 in 1871–5 and more rapidly to 16.1 in 1901–5. Support for the optimist was also found in the fact that the improvement was most marked in the decline in mortality in children and young adults, but not in infant mortality. After remaining at around 150 per thousand until 1870 the infant mortality rate fell to 137 per thousand by the early 1880s, but then rose to 145 in the early 1890s and was still over 140 by 1900.[31]

The overall improvement could have been a reflection of higher living standards, but it could also have resulted from other factors such as sanitary reform, improved medical care or even changes in the nature of specific diseases. The problem of allocating credit to these factors is complicated by the differing experience of different communities, and within communities of variations by age, sex and occupation. Thus although rural communities were usually poorer, their inhabitants did significantly better than their urban counter-

20

parts. On the other hand a dweller in a poor urban parish was likely to have a much shorter life than the middle class occupant of a home in a wealthier district. Thus as Chadwick showed in his report of 1842 a member of the gentry or professional classes living in Rutland had a life expectancy of fifty-two years whereas a labourer or artisan had thirty-eight years. However, a member of the gentry or professional classes in Manchester also had a life expectancy of thirty-eight years but an artisan or labourer only seventeen years. As the First World War approached a general labourer was more than twice as likely to die as the average citizen of his age and almost four times more likely to die than a clergyman. The national average infant mortality rate was around 110 per thousand, but for the upper and middle classes the figure was 76 and for an unskilled labourer 153.[32]

To discuss the link between improving death rates and poverty it is necessary to consider diseases which were especially associated with those regarded as the lower classes. Typhus increased with the onset of industrialization. Transmitted by the body louse, it flourished in the overcrowded slum districts of early nineteenth-century towns. In such areas the numbers of poor, and consequent overcrowding, were continually increased by the pressure of new migrants. Typhus was often at its worst during times of economic downturn, or in winter, and was thus regarded by many contemporaries as a useful guide to destitution. Typhus declined in the second half of the nineteenth century and progress was especially rapid in the final quarter. Typhus may have declined because of higher living standards, particularly improvements in diet. However, it could also have been influenced by sanitary improvements, particularly in the area of water supply, and, in the case of London, its decline has recently been linked to the decline of Irish migrants. It is also possible that changes in the lice population may have exercised an independent influence.[33]

The link between poverty and mortality is strongest when applied to tuberculosis. Regarded as almost a fact of life by the poor in the mid-nineteenth century, the disease was clearly linked to malnutrition and housing. Here also the pattern of improvement covers the second half of the century with the most marked change being in the final quarter. Improvement commenced before the bacillus had been identified and appears to owe little to medical advance. With housing standards appearing to make only limited progress, the tendency has been to give most credit for improvement to better diet and changes in milk supply.[34]

A belief in dietary improvement would appear to support the views of Giffen and Wood. The issue is important because food always appears to be the major item of working-class expenditure. Rowntree's poor in York spent 51 per cent of their income on food and this appears to be broadly in line with other budgetary evidence. Although Burnett finds that the 1860s were the last decade of 'widespread bad feeding', he finds evidence of serious undernourishment in rural areas in 1900. The research of D.J. Oddy into late-Victorian and Edwardian budgets has shown the severely limited diets of the poor during the period, with consumption of bread and potatoes dominating the diet of the working class well above the level of secondary poverty. Although cheaper meat was becoming available as the result of canning and refrigeration, he appears to confirm the view of contemporary social researchers that meat provided a flavouring rather than a main course in the meals of the poor. This accounts for the significance of bacon in working-class diets, in that, although not cheap, by cutting it thinner it would go further. The majority of working-class diets appear to have remained deficient in milk and dairy produce. Moreover, in the case of milk, the growing use of tinned, condensed milk was providing an inferior substitute and the quality of contemporary margarine apparently left much to be desired. The rise in sugar consumption noted by the optimists was often taken in the form of jam or treacle and as such was largely a substitute for the deficiencies in protein and fat intake. Jam and bread was a major feature of the diet of the children of the poor. For those aspiring to something better, suet pudding with jam or treacle provided the lunchtime alternative, while there was a tendency among those slightly better off to use flour in the form of pastry to relieve the monotony of a continuous reliance on bread. Major absentees from working-class diets appear to have been fresh vegetables, fruit and fish. To some extent this may have represented prejudice rather than poverty, but there can be little doubt that generally the working-class diet at the close of the nineteenth century remained deficient in protein and important vitamins. Moreover, with the male worker obtaining the greater part of the protein available, the position of other members of the family was more serious than the family budget would suggest. To these problems must be added the continued adulteration of food, the inadequate cooking facilities and the limited culinary skills of the average housewife at this time.[35]

It is difficult to select a typical budget for any income group. Those in dire poverty appear to have survived the latter part of any week on a diet of little more than bread and tea.[36] Lady Bell provided an example of a family who survived around the level of the poverty line. Her survey presented budgets for a six-week period for a man, wife and twelve-year-old daughter. During this period the man was in continuous employment, earnings ranging from 18s. 6d. to 23s. 9d. The mother was described as an exceptionally good manager, and in five weeks out of six she repaid debt, to a total of 4s. 6d. over the period as a whole. The only extras recorded were a rent of 5s. 6d. per week, which was high, even in a town of high rents generally, and an expenditure of 9d. per week on tobacco. Table Three gives a survey of weekly expenditure on food during the six-week period.

Other items of expenditure consisted of fuel, lighting, cleaning materials, insurance and a total of 11s. 11d. for clothes, of which 5s. 11d. was for a purchase of boots for the husband. For Lady Bell this was an example of 'what can be done on the modest amount available'. Although she had to point out that in difficult times even this careful family were forced into debt. The budget provides a good instance of the limited diet of even a small family on low income. Faced with such evidence of limited dietary improvement the question has been asked, 'whether small improvements in nutrition combined with smaller completed families did allow some improvement in health?'[37]

If small improvements are to be considered significant, and, if sufficiently widespread, there is no reason why this should not have been so, the question of housing should perhaps figure more widely than it has tended to do. Although, late nineteenth-century reformers correctly presented the housing question as one of the most pressing of contemporary problems, it must not be forgotten that houses built in this period were generally superior to those built earlier. Moreover, some of the worst had been replaced by the development of urban central business areas:

> There can be little doubt that in terms of sanitary standards and public
> health the nineteenth century made remarkable progress in slum
> clearance. The utterly fantastic, labyrinthine slums of the past, with their

Table Three
Mrs A.B.'s Budget

Item	Weekly cost	Quantity	
Meat	1s. 6d./1s. 10d.	3/3½ lb	
Flour etc.	1s. 9½d.	1¼ st }	= approx 30 lb bread
Butter	1s. 1d./1s. 2d.	1 lb }	Danish
Lard	2½d.	½ lb	
Bacon	9d.	1 lb }	5½ lb over six weeks
Sugar	8d.	4 lb	
Tea	9d.	½ lb	
Potatoes	3d.	½ st	
Milk	2d.	1 pt }	average over period
Yeast	1d.		
Other food purchases			
Eggs	10d. }	total spent on three recorded puchases	
Tinned milk	10d. }	3 tins recorded in three weeks	
Onions	1d. }	one purchase	

Source: Lady F. Bell, *At The Works*, pp. 78–80.

tumbledown, old housing stock, subterranean dwellings, narrow
courtways and densely packed tenements were swept away, and street and
other 'improvements', commercial construction, railways and other forces
of urban development transformed the topography of the major British
cities.[38]

Such changes were not painless and slums and massive overcrowding
remained. However, G.H. Wood's point that the quality of housing
was improving, albeit slowly, has some support. In considering
overcrowding the 1891 census found the three worst urban examples
in England and Wales were in the north-east. Yet even in this area
local historians have noted significant improvement as the century
progressed. G.H. Wood admits, however, that to some extent
improvements in housing were combined with higher rents. Rent

was normally the second largest item of working-class expenditure and it would appear likely that in many cases higher rents may have bought better accommodation at the expense of dietary improvement.[39]

A major Local Government Board survey of 1893–5 showed not only the progress which had been made in all aspects of sanitary circumstance but also exposed the limitations of that advance. Repeated recommendations concerning sewerage, dwellings, excrement and refuse disposal, and concern over urban cowsheds and milk shops illustrated the continuance of public health and housing problems. Despite its improvement the mortality rate from tuberculosis remained high. For males the disease was worse in urban than in rural communities, but for women this distinction was less marked. It is argued that to some extent this must indicate the significance of inadequate housing as this was a factor which both urban and rural housewives shared. However, it could also reflect the difference in diet between the sexes, with the breadwinner receiving the best food and the mother limiting her intake in the interests of the children.[40]

Although the decline in the death rate does give support to the optimist, this must be qualified in the case of the poor by the continuing high infant mortality rate among this group and in the continued significance of tuberculosis. In both cases there appears to be a correlation between poverty, malnutrition and overcrowding. This view is reinforced by the widespread comments on rickets and skin disorders and the significant differences in the height and weight of middle-class and working-class children revealed by early school medical inspections.[41]

Other statistics quoted by contemporary supporters of improvement have limited value. If, as seems almost certain, progress was not shared equally by the poor, the evidence of rising working-class savings and increased membership of self-help organizations provide a poor guide to improvement in the lowest paid groups. In the case of the diminution of crime or levels of pauperism, as suggested above, both are suspect. Not only are there problems in the methods adopted in calculating such figures, but both appear to be unduly reflective of changes in administrative practice. Indeed, pauperism, which might be expected to give some guide to extent, was reporting a level only around one-quarter of that suggested in primary poverty by the poverty surveys at the end of the century.

The qualitative evidence cited by Giffen as evidence of the terrible conditions at the start of Victoria's reign was again commonplace at the close of the century. Such evidence reflects an awareness of poverty rather than a measure of its quantity. This evidence certainly supports a belief in the continuance of poverty, but is more a guide to what contemporaries regarded as its distinguishing features than an aid to calculating its extent.

While the extent of poverty cannot be measured, a general picture does emerge from the mutually supportive nature of much of the evidence. It seems unlikely that the condition of the poor changed markedly in the first half of the nineteenth century. From the 1860s the coincidence of favourable trends in real wages, upgrading of occupational structure and lowering of the death rate, with less marked improvement in diet and housing, support the idea of progress.

However, there must be considerable doubt over the extent to which improvement filtered down to the poorest. Certainly it cannot have reached those who continued in a state of primary poverty and could only have had a marginal effect on those surviving just above the poverty line. Local variation is a marked feature of all available studies. In addition there is evidence of extreme variation with economic fluctuation, differences in the prospects for individual occupations and, for individual workers, according to their sex and age. Nevertheless, had Booth and Rowntree surveyed the same communities using the same methods over the final decade of the century a more optimistic picture would probably have emerged. However, in the conditions of the time, greater awareness of poverty had the effect of increasing the relative importance of the issue, which to the concerned was similar to an increase in extent. The recognition of the size of the problem encouraged discussion of its causation.

The Causes of Poverty

The fundamental causes of poverty appear to have changed little with the passage of time. Changes occur in the significance which is accorded to the various factors and, as indicated in the introduction to this chapter, the most noticeable change appears to be the role accorded to the conduct of the individual. The only attempts at measuring the importance of the various causes is provided by the social surveys. To some extent the surveys mark the transition from the stress on personal to environmental factors. It is almost impossible to provide objective standards for measuring personal failings and, as the surveys of Booth and Rowntree indicate, personal and impersonal factors may have combined to thrust a family into poverty. Booth found personal factors contributing to the problems of all four of his classes in poverty, although this was more pronounced in the poorest classes A and B. Rowntree regarded personal failings as a significant cause of secondary poverty, which must partly explain his vagueness on that issue. Finally, Bowley and Hurst in the most statistically-orientated survey contented themselves with stating that personal causes had probably been 'exaggerated'.[42]

The clearest attempts to measure the impersonal causes are the analyses of primary poverty provided by Rowntree and Bowley and Hurst. Their findings are summarized in Table Four below. Both surveys agree that the major cause of primary poverty resulted from the combination of low wages and family size. Booth also found these significant causes of poverty, although in classes C and D irregularity of earnings was of much greater significance.[43]

Table Four
Causes of Primary Poverty
(%)

	Rowntree	Bowley and Hurst
Death of chief wage earner	15.36	14
Illness/old age	5.11	11
Chief wage earner out of work	2.31	2
Irregularity of work	2.83	2
Largeness of family (more than four children)	22.16	
In regular work but low wages	51.96	
Insufficient income for three children		26
Insufficient income for four children		45

Sources: S.B. Rowntree, *op. cit.*, pp. 120–1.
A.L. Bowley and J. Burnett-Hurst, *op. cit.*, summary of four towns, pp. 46–7.

27

Low pay could be the result of occupation, sex or age. It was characteristic of the rewards for unskilled manual labouring groups and also of areas where traditional skills were being undermined by competition from machines. The low paid, therefore, included a complex range of activities requiring varying degrees of skill and physical strength. Pay was influenced by the age and experience of the individual worker, the fluctuating supply and demand for labour in the locality and the manner in which particular trades were organized. Wage evidence shows a wide differential between skilled and unskilled rates persisting throughout the century and it also shows the markedly poorer rewards for women and children. Even at the end of the century John Burns noted the marked differences between the delegates attending the TUC conference in 1890. Whereas the skilled representatives often 'looked like respectable city gentlemen', those representing the unskilled 'looked like workmen'.[44] Low paid groups in general lacked the organized bargaining power of the skilled worker. A major factor was that their occupations were especially open to the entry of competitors, an issue of crucial importance in a century where the work-force was not only expanding numerically, but was also becoming increasingly mobile.

The slow decline of unskilled male occupations was not as significant to the individual worker as the up-swing in the poverty cycle when the wife and children could seek employment. Despite the abundant evidence of the low level of earnings for women and children throughout the century, it has been estimated that at the close of the century the average household contained two wage earners producing an income of approximately one-and-a-half times that of the male breadwinner.[45]

The extent to which women and children could contribute to the family income may have changed little over the century. In the case of children opportunities became more limited as the century progressed. For the poor the benefits of factory legislation and compulsory education were not always immediately obvious. However, the limitation on the employment of children could be expected to have worked to the benefit of the low paid generally and of women in particular.[46]

The majority of girls and single women throughout the nineteenth century found their employment in domestic service and this was a major outlet for migrants from the countryside. Outside of textiles, and opportunities here did not expand in line with the rising female population, work for married women was largely in the ancillary domestic services of seamstresses, washerwomen and charladies. In the late-Victorian and Edwardian period Bowley noted the rise of an intermediate class who included, 'clerks and others in retail, wholesale and distributive trade, and the younger and less successful persons in teaching and other professions'. The impact of this rising intermediate group on the numbers of the unskilled is impossible to quantify. The expansion in retailing and teaching, together with the impact of the typewriter on office work has been heralded as providing new employment for women. Certainly Bowley's areas of expansion did provide opportunities for the better educated single woman. However, even within this group progress largely awaited the labour shortages of the First World War. For the female poor employment continued to be concentrated in the overcrowded and undervalued sections of the labour market; domestic service remained the most likely choice, while for others the decline of outwork in the early part of the century was replaced by the sweatshops of the later years. Work on census enumerators' books and the social surveys both suggest that the income of many working-class families could be augmented by the taking-in of lodgers and that this could extend to the poorer families. However, the prospect of income from this source varied with the supply and demand for accommodation in a locality and could change considerably over time.[47]

The burden of children in the cycle of poverty was always significant. The decline in the birth rate in the latter part of the century occurred later for the working class as a whole and for the unskilled manual labourer it appears to have had least effect. The Annual Report of the Registrar General in 1912 commented upon the exceptional fertility of the mining counties. There was a widespread contemporary belief that a high birth rate was a feature of classes engaged in manual labour. The most likely explanation, however, was not related to physical fitness, as high rates were found among the presumably less fit slum dwellers. The rational explanation would appear to be that groups who reached their maximum earnings at an early age tended to marry earlier, thus lengthening the wife's potential childbearing years. Moreover, it was precisely these groups who saw children as necessary to assist the parents in old age, and the fact that infant and child mortality was highest among the poor gave an added incentive to procreation.[48] Although the Malthusian fears of the early part of the century had largely disappeared by its close, they could still be echoed by the observers of the poor. Hence Lady Bell's comment, 'We are gloomily told that the birth rate is declining. But in many a case, unless the birth rate declines in his particular home, the worker has not enough to live upon.'[49]

The other major factors causing poverty were concerned with interruptions to earnings. In many cases these were the result of death or illness. One result of the higher death rate for males, which persisted throughout the century, was the plight of widows. For those with a family to support, employment opportunities were exceptionally limited. In the studies by Rowntree and Bowley and Hurst the death of the wage earner was the second most important cause of primary poverty. For Charles Booth the only section of his 'very poor' for whom he expressed sympathy were the 'poor women' among them. In an area of heavy industry with few opportunities for female employment, Lady Bell found that 'many women on losing their first husband seek a second'. For Francie Nichol, faced with that situation, marriage, however unsatisfactory was 'preferable to the workhouse, the only alternative'. It has been estimated that around half of all pauper children were fatherless, and widows and their families were always a major concern of the Poor Law.[50]

Rowntree and Bowley and Hurst grouped sickness and old age together in calculating their contribution to primary poverty. Although on low wages, family size and loss of a wage earner the surveys were sufficiently close to be supportive, Bowley and Hurst found this aspect approximately twice as significant as did Rowntree. Even allowing for the differences in community studied such a degree of variation is surprising. In practice the combination of what would now be regarded as separate causes produced an unavoidable complication. In the nineteenth century there was no recognized age of retirement and for the manual worker increasing age was often accompanied by declining health. The records of friendly societies show that increasing expectation of longer life did not necessarily mean better health. Lady Bell represented old age as, 'that dark prospect of the night coming in which no man can work'. For some the hope was for a lighter job with a diminished income. These were the fortunate few, the majority of the unskilled spent their later years in an increasingly unsuccessful struggle to compete on the casual labour market. Eventually their first line of support had to be their family. However, they too were often unable to cope, especially during periods of bad trade. At such times the number of aged poor seeking Poor Relief usually increased and did not necessarily diminish as quickly once the depression was over. For Charles Booth the greater the age the greater the likelihood of resort to the Poor Law. The increasing length of life brought the poverty of the aged to the forefront of discussion in the latter part of the century and posed serious problems for the Poor Law.[51]

The impact of ill-health is impossible to estimate. The connection between poverty and ill-health was always recognized, although there was considerable debate over which was the more dominant factor. Progress was always rendered more difficult by lack of statistics. At first medical ignorance and later administrative limitations prevented the gathering of basic information. The need for the notification of infectious diseases was not nationally recognized until 1889, and even then was compulsory only in London. Thus reformers were forced to make use of mortality rates to make connections between unhealthy areas and dangerous occupations. Since these figures were influenced by a variety of considerations the correlation could never be exact, although as shown above they served the purpose of such as Chadwick to further demands for reform.[52]

The mortality figures suggest progress but there can be no doubt of the extent of the surviving problem late in the century. The cost to the ratepayer, the employer and the nation caused a wide range of enquiries to unite in suggesting the massive problems which remained.

Much of the concern was for the male worker. Thus in 1878 the Registrar General cited health and long life as major factors in determining the economic value of the working population: 'The longer men live, and the stronger they are, the more work they can do. Epidemic diseases in rendering life, render wages, insecure.'[53] For Lady Bell ill-health was a major problem among the Middlesbrough ironworkers, 'One is apt to be surprised at first, considering that it is presumably the strong and stalwart who have taken up this work, to find how many of the labourers are more or less ailing in different ways.'[54]

Not all comment was concentrated on the breadwinner. Interest in factory and pauper children in the early-Victorian period

31

continued and was extended, via concern for education, to a more widespread concern with the future of the race. Thus Charles Booth considered the children at Board schools in poor areas:

> Still in all poor schools we shall find many whose puny and sickly looks show too clearly that they are either feebly born, or are living under unwholesome or bad conditions at home. Usually such children come from drinking homes, or from those where the family has over-run the means of subsistence.[55]

For Bowley and Hurst writing on the eve of war, and fully aware of the significance of the poverty cycle, the numbers of children growing up in a state of primary poverty was a major concern; 'But of . . . the children who appear in our tables 27 per cent *are living in families which fail to reach the low standard taken as necessary for healthy existence.*'[56]

For the families of the poor when ill-health occurred it was the woman of the house, supported by female kin and the neighbours, who faced the additional burdens of nursing, elementary doctoring and midwifery. While many commentators recognized the need for housewives to be good managers they were to receive little detailed analysis of their problems. Where they were discussed it was the potential consequences of the working housewife which most disturbed contemporaries. Whether as a result of disinterest or reticence the health problems of the housewife were largely ignored by male commentators and among the social surveys only Lady Bell gave adequate consideration to the fact that personal ill-health was a major problem for the housewife, often rendering a difficult task almost impossible.[57]

To some extent the ill-health of the poor was the result of inadequate medical facilities. However, throughout the century there appears to have been a widespread distrust of the medical profession by the working class. In part this was obviously a desire to avoid expense, but for the poor, relying on charity and the Poor Law, or even for those fortunate enough to be members of a friendly society, the doctor was never regarded as wholly sympathetic. Hence doctors were usually called only when the situation was desperate and often return to work was dangerously hurried. Such a policy could have tragic consequences in the treatment of complaints such as tuberculosis. A further feature of the reluctance to use the medical profession was the resort to quacks and patent medicines as substitutes. For the poor serious illness usually ended with application for assistance from charity or more likely the Poor Law. The impact of the sick on the Poor Law will be shown to have been of considerable importance, in that they placed an unexpected and disproportionate strain upon its resources and challenged its most fundamental principles.

The final area regarded as creating poverty was the reduction in earnings resulting from unemployment or underemployment. The term unemployment suggests a fault in the economic system and is essentially a term of the twentieth century. In the nineteenth century the terms used to cover those without work normally related to the individual. Those receiving Poor Relief were able-bodied paupers, others were more sympathetically termed unemployed. Early concern was largely with the plight of rural labourers. Here the traditional problems of seasonal unemployment and chronic underemployment were exacerbated by the rapid increase in population, the decline of the domestic industry and in some cases by enclosures and the loss of common rights.[58]

The growth of industrialization made later discussion turn increasingly to the urban workless. Comment was loudest on those occasions when cyclical downturns in the economy combined with such additional problems as the severe seasonal unemployment associated with a bad winter. At such times humanitarian concern, fear of disorder and the mounting cost of Poor Relief produced greater public reaction. For the construction industry, shipbuilding and water transport workers, such as seamen and dockers, the combination of a downturn in trade and a hard winter could have a devastating effect upon their local community.[59]

These industries also employed considerable numbers of unskilled casual labour, often hiring workers daily or even twice daily. Casual workers also included many who sought employment in the declining outwork industries and, in the case of the handloom weavers, the uncertainties of the casual worker overlapped with the threat of unemployment caused by advances in technology. For the factory owners outworkers could act as a reserve labour force to be brought into play when demand was full. Indeed, the casual labour force usually appears to have been larger than normal demand required. London was particularly attractive to the casual labourer and, as a generalization, it seems that casual labour was a special problem in the bigger cities and ports. The widespread acceptance of the need for a surplus of casual labour almost certainly helped to limit discussion of the problem of underemployment.[60]

Evidence on the extent of unemployment is very limited. The only statistics giving coverage of the second half of the century are provided by the trade unions representing skilled workers, which offered unemployment insurance. By their nature these figures underestimate the number of unemployed, but as the unions concerned tended to suffer a greater than average burden of cyclical unemployment they overestimate the influence of the trade cycle.[61] Even with the greater interest taken in the problem of unemployment in the final quarter of the nineteenth century conclusions must be tentative. The general belief is that the average rate of unemployment for the period of 1880–1914 was 4.8 per cent, rising to a peak, in bad years, of around 10 per cent. There is no suggestion that the overall problem had changed significantly during the nineteenth century, rather it appears to have received greater attention in the later years. For much of the century the impact of unemployment was regarded as a purely temporary phenomenon or, as a problem for a particular industry or locality. One consequence of this fact is that the social surveys differ considerably in their judgement on this issue. Apart from Booth's survey of London and to a lesser extent the Rathbone survey of Liverpool, there is a tendency to underplay the impact of unemployment. Rowntree examined York with its more secure occupational structure in a good year and Bowley and Hurst took their measurements in the build up to the First World War. Lady Bell, who might have provided useful information on this cause, decided to ignore the issue on the grounds that it was being adequately treated elsewhere. However, she did not apply the same criteria to drink and gambling, to which she devoted an entire chapter. To Booth irregularity of employment always appeared as the most significant cause of poverty, although as will be shown he had strong reservations concerning the desire for regular work in classes A and B.

Many of those classed as 'insufficiently employed' were not regarded as deserving of sympathy, rather they suffered because of a variety of personal failings. Where personal factors were involved the tendency was not to stress low earnings but rather to emphasize wasteful expenditure. Hence, the breadwinner was often represented as keeping too large a proportion of his salary to spend on gambling, smoking and above all drinking. Similarly the housewife could be seen as a bad manager, inefficient in cooking and sewing, resorting to expensive convenience foods and balancing the family budget by a mixture of credit and debt. Large families were the result of improvident early marriages. Widows, unless possessed of a large family, were regarded simply as a further branch of the able-bodied poor, many of whom had made their short-term problems worse by excessive expenditure on their husband's funeral. Old age, temporary sickness and short-term unemployment were all problems for which provision should have been made by savings and friendly societies, and where such means proved inadequate, the burden was expected to fall first upon their relatives. Diseases which were particularly associated with the poor were often explained as resulting from their ignorance and lack of personal cleanliness, while long-term unemployment in the case of a normal, healthy individual, was regarded as being the result of ingrained idleness.[62]

Booth divided those below his poverty line into two classes, which he labelled A and B. He was especially unsympathetic to the lowest group, class A. These he described as consisting of, 'occasional labourers, street-sellers, loafers, criminals and semi-criminals'. As a class they were difficult to enumerate as 'there was little family life among them and many were inhabitants of common lodging houses' or were 'homeless outcasts who on any given night take shelter where they can'. Although class A were estimated to form slightly less than 1 per cent of London's population, Booth's description of the group was guaranteed to capture the reader's attention:

> Those I have attempted to count consist mostly of casual labourers of low character and their families, together with those of a similar way of life who pick up a living without labour of any kind. Their life is the life of savages, with vicissitudes of extreme hardship and occasional excess. Their food is of the coarsest description, and their only luxury is drink. It is not easy to say how they live; the living is picked up . . . . From these come the battered figures who slouch through the streets, and play the beggar or the bully, or help to foul the record of the unemployed; these are the worst class of corner men who hang round the doors of public houses, the young men who spring forward on any chance to earn a copper, the ready materials for disorder when occasion serves. They render no useful service, they create no wealth; more often they destroy it.[63]

35

Booth expressed little additional sympathy for the majority of his 'very poor' in class B. The greater part of this group he described as casual labourers, who on average probably obtained less than three days' work a week:

> . . . but it is doubtful if many of them could or would work full time for long together if they had the opportunity. From whatever section class B is drawn, except the sections of poor women, there will be found many of them who from shiftlessness, helplessness, idleness or drink, are inevitably poor. The ideal of such persons is to work when they like and play when they like; these it is who are rightly called the 'leisure class' amongst the poor – leisure bounded very closely by the pressure of want, but habitual to the extent of second nature. They cannot stand the regularity and dullness of civilised existence . . . .[64]

Booth expressed more concern for his classes C and D, who roughly corresponded to Rowntree's group in secondary poverty. Class C he saw as the 'victims of competition' on whom 'falls with particular severity the weight of recurrent depressions of trade'. Class D were normally in regular employment but with a low income. Regularity of work, however, enabled them to develop a more organized lifestyle and consequently they subsisted with more dignity. Class C he believed tended to be 'shiftless and improvident' because of the irregularity of their earnings.[65]

Booth's views on classes A and B confirmed a widespread Victorian belief on the nature of the residuum. In the eighteenth century it was often held that low wages were necessary to keep the predominantly agrarian labour force at work. Such views had less validity in the advancing industrialized society of the nineteenth century. However, the issue of 'leisure preference' sometimes termed 'the backward sloping labour curve' continued to be applied to those groups who had felt the impact of technology least. Such views were transferred from the agricultural labour force to those who survived in the outwork industries and came to be widely used in connection with casual labouring groups. It was applied also to those sections of the work-force whose patterns of consumption remained bound by custom, such as coalminers. Dockers as both casual workers and inhabitants of traditional environments were especially open to such criticism.[66] Booth accepted the contemporary view that some measure of surplus labour was necessary for the efficient functioning of the industrial system. The problem he believed was that the surplus had grown too large, a situation which could best be remedied by removing class B from the labour market and settling them in industrial groups outside the cities in government-run communities. Those who failed to perform adequately would be placed in the workhouse. Although views on the problem of those without work were to advance considerably by the first decade of the twentieth century, both the Webbs and Beveridge saw the need for some form of corrective establishment for those who deliberately avoided work.[67]

Deliberate idleness was often associated with heavy drinking habits. Although Rowntree differed markedly from Booth in his analysis of primary poverty, he saw personal weakness as a significant factor in the creation of secondary poverty. He believed that drink was the major single cause of secondary poverty in York, with labourers spending between one-sixth and one-third of their earnings on this item. Although Rowntree saw drink as being encouraged by poor housing, monotonous work, inadequate education and limited alternative leisure activities, he was convinced that immediate improvement could only be brought about by a change in the individual lifestyle. Rowntree's views were in accord with the findings of both Charles Booth and Lady Bell. The latter concluded that about half the men in the families surveyed 'drank too much' and pointed to the continued use of fines for ironworkers being found unable to work as the result of intoxication.[68]

Evidence on the extent of drinking was always difficult to obtain and is inevitably largely impressionistic. To some extent it is also coloured by the zeal of the temperance advocate. The available statistical evidence presents serious problems, but it does suggest that drink had been an even more severe problem earlier in the century. Excise figures suggest that per capita consumption of alcohol had peaked in the 1870s and that the wider range of consumer goods available in the latter part of the century was diverting some working-class income away from drink. However, no historian doubts that the widespread condemnation of heavy drinking expressed throughout the nineteenth century was soundly based:

> In conclusion, expenditure on drink did affect working-class living
> standards, by depressing the level of nutrition enjoyed, and being largely
> responsible for 'the disproportion shown . . . between average earnings

and results in the comforts of home' . . . . But the extent to which drink inhibited rising living standards declined from the 1870s onwards.[69]

The belief that poverty was to a considerable extent the result of individual weakness was closely connected with the vague but important Victorian concept of respectability. While this was an area whose boundaries were largely drawn by the individual, it was an essential indicator of status. Respectability appears as a complex mixture of personal and economic factors in which the line was always drawn below the level of the commentator. Skilled workers had no doubt of their respectable status. Higher earnings gave better homes which often involved some degree of segregation from those of more lowly status. Dress, friends, religion, leisure activities, diet, parentage and education could all carry the mark of respectability. This applied also to membership of self-help organizations such as friendly societies, where respectability was associated with evidence of self-reliance and greater security. Inevitably there were inconsistencies here as some of the lesser friendly societies were associated with public houses and were held to encourage drinking. The desire to be self-reliant showed itself in the growing membership of friendly societies and the widening of savings as the century progressed. Even the humblest sought to avoid the ultimate disgrace of a pauper funeral by weekly insurance contributions. For the poor such payments were often made at the expense of more immediate necessities and lapsed policies were commonplace.[70]

Beyond financial considerations working-class respectability could show itself in a variety of cultural and social considerations. Pride in skill at work and cleanliness in the home were widespread. For some the avoidance of drink was important, while for others respectability was marked by the public house in which you drank. Some distinctions were the outcome of local convention. The belief that the husband should be able to maintain his wife at home was accepted not only by the skilled but was widely held in areas of heavy industry, where the limitations of the labour market produced a virtue out of necessity.

As the concept of respectability descended the social scale the role of debt became increasingly significant. A clean rent book was often accepted as a sign of respectability by the visitors of organized charity, although missing the rent was preferable to relying on the Poor Law in many cases. The Rathbone survey of Liverpool reveals that debt acted as a reserve social service. Groceries and clothing were often bought on credit and provided what were often dubious bargains. For those in greater need there was the non-payment of regular bills such as rent and coal, accompanied by borrowing from friends and relatives. As problems increased there was always the pawnshop. For some this was a regular procedure, but in times of economic hardship this was a service with a wider range of customers and the items pawned came progressively closer to the essentials of family life. Finally, there was resort to the money-lender, accompanied by exorbitant interest rates and the physical dangers of failing to meet repayments.[71]

For such as Jack Lawson, in the mining community of Boldon Colliery it was respectable to purchase from the co-operative store which gave no credit and groceries bought on credit had to be smuggled into the house. However, at a lower level being able to obtain credit was a mark of respectability. Robert Roberts describes the process in Salford:

> A wife (never a husband) would apply humbly for tick on behalf of her family. Then in our shop, my mother would make an anxious appraisal, economic and social — how many mouths had the woman to feed? Was the husband ailing? Tuberculosis in the house perhaps? If TB took one it always claimed others; the breadwinner next time maybe. Did the male partner drink heavily? Was he a bad timekeeper at work? Did they patronise the pawnshop? If so, how far were they committed? Were their relations known good payers? And last had they 'blued' some other shop in the district, and for how much? After assessment credit would be granted and a credit limit fixed, at not more than five shillings worth of foodstuffs in any one week, with all fancy provisions such as biscuits and boiled ham proscribed.[72]

For Francie Nichol residing only a few miles from Jack Lawson, but several degrees lower on the perceived social scale, it was not a question of applying for credit, having clothes to pawn was the guarantee of independence.[73]

The habit of judging respectability by reference to family and companions had its impact on social behaviour. There was a stigma attached to those who allowed their relatives to become a burden on the ratepayer. While the good neighbour was one who respected privacy in normal times, failure to offer help in times of crisis meant serious loss of face. It was as important for the working classes as for other social classes not to marry beneath their station. Children were discouraged from mixing with those thought less repectable whatever the cost:

> There is no desire more firmly planted in the minds of the respectable
> working woman than to keep her children from undesirable associates and
> from hearing what goes on in a low class district. She knows better than
> anyone else the harm which such association can do. She will sacrifice,
> not only money, but health itself to this desire, by keeping her children
> within stuffy little rooms rather than let them play in the street.[74]

While this sentiment was one which illustrated the official view, there can be little doubt that it reflected some measure of working-class practice. The middle-class concept of the residuum existed in an equally ill-defined form in the working class concept of the 'rough'.

The environmental causes of poverty introduced by the social surveys are similar to those which would be found in any modern discussion of poverty. The strength of the Victorian belief that the major cause was the result of personal, avoidable failings shown most clearly in Booth's description of the 'very poor' and somewhat more vaguely in Rowntree's concept of secondary poverty had powerful repercussions on the provision of relief.

The Relief of the Poor

The belief that a considerable number of the poor were responsible for their situation was a powerful limiting factor on the pattern of relief offered. Such a view fitted in well with the variety of opinions advanced in favour of the curtailment of all forms of non-essential state intervention. The precise commitment of individual economists to the philosophy of *laissez-faire* is a matter of debate. However, there can be little doubt that as popularized, and inevitably simplified, in the minds of contemporaries such views could present an intellectual foundation for those favouring the limitation of state intervention. At the very least there existed a strong belief 'that what were thought to be hampering or anti social impediments should be removed'.[75]

In its simplified form the classical economists' attack on mercantilist restrictions and praise for the working of a free market, in which individual self-interest responded to the laws of supply and demand to produce a self-regulating mechanism, had an obvious appeal to those impatient of state intervention. Such views were reinforced by Malthusian fears of overpopulation and Ricardian support for the supremacy of capital. Further intellectual justification was provided by the views of the Benthamites. While the principle of 'the greatest happiness of the greatest number' can be seen as supportive of *laissez-faire* and state intervention, it was most widely accepted when 'working with the grain' of current belief. In practice State intervention received its strongest support where it could be justified as providing the appropriate framework to encourage individual action.[76]

Such doctrinal beliefs could be expected to be popular in a society which suspected any expansion of State activity as providing increased possibilities for patronage. More fundamentally, a parliament representative of property owners knew full well that the electorate strongly resented any increase in expenditure at either national or local level, a view strengthened by the not unjustified belief that the existing system of both taxation and rating was manifestly unfair. Hence, the trend of mid-Victorian finance has been described as, 'towards the reduction to a minimum of the economic control of the State, towards rigorous balancing of the public budget, and the reduction of public expenditure to the least amount compatible with the provision of defence and police.'[77]

The influence of such beliefs will be shown to have been of significance in supporting the attack on the Old Poor Law and in framing the principles of its Victorian successor. The acceptance of the role of the individual also encouraged the emphasis which was increasingly placed on the middle-class virtues of hard work and thrift. As transmitted to the working classes such values were expressed in the support and encouragement given to self-help activities, with the corollory that anything held to promote wasteful activity should be penalized.

Middle-class exhortations to self-help had a long history, but the institutions of self-help, often assisted by the teachings of organized religions, have an even longer record.[78] Samuel Smiles' best known works, *Self Help: with Illustrations of Character and Conduct* (1859) and *Thrift* (1875) were best sellers, not because of any originality, but because they were produced at a time when confidence in individualism was approaching its peak. A good illustration of the accepted role of self-help institutions was provided by the evidence of J.M. Ludlow to the Royal Commission on Friendly Societies in the early 1870s:

When we group together the various bodies of which the Registrar of
Friendly Societies is the pivot, we perceive that they really form one
whole, as representing the different modes in which the workings of the
spirit of self-help among what the acts often term the 'industrious classes'
has been recognized and deemed worthy by the legislature, – the various
means by which that portion of the population which is most within the
risk of pauperism endeavours to escape from it.[79]

Among the range of activities mentioned by Ludlow were the
variety of friendly societies, the building societies, the co-operative
stores, trades unions, savings banks, the scientific and literary
societies by which man sought to 'improve his mind' and,
grudgingly, the loan societies. Borrowing in time of difficulty being
frequently 'his first recourse, perhaps a fatal one'. As he was
concerned with all of these organizations, the Registrar of Friendly
Societies was, he concluded, 'virtually a minister of self-help to the
whole of the industrious classes'. He was therefore 'the embodiment
of the goodwill and protection of the State, in all that goes beyond
the police, the poor law, justice and the school'. To this list of
activities most contemporaries would have added the wide range of
temperance organizations which were so obviously partners in the
self-help programme.

The best known example of self-help activity was the friendly
society. Although the estimate of the membership of such organizations given by the Royal Commission of 1871–4 is now thought
to be exaggerated, there seems little doubt that they were the largest
nineteenth-century working-class organization. Friendly societies
had grown rapidly with the coming of industrialization. Early
societies were usually local with a small membership, but as the
nineteenth century advanced the movement became dominated by
large affiliated organizations, such as The Oddfellows and The
Foresters and such large commercial insurance companies as the
Prudential and the Hearts of Oak. Friendly societies provided
mutual assistance by insuring against some of the main factors
producing loss of earnings, such as sickness, accidents at work and
death. In addition the trades unions representing skilled workers,
which also provided friendly society benefits, often added insurance
against unemployment. The absence of statistics, inadequate
actuarial skills and limited membership meant that many of the
smaller local societies often found themselves in financial difficulties
at the time when their assistance was most needed. This was a

feature of societies with an aging membership where demands placed undue strain upon income and discouraged younger members. Benefits were in direct ratio to subscriptions. All demanded regular payments of subscriptions and the rules of many societies sought to limit risks by refusing membership to known drunks, residents of certain districts, and workers in dangerous trades. Although their leadership appears to have been dominated by skilled workers, many seem to have considerably widened their range of members as the nineteenth century progressed. The need for regular contributions often reinforced by regulations requiring a minimum level of annual earnings, put these organizations out of the reach of many of the poor, including those who were often in most need of their services. Friendly societies were proud of their independence and firmly resisted any state intervention which competed for working-class subscriptions, even though in the case of old age pensions it would have been to their considerable financial advantage.[80] The growing prosperity during the second half of the nineteenth century meant that many contemporaries would have agreed with Giffen's conclusion:

> From being a dependent class without future and hope, the masses of working men have in fact got into a position from which they may effectually advance to almost any degree of civilisation. Every agency, political and other, should be made use of by themselves and others to promote and extend the improvement. But the working men have the game in their own hands. Education and thrift, which they can achieve for themselves, will if necessary, do all that remains to be done.[81]

In practice it was recognized that not all of the risks of working-class life could be covered by individual effort. Humanitarian concern, however haphazard and difficult to define was always a factor. So also was the desire to maintain social control. Intervention here could cover a range of possible motives, varying from concessions in the face of social unrest to attempts to direct the poor along the path to social improvement. For anyone who could present their misfortune as being the result of forces beyond their control, the most flexible form of relief was charity. Long-term sickness or disability, extreme age, the loss of parents could all provide cases, where, often despite the practice of self-help, further assistance was needed. Such poor were regarded as respectable and therefore deserving of charitable assistance.

43

Charity in the Victorian period took many forms. Norman McCord gives a useful threefold classification. First there was the wide range of individual charity involving family, neighbourhood and workplace whose extent it is impossible to estimate. Secondly, there were the exceptional efforts made at times of disaster; ranging from nationally recognized calamities such as the Hartley Colliery disaster, or at a regional level the Mansion House Fund operating at times of severe unemployment in London, to local soup kitchens offering assistance in bad winters, boots' funds for local school-children and Christmas treats for the aged. Finally, there were the permanent charitable organizations, whose number and variety defy easy classification. Such charities provided a wide range of institutional support for the sick, the aged and the orphan, and they also provided a diversity of educational and leisure activities. Other organizations assisted all manner of deserving individuals, ranging from aged clergy to fallen women. In general larger communities, especially those possessing a sizeable middle class, were best served by charity with London topping the list.[82]

Derek Fraser presents a sound analysis of the motives for this massive amount of charity. In the first instance charity could act as a social sedative, limiting demands for more drastic change. Secondly, it could arise from religious or humanitarian sympathy for those in misfortune. Thirdly, it could benefit the giver by satisfying some inner religious or psychological requirement or providing valuable publicity and social esteem. For the middle-class woman it afforded one of the few acceptable outlets for her abilities. The list of famous women engaged in social work of this kind appears greater than that for any other contemporary activity and the famous were merely the standard bearers for a vast army in the localities. Finally, charity was regarded as being of benefit to the poor by keeping the deserving from contact with the undeserving paupers and by assisting them on the road to self-reliance.[83]

There was always a recognition of the fact that some of the less deserving would seek to profit from charity, and in this respect the wide range of uncoordinated agencies could be seen as a disadvantage. Indiscriminate relief could discourage the spirit of self-help and so defeat one of the main objectives of charitable relief. By the mid-nineteenth century a number of schemes had been proposed aiming at the suppression of such undesirable practices. The best known of these arrangements was the Charity Organization Society founded in London in 1869, with the deliberate aim of removing the evil of indiscriminate relief.[84] The Charity Organization Society believed that by careful investigation of the individual case charity could be confined to the deserving case. It made its principles admirably clear.

> The principle is that it is good for the poor that they should meet all the ordinary contingencies of life, relying not upon public or private charity, but upon their own industry and thrift, and upon the powers of self-help that are developed by individual and collective effort. Ample room will still be left for the exercise of an abundant charity in dealing with exceptional misfortune, and also in connection with large schemes for the benefit of the working class which may require, in the first instance at all events, the fostering of wealth and leisure. But it is a hurtful misuse of money to spend it in assisting the labouring classes to meet emergencies which they should themselves have anticipated and provided for.

The emergencies which the working man was expected to anticipate showed a good understanding of the major causes of contemporary poverty; temporary sickness, slackness, early marriage and a large family and old age. These were the ordinary contingencies for which the individual should provide and any state or charitable assistance would be positively harmful. 'A spirit of dependence fatal to all progress will be engendered in him . . . the road to idleness and drunkeness will be made easy to him and it requires no prophesying to say that the last state of a population influenced after such a fashion as this will certainly be worse than the first.'[85] Thus for the Charity Organization Society relief should be given only after the completion of an individual case study to ensure that the claimant was deserving and to assess the best way in which assistance should be provided. Since a prime objective was to encourage a return to self-reliance, the drunken, immoral or idle should only be given assistance where it could be shown that they were attempting to reform. In the interest of discouraging the undeserving applicant, payment of rent arrears and funeral expenses were normally refused and loans were provided only where a claimant could obtain the backing of a respectable householder as surety. Having proved his worthiness the borrower was expected to repay loans by regular instalments. Assistance was rarely given in money, support was usually sought from family and past employers and where possible individuals were provided with practical means of earning their living.

The principles of voluntary action, whether of self-help or charity, were in accord with both the values and the pockets of an individualist society. There was an obvious confidence that existing society required no significant change. Since the majority of social problems were the responsibility of the individual it followed that the role of the State was minimal. At times Victorian voluntary action appears to have performed on an almost heroic scale. It pioneered new methods and catered for areas of concern initially ignored by the State. Thus it was an important source of future progress as well as providing contemporary benefit. However, the supporters of voluntary action underestimated the scale of the problem which they faced. Moreover, since voluntary action saw itself as catering for the deserving, it followed that the role of the State was in the care of the undeserving. If voluntary action looked after the respectable the State was to supervise the 'rough'. The belief that deserving and undeserving could be separated was an essential belief of the Charity Organization Society and the Victorian Poor Law. The stigma associated with Poor Relief was firmly rooted in this division. For the Charity Organization Society the test of respectability was the examination by case study, for the Poor Law the test of destitution was the offer of the workhouse. Of course, in practice, poverty was so complex as to defy such easy categorization. Where charitable resources were inadequate there was often no alternative to application for Poor Relief. An important consequence was that some paupers came to be regarded as more deserving than others. Thus children, the sick, and, later in the century, the aged were regarded with more sympathy than the able-bodied. Hence the former group might benefit from outdoor relief or more favourable indoor treatment. In theory the able-bodied applicant for Poor Relief was a wastrel requiring firm institutional correction. In practice the situation was very much more complicated. However, the theory had perhaps more influence than the reality. The Victorian workhouse carried the image of being the resort of the least deserving and what was statistically the least significant component of the contemporary provision of relief became its best-known feature.

NOTES

1. For the inter-war period see K. Laybourn, *Britain on the Breadline*, (1990), ch. 2. For developments since World War Two compare B.S. Rowntree, *Poverty and the Welfare State*, (1951); W.G. Runciman, *Relative Deprivation and Social Justice*, (1966); P. Townsend, *Poverty in the United Kingdom. A Survey of Household Resources and Standards of Living*, (1979).

2. P. Colquhoun, *A Treatise on Indigence*, (1806), 7–8. For similarity of definition with that of Bentham see G. Himmelfarb, *The Idea of Poverty. England in the Early Industrial Age*, (1984), 85–6 and J.R. Poynter, *Society and Pauperism. English Ideas on Poor Relief 1795–1834*, (1969), 320. Colquhoun is quoted more extensively in Himmelfarb and M.E. Rose, *The English Poor Law 1780–1930*, (1971); S.E. Finer, *The Life and Times of Sir Edwin Chadwick*, (1952), 74–5 discusses the link between Bentham and the Poor Law Report of 1834.

3. The major social surveys used in this chapter are: Charles Booth, *Labour and Life of the People, London*, 2 vols., (1891); and *Life and Labour of the People in London*, 13 vols., (1902–3); B.S. Rowntree, *Poverty: A Study of Town Life*, (1901); Lady F. Bell, *At the Works*, (1907, reprinted 1969); and A.L. Bowley and J. Burnett-Hurst, *Livelihood and Poverty*, (1915).

4. B.S. Rowntree, *op. cit.*, (1901), 45–7.

5. For a good critical introduction to the social surveys see E.P. Hennock, 'The measurement of poverty: from the metropolis to the nation', *Economic History Review*, xl, (May, 1987).

6. For the rural labourer see B.S. Rowntree and M. Kendal, *How the Labourer Lives: A Study of the Rural Labour Problem*, (1913).

7. B.S. Rowntree, *op. cit.*, (1901), 136–8.

8. R. Giffen, *Essays in Finance: Second Series*, (2nd ed. 1887), 468–73; quoted in W.H.B. Court, *British Economic History 1870–1914 Commentary and Documents*, (1965), 285–8. Giffen informed the Royal Commission appointed to inquire into the Depression of Trade and Industry 1886 that the way forward was to reduce wages, although he subsequently apologized for this statement to Henry Broadhurst, Secretary to the Parliamentary Committee of the Trades Union Congress (see Broadhurst Collection, 1886 in British library of Political and Economic Sciences). I am grateful to Dr K. Laybourn for this information.

9. G.H. Wood, 'Real wages and the standard of comfort since 1850', *Journal of the Royal Statistical Society*, (1909); reprinted in E.M. Carus-Wilson (ed.), *Essays in Economic History*, vol. 3, (1962).

10. On the problem of calculating real wages see M.W. Flinn, 'Trends in Real Wages, 1750–1850', *Economic History Review*, xxvii, no. 3, (1974).

11. For an introduction to family budgets see J. Burnett, *A History of the Cost of Living*, (1969), 273–4. For the census see N.L. Tranter, *Population and Society 1750–1940*, (1985), 8–14. On enumerators' books see W.A. Armstrong, in H.J. Dyos (ed.), *The Study of Urban History*, (1968). On Poor Law statistics see M.E. Rose, *The Relief of Poverty 1834–1914*, (1972), 13–15.

12. For a useful discussion of these issues see D. Bythell, 'The History of the Poor', *English Historical Review,* 89, (April, 1974).

13. Novels are considered by: K. Tillotson, *Novels of the Eighteen Forties,* (1954); L. Cazamian, *The Social Novel in England* (trans. M. Fido, 1973); and G. Himmelfarb, fn. 2 above. For Mayhew see Bibliography. A useful introduction to working class autobiography is provided by J. Burnett, *Useful Toil,* (1974). For a work making use of oral history see S. Meacham, *A Life Apart. The English Working Class 1890–1914,* (1977).

14. R.M. Hartwell, 'The Rising Standard of Living in England, 1800–1850', *Economic History Review,* xiii, (1961); reprinted in A.J. Taylor (ed.), *The Standard of Living in Britain in the Industrial Revolution,* (1975), 118. Taylor's introduction to this volume provides the best survey of the debate to that time.

15. G.N. von Tunzelmann, 'The Standard of Living Debate and Optimal Economic Growth', in J. Mokyr (ed.), *The Economics of the Industrial Revolution,* (1985), 207. For a survey of the current position see N.F.R. Crafts, *British Economic Growth during the Industrial Revolution,* (1985), ch. 5.

16. For surveys of the second half of the century see P. Mathias, *The First Industrial Nation,* (2nd ed., 1983), 343–8; E.J. Hobsbawm, *Industry and Empire,* (1969), ch. 8; S.G. Checkland, *The Rise of Industrial Society in England, 1815–85,* (1964), 228–9.

17. For regional variations see: G. Barnsby, 'The Standard of Living in the Black Country during the Nineteenth Century', *Economic History Review,* xxiv, (1971); and the criticism of C. Griffen, *ibid.,* xxvi, (1973); R.S. Neale, *Bath. A Social History 1680–1850,* (1981); A.T. McCabe, 'The Standard of Living on Merseyside 1850–75, in S.P. Bell (ed.), *Victorian Lancashire,* (1974); T.R. Gourvish, 'The Standard of Living, 1890–1914, in A. O'Day (ed.), *Edwardian England,* (1979).

18. For example: P.H. Lindert and J.G. Williamson, 'English Workers' Living Standards during the Industrial Revolution: A New Look', *Economic History Review,* xxxvi, (1983).

19. See D.J. Oddy, 'Working-Class Diets in Late Nineteenth-Century Britain', *Economic History Review,* xxiii, (1970).

20. For the agricultural labourer compare Lindert and Williamson, cited in fn. 18 above with K.D.M. Snell, *Annals of the Labouring Poor,* (1985). Urban poverty receives excellent coverage in J.H. Treble, *Urban Poverty in Britain, 1830–1914,* (1979).

21. Joseph Adshead, *Distress in Manchester. Evidence (tabular and otherwise) of the state of the labouring classes in 1840–42,* (1842), 29–30.

22. See e.g. A.S. Wohl, *Endangered Lives Public Health in Victorian Britain,* (1983), ch. 11.

23. J. Foster, *Class Struggle and the Industrial Revolution,* (1974), 91–9, 255–9; M. Anderson, *Family Structure in Nineteenth-Century Lancashire,* (1971), 31.

24. On price movements see J. Burnett, *op. cit.,* (1969), 196–205. On wages in the second half of the century, E.H. Hunt, *Regional Wage Variations in Britain, 1850–1914,* (1973), is the standard authority.

25. See I. Gazely, 'The cost of living for urban workers in late-Victorian and

Edwardian Britain', *Economic History Review,* xlii, (1989) who concludes, 'The poorest households did not fare proportionately better than their richer counterparts because of falling living costs.'

26. A.L. Bowley, *Wages and Income since 1860,* (1937), 42.

27. On the size of the agricultural labour force see P. Deane and W.A. Cole, *British Economic Growth,* (1962), 143.

28. On differentiation among the unskilled see: D.E. Baines, 'The labour supply and the labour market, 1860–1914', in R. Floud and D. McCloskey (eds.), *The Economic History of Britain since 1700,* vol. 2, (1981), 164–5; S. Meacham, *op. cit.,* 142; A.C. Bowley and G.H. Wood, 'The statistics of wages in the United Kingdom during the nineteenth century', *Journal of the Royal Statistical Society,* lxx, (1906).

29. G. Best, *Mid-Victorian Britain 1851–70,* (1979 edn.), 114–8.

30. G. Stedman Jones, *Outcast London,* (1984 edn.), 387. J.A. Banks in R. Lawton (ed.), *The Census and Social Structure,* (1978), 194.

31. A.S. Wohl, *op. cit.,* 46–7; N.L. Tranter, *op. cit.,* 48; R. Woods, 'Mortality patterns in the nineteenth century', in R. Woods and J. Woodward (eds.), *Urban Disease and Mortality in Nineteenth-Century England,* (1984), 37–64.

32. E. Chadwick, 'Report on the Sanitary Condition of the Labouring Population of Great Britain, (1842), 223–7; Supplement to '69th Annual Report of the Registrar General', Pt. 2, (1908); Appendix-Letter Dr J. Tatham; *74th Annual Report of Registrar General,* (1913), Table 288.

33. On typhus see: A.S. Wohl, *op. cit.,* 125–6; B. Luckin, 'Evaluating the sanitary revolution: typhus and typhoid in London 1851–1900', in Woods and Woodward, *op. cit.,* 102–19.

34. On tuberculosis see G. Cronje, 'Tuberculosis and mortality decline in England and Wales, 1851–1910', in Woods and Woodward, *ibid.,* 79–101.

35. For a description of diet see the works of J. Burnett, *op. cit.,* (1969); *Plenty and Want. A Social History of Diet in England from 1815,* (1966); and his article 'Country Diet' in G.E. Mingay (ed.), *The Victorian Countryside,* vol. 2, (1981). For quantification see D.J. Oddy, *op. cit.,* (1970) and his later article extending and slightly modifying his figures in D.J. Oddy and D. Miller (eds.), *The Making of the Modern British Diet,* (1976).

36. See e.g. W.H.B. Court, *op. cit.,* 312.

37. J. Woodward, 'Medicine and the city: the nineteenth-century experience', in Woods and Woodward, *op. cit.,* 68.

38. A.S. Wohl, *op. cit.,* 326–7.

39. *Census General Report,* vol. cvi, (1893–4), 23; N. McCord, *North-East England,* (1979), 161; F. Manders, *History of Gateshead,* (1973), 169–70; G.H. Wood, *op. cit.,* (1909) section on rents. For rent as a proportion of income see: Mrs Pember Reeves, *Round about a Pound a Week,* (1913), 22–3. Bowley and Hurst, *op. cit.,* (1915), 23–40 believe one-eighth of income was general for working class, while Rowntree, *op. cit.,* (1901), 165, found the poor spent 29 per cent of their income on rent.

40. Local Government Board Inland Sanitary Survey, (1892–5); for details of tuberculosis see fn. 34.

41. S. Meacham, *op. cit.*, 156–8 and A.S. Wohl, *op. cit.*, 10–42.
42. C. Booth (1891), i, 146–7; B.S. Rowntree (1901), 142; Bowley and Hurst (1915), 46.
43. Cited by E.P. Hennock, 'Poverty and social theory in England: the experience of the eighteen-eighties', *Social History*, i, (1976), 81.
44. Quoted from Postgate, *The Builders' History*, (1923) by S. Meacham, *op. cit.*, 25.
45. E.H. Phelps Brown *The Growth of British Industrial Relations*, (1959), 19, cited in E.H. Hunt, *op. cit.*, (1973), 106, fn. 1. Chapter 3 of this work is a useful guide to this aspect in general.
46. P.E.H. Hair, 'Children in Society 1850–1980', in T. Barker and M. Drake (eds.), *Population and Society in Britain 1850–1980*, (1982), 46–50.
47. For Bowley see W.H.B. Court, *op. cit.*, 317. For sweated labour *ibid.*, 385–95. On female employment see Meacham, *op. cit.*, ch. 4. For limited opportunities in an industrial area see Lady Bell, *op. cit.*, 179–80. On lodgers see Bowley and Hurst, *op. cit.*, 177 and Lady Bell, 117–8.
48. *Seventy-Third Annual Report of the Registrar General*, (1912), table XV: Legitimate Birth Rates in Social Classes.
49. Lady Bell, *op. cit.*, 244.
50. *Ibid.* 193. J. Robinson, *The Life and Times of Francie Nichol of South Shields*, (1977), 7.
51. *Ibid.*, 108. C. Booth, *The Aged Poor in England and Wales*, (1894), 43.
52. A.S. Wohl, *op. cit.*, 46–7, 135–7.
53. *Thirty-Ninth Annual Report of the Registrar General*, (1878), ix–x.
54. Lady Bell, *op. cit.*, 92.
55. Charles Booth, *op. cit.*, (1902–3); Poverty, vol. 3, 205–15 makes several adverse comments on the health of such children.
56. Bowley and Hurst, *op. cit.*, 47; also Rowntree *op. cit.*, (1901), 211–2.
57. Lady Bell, *op. cit.*, ch. 8.
58. K.D.M. Snell, *op. cit.*, chs. 1 and 4. Pamela Horn, *The Rural World*, (1980), ch. 3.
59. For urban unemployed see J. Treble, *op. cit.*, ch. 2.
60. D. Bythell, *The Handloom Weavers*, (1968); D. Landes, *The Unbound Prometheus*, (1969), 118–19; G. Stedman Jones, *op. cit.*, 19–158 is the most thorough discussion of the problem of casual workers in London.
61. J. Harris, *Unemployment and Politics 1886–1914*, (1972), Appendix B. Also W.R. Garside, *The Measurement of Unemployment in Great Britain*, (1980), pt. 1, ch. 1.
62. On the role of working-class women see C. Chinn, *They Worked All Their Lives. Women of the Urban Poor in England, 1880–1939*, (1988).
63. C. Booth, *op. cit.*, (1891), i, 37–8.
64. *Ibid.*, i, 42–5.
65. *Ibid.*, i, 55–6.
66. P. Mathias, *op. cit.*, 195.
67. C. Booth, *op. cit.*, (1902–3), iii, 148–69; J. Garraty, *Unemployment in History*, (1978), 111–12.
68. B.S. Rowntree, *op. cit.*, (1901), 140–3. C. Booth, *op. cit.*, (1891), i, 146–8; Lady Bell, *op. cit.*, 246–54.

69. A.E. Dingle, 'Drink and Working-Class Living Standards in Britain 1870–1914', in Oddy and Miller, *op. cit.*, 131. This article is of general value on this topic.

70. On the concept of respectability see F.M.L. Thompson, *The Rise of Respectable Society 1830–1900*, (1988), 199–200, 202–3, 352–3.

71. W.H.B. Court, *op. cit.*, 309 gives example from the Rathbone survey. For purchases on credit see Lady Bell, *op. cit.*, 70–1. J. Robinson, *op. cit.*, 16–18. On pawnshops see Melanie Tebbutt, *Making Ends Meet. Pawnbroking and Working Class Credit*, (1983).

72. J. Lawson, *A Man's Life*, (1932), 34–5; R. Roberts, *The Classic Slum*, (1971), 61; Hamish Fraser, *The Coming of the Mass Market*, (1981), ch. 7.

73. J. Robinson, *op. cit.*, 28.

74. 'Report of Children in Receipt of Poor Relief in England and Wales', (1910), Cd. 5037, 32, quoted in S. Meacham, *op. cit.*, 27.

75. L.C. Robbins, *The Theory of Economic Policy in English Classical Political Economy*, (1952), 19.

76. For a useful introduction to this discussion see A.J. Taylor, *Laissez-Faire and State Intervention in Nineteenth-Century Britain*, (1972), ch. 2 and 4. The phrase 'working with the grain' is from O.O.G.M. MacDonagh, 'The Nineteenth-Century Revolution in Government: A Reappraisal', *Historical Journal*, 1, (1958).

77. W.H.B. Court, *Concise Economic History of Britain*, (1965), 191.

78. For a useful introduction to this topic see J.F.C. Harrison, *The Common People*, (1984), 271–304.

79. 'Royal Commission on Friendly Societies (1871–4)', evidence of J.M. Ludlow, registrar, quoted in G.M. Young and W.D. Handcock (eds.), *English Historical Documents*, xii, 1833–1874, (1956), 314–5.

80. On Friendly Societies see P.H.J.G. Gosden, *The Friendly Societies in England 1815–75*, (1961).

81. As note 8 above.

82. N. McCord, 'The Poor Law and Philanthropy', in D. Fraser (ed.), *The New Poor Law in the Nineteenth Century*, (1976), 90.

83. D. Fraser, *The Evolution of the British Welfare State*, (2nd edn. 1984), ch. 6, pt. 1.

84. For an introduction to the COS see J. Fido, 'The Charity Organisation Society and Social Casework in London 1869–1900', in A.P. Donajgrozki, *Social Control in Nineteenth-Century Britain*, (1977).

85. 'Eighth Annual Report of the Charity Organization Society', (1876), App. iv, 24–5. Useful examples of the COS at work, are included in K. Woodroofe, *From Charity to Social Work in England and the United States*, (1962), ch. 1 and 2.

CHAPTER TWO

THE ORIGINS OF THE NEW POOR LAW

The New Poor Law was created in response to a growing belief among contemporaries that its predecessor had become both corrupt and inefficient. The foundation of both Old and New Poor Laws lay in the Elizabethan codification of existing laws and practices in the period 1597–1601. For the reformers of the early years of the nineteenth century, the final piece of legislation, the 43rd of Elizabeth, was to acquire an unprecedented respect. The Elizabethan legislation defined three categories of poor to be relieved: those without work, those who refused to work, and those unable to work. The individual parish was authorized to levy a rate to cater for each of these groups. For those without work, materials were to be purchased to provide them with employment, while the idler was to be taught the error of his ways in a house of correction. The impotent poor: the sick, the infirm and the orphan, were to be relieved in almshouses. In practice, around 15,000 parishes worked within this broad framework to develop solutions in accordance with their individual social and economic pressures and the whims of their administrators. For Derek Fraser the result was that each parish became 'a sort of petty kingdom with its own sovereign will'.[1] Thus historians have found that even adjacent parishes could differ

markedly in their treatment of the poor.[2] Legislation is therefore
believed to be a poor guide to the pattern of administration,
representing at best the desire of the central authority to encourage
the use of what was currently regarded as sound practice.

The most significant items of legislation were concerned with the
Law of Settlement and the workhouse. Settlement was always
difficult to define. As each parish was responsible for its own poor,
problems arose in deciding the fate of any pauper who had in the
course of his life moved from one parish to another. While parishes
might at times desire to attract able-bodied labour few wished to
retain the sick or the aged. Initial legislation in 1662 was intended
to provide an administrative procedure based on the best of current
practice. It provided the basic rule that removal should take place
within forty days of taking up residence in a parish. In practice the
law was difficult to interpret and was complicated by repeated
legislative amendments. The right to claim settlement in a parish
could be based upon birth, apprenticeship, employment and, in the
case of a woman, marriage. Where a new arrival could not claim
settlement, the overseer of a parish could obtain an order from the
magistrates removing potential claimants back to the last parish in
which they had the right of settlement. The complexity of the law
made it of more benefit to lawyers than to the ratepayers. There was
undoubtedly harassment of vulnerable categories of potential
claimant. Single women, widows with families and labourers with
large families were always liable to prompt removal. The removal of
the sick and women in the later stages of pregnancy produced many
scandals. In 1795 the law was made more humane, with the
provision that removal could only be sought after Poor Relief had
been claimed, and orders of removal were suspended during periods
of sickness.[3]

For Adam Smith the Law of Settlement hindered the mobility of
labour, but the extent to which this was the case must be doubted.
In rural areas labourers normally worked within travelling distance
of their home, while the rapidly growing urban communities, which
generally required additional labour, sought to avoid the expense of
litigation by the use of certificates and agreements with the parish of
settlement to provide relief payments should the migrant worker
need to claim. In cases of controversy most urban overseers found the
threat of litigation was often all that was required to enforce
payment. Nevertheless, the volume of correspondence concerning

the non-resident poor in the letter books of many urban parishes shows the difficulties which occur over such practical matters as arranging payment and the particular problems which arose when payments continued for a prolonged period.[4]

An important issue connected with the Law of Settlement was the creation of the 'close' parish. In such a community all property was owned by one or two landlords who were thus in a position to pull down empty cottages and prevent the erection of new homes. 'Close' parishes relied for their labour force on their 'open' neighbours. Such a policy had the merit for the ratepayers of the 'close' parish of reducing the prospective claimants for relief. These practices could also be introduced as a means of restricting access to the common lands of the parish or to limit expenditure on housing. The obvious defects were the burden placed on neighbouring parishes, the fact that the practice encouraged casualization of the labour force and that it decreased the supply of housing at a time of population expansion. To irate ratepayers who felt victimized by such a policy, the 'close' parish was a further argument in favour of Poor Law reform.[5]

The workhouse had its origin in the Elizabethan Poor Law. Generally the individual parish had limited financial resources and where it possessed a workhouse it served both as almshouse for the impotent and corrective establishment for the able-bodied. The availability of even general workhouses was limited and unevenly distributed. There appear to have been more urban than rural workhouses, although late eighteenth-century writers saw poverty as being largely a rural problem. The first official return of 1776 listed around 2,000 workhouses, each having between twenty and fifty inmates. Although some of these workhouses covered more than one parish, and it was often the case that a parish possessing a workhouse with space would accept paupers from neighbouring parishes, it is obvious that the workhouse was not the principal means of relief. A return of 1802–3 found 3,765 workhouses in 14,611 parishes. The average number of inmates was twenty-two per institution and only around one pauper in twelve was in receipt of indoor relief. However, this small percentage absorbed approximately one-quarter of the total expenditure. With the rapid increase in rates at this time workhouses began to be regarded with decreasing favour.[6]

Beyond the statistical averages the term workhouse appears to have been applied to a variety of institutions, varying from rented houses intended merely to provide shelter, to large establishments which were workhouses in every sense of the word. Experiments in the provision of larger institutions often involved a combination of groups of parishes. One of the best known early examples was the Corporation of the Poor founded in the city of Bristol in 1696. Here a local Act provided for the erection of a 'pauper manufactory' to provide a means of the poor earning their keep. In 1722–3 Knatchbull's Act encouraged the early eighteenth-century practice of parishes using workhouses as places where the inmates were expected to earn the cost of their maintenance. The Act also permitted the refusal of relief to those who refused to enter the workhouse. In addition parishes were allowed to combine, with the consent of the majority of their inhabitants and the approval of the local magistrates, for the purpose of providing a workhouse. This prototype for the Victorian Poor Law was, however, completely undermined later in the century. Gilbert's Act of 1782 while providing for parishes combining to defray the cost of providing workhouses, regarded such institutions as existing for the relief of the impotent poor. The able-bodied, who were prepared to work, were to be provided with outdoor relief and the idlers taken before the magistrates.[7]

Rising costs in the latter part of the Napoleonic Wars and the succeeding depression encouraged the always strong desire for economy. There appear to have been few new workhouses erected in this period and a growing use of contractors. These tendered for the task of providing for the indoor poor, and occasionally for the outdoor poor as well. In some cases the tender was on a per capita basis but in others it was for a global sum. In the latter case contractors could be forced by competition into bids which were very low and in any emergency, such as a hard winter, it was not unknown for them to be unable to complete their contract. In cases of contracting or 'farming' the poor profit was often sought by rigorous and even scandalous economy. Although the abuse of contractors was probably exaggerated by reformers, their malpractices helped to further blacken the image of the Old Poor Law.[8]

The major source of relief provided was the cheaper and more flexible payment of outdoor relief. Normally such payments were in cash as the limited administrative resources of the average parish baulked at the burden of supervising payments in kind. One exception to this was the payment of rents. This was a practice popular with many of the richer ratepayers who were themselves landlords, and could be defended as a means of seeing relief was not wasted on drink. There appears to have been a growing tendency in the eighteenth century for parishes to provide some form of medical relief. In some cases the parish paid doctors bills' in others there was a recognized parish doctor who might be recompensed on the number of cases treated or work to a fixed overall contract. In addition to doctors' parishes appeared to have paid many unqualified practioners such as bone-setters and midwives. A recent local study of West Riding sources found approximately one-quarter of all complaints being treated by unqualified personnel. Parish funds could also be used to make payment to local charities and infirmaries to secure medicine and hospital treatment for paupers. The extent to which this happened varied with parochial attitudes and the availability and willingness of the voluntary sector to cooperate. The limited evidence available suggests variation not only be area but that policy could change within an area at different times. From the viewpoint of parish administrators such payments might by expected to curtail expenditure on local doctors and in times of crisis would be regarded as a possible sacrifice to economy.[9]

A similar picture of slow and sporadic development appears to apply to the treatment of lunatics. Where possible the lunatic was given outdoor relief. Where they were unable to be cared for at home the trend was to house them in a workhouse, or, if dangerous, in a private lunatic asylum. Once accepted as paupers, lunatics became long-term charges on parish funds and could become an expensive item. In general medical relief does not appear to have formed a major item of expense for the Old Poor Law although it appears to have made a more varied and imaginative use of existing facilities than its successor.[10]

The difficulty with records detailing expenditure on the sick is that in recording what was done they present a more positive picture than was perhaps deserved. Equally, records concerning the search for economies in the treatment of illegitimacy and the apprenticeships of the young, particularly those detailing arrangements with early factory masters, present the Old Poor Law in a less than favourable light. Oxley warns that the extent of abuse in both cases should not be exaggerated, although the cases recorded suggest that considerable hardship was inflicted. Other signs of the search for economy can be illustrated by attempts to ensure a more strict

THE POOR-LAW ACT.

PUBLIC MEETING

AT

BRADFORD, YORKSHIRE.

MONDAY, MARCH 6, 1837.

OPPOSITION of the most decided character continues to prevail, in the North, to this unchristian Law. By a requisition, embracing all parties and sects, the Constable of Bradford summoned a Meeting, which was held on Monday, March 6th, at noon, in the open air, in a field near the Court-House; and was attended by thousands of that dense population. Upon the platform, which had been erected for the purpose, were two of the acting Magistrates, Matthew Thompson and J. G. Paley, Esqrs., and with them, Clergymen, Dissenting Ministers, Tradesmen, Manufacturers, and Operatives; all apparently zealous in the cause of the poor.

Upon the motion of Mr. Thomas Hill, seconded by Mr. V. Rochfort, (both liberals,) Joshua Pollard, Esq. of Crow-trees, (a Conservative) was unanimously called to the Chair; and, in opening the proceedings, expressed his peculiar gratification to be President of a Meeting, summoned for the support of the noblest cause—that of the widow, the fatherless, and the poor. (Cheers.) He trusted, that in using that great constitutional privilege, which, as Britons, they would never relinquish,—the right of petitioning, or protesting, against unjust laws; his fellow-townsmen would ever seek to conquer by force of argument and proof, and not by senseless and impotent clamour. (Cheers.) Bespeaking a fair hearing for all, he would now call upon one of their respected magistrates to move the 1st resolution.

A pamphlet containing a report of an anti-Poor Law meeting at Bradford. From the Ferrand family and estate archive, 1837

'Poor Law Divorce', *The Pictorial Times*, a satirical judgement on the insistence of the Poor Law that elderly couples should be kept in separate male and female accommodation

'Able-bodied Poor', *The Pictorial Times*. Here reference is made to the Victorian concept of those who were judged to be 'deserving' cases and therefore should be helped against those, such as the able-bodied poor, who were considered to have in some way contributed to their own poverty and were therefore 'undeserving' of relief

LIST OF

PERSONS RECEIVING RELIEF

FROM

The Corporation of the Poor,

To JULY 31st, 1834.

Parish of St Michael.

SICK AND CASUAL CASES.

NAMES OF PAUPERS.	Ages of Men	Ages of Women	No. of Children	Age of Children receiving Pay	RESIDENCE	EMPLOYMENT	Weekly pay s. d.
Bailey, Joseph	23				12, Griffin-lane		2 4
Barry, Ellen		16			30, Host-street		2 0
Bryant Ann, widow		54			Johnny Ball-lane		2 0
Bray's Hugh, wife Ann	67				Horfield-road	Mason	2 0
Cozy Martha, and bastard			1		9, Maudlin-lane		2 0
Cleaver William, and wife	24	60			Host-street	Laborer	3 0
Challengee Elizabeth, widow		60			1, Trenchard-street	Needlewoman	2 0
Clark Joseph, and wife Mary	39	65			St. Michael's Church Yard		2 0
Dudley, Ellen		60			Pondfy's-court, Christmas-street		2 0
Fenning Elizabeth, widow					2, Trenchard-street		2 0
Godden Ann, and 2 children			2		Old Park		4 6
Galloway, Elizabeth		33			11, Griffin-lane		2 0
Griffith's John, wife and 2 children					4, Trenchard-street		5 0
Guscott Isaac, and 2 children					3, Steep-street		6 0
Griffin, Richard					17, Horfield Road		1 6
Harris Mary, widow					17, Host-street		2 0
Huggins Abraham, and 3 children	42		3		10, Salmon-street		4 6
Hole, Ann		30			2, St. Michael's Steps		2 0
Hatfield Jane, widow		79			8, Walker-street, Kingsdown		2 6
Johnstone George, and bastard	74		1	9	Host-street		2 0
James, Emma		18			18, Host-street		1 6
Jones Jane, widow		50			24, Host-street		2 0
Lewis James, and family					Alfred Buildings		4 6
M'Laughlin, Catharine		18			Host-street		1 6
Moore's John, wife Elizabeth					Watt's, Host-street	Seaman	1 6
Mahony Dennis, wife and 2 children			2		20, Trenchard-street		3 0
Marsh, Julius	84				9, Trenchard-street		3 0
Nicholson Eliza, widow		35		1	3, Johnny Ball-lane		1 4
Neale Ann, widow		63			1, Steep-street		1 0
Owen's Ann, child Edward			1	5	Frog-lane		1 4
Potter Alfred, and 2 children			2		12, Griffin-lane		3 4
Ryan, Catharine					4, Tankard Close		2 0
Reeves, Hannah					22, Trenchard-street		2 0
Steel's Samuel, wife Frances					Maudlin-lane		2 0
Tucker Ann, widow		69			4, Griffin-lane		2 6
Terrett Ann, widow		82			6, Griffin-lane		2 0
Walker, Eleanor		54			Church-lane		1 0
Williams Godfrey, and 3 children			3		Queen-street		4 6
Wren's William, wife and child	51		1		St. Michael's Steps		3 6
Wilkinson James, wife and 2 children	33		2		72, Trenchard street		3 0

NAMES OF PAUPERS.	Ages of Men	Ages of Women	No. of Children	Age of Children receiving Pay	RESIDENCE	OCCUPATION	Weekly pay
Gillett Sarah, widow		73			Host-street	Nurse	2 0
Gillis Elizabeth, widow and child			1	8	Christmas-street	Shoebinder	1 6
Graham Johanna, widow		81			Narrow Lewins-mead	Knitter	2 6
Gale, Thomas	68				8, Trenchard-street	Carpenter	2 0
Harris Mary, widow and 3 children		40	3	8, 6, 4	17, Host-street	Dress maker	4 6
Hanley Sarah, widow		54			Ditto	Sempstress	2 0
Howell, James	83				Kingsdown	Carpenter	2 0
Hole Ann, widow and child		30	1	9	St. Michael's Steps	Washing	2 0
Hill, Ann		39			Maudlin-lane	Charwoman	1 6
Halliney Mary, widow and child		60	1	11	8, Host-street	Fruitseller	1 6
Horn Sarah, and 3 children		44	3	8, 5, 3	St. Michael's-hill		4 6
Hawkes, Elizabeth		36			Christmas-street		2 0
Hatfield, Jane		70			Salmon-street		2 0
James, Mary		70			Stoney-hill	Cakewoman	2 6
Jefferies Mary, widow and 3 children			3	7, 4	22, Host-street	Servant	3 0
Jones Timothy, and wife	62	60			Maudlin-lane	Laborer	3 0
James, Thomas	78				8, Queen-street		2 0
Jenkins, Sarah		70			St. Michael's Steps		2 0
Leah Elizabeth, widow		69			Tankards Close		2 0
M'Kenly Elizabeth, widow & 2 chil.		28	2		Trenchard-street	Mangler	3 6
Miller, Sarah		62			Old Park	Shoemaker	2 6
Moore Mary Ann, widow		44			Upper Maudlin-lane		2 0
M'Laughlin Daniel, widower & 3 chil.	47		3		3, Griffin-lane		5 0
Nicholson Elizabeth, widow & 2 chil.		38	2	10, 8	Johnny Ball-lane	Shoebinder	3 0
Nicholls Elizabeth, widow and child		47	1		28, Host-street	Charwoman	1 6
Osler, Elizabeth		63			Old Park	Dressmaker	2 6
Perry Ruth, widow		68			Salmon-street	Beadwoman	1 6
Potter Elizabeth, widow & 2 children		38	2	8, 5	12, Griffin-lane	Plainwork	2 0
Pyle, Elizabeth		68			22, Maudlin-lane	Charwoman	2 0
Reed's Mary Ann, child					9, Trenchard-street		1 0
Ryan Catharine, widow and child		52	1		Host-street	Washing	1 6
Reene Sarah, and 2 children			2	5, 2	Old Park	Needlework	2 0
Roberts, Mary		66			Church lane	Breeches maker	2 0
Semlett, Mary		73			Maudlin lane	Sempstress	2 6
Simmons, James	64				1, Trenchard-street	Gardener	2 6
Scott Ann, widow and child			1	10	St. Michael's Steps		2 6
Skinner William, wife & 3 children	42		3		Salmon-street	Shoemaker	4 6
Thomas Ann, widow		66			Steep-street	Hawker	2 0
Tucker, Ann		68			11, Griffin lane	Shopkeeper	2 6
Trews, Susanna		80			St. Michael's Bath	Charwoman	2 6
Turtle Elizabeth, widow and child		39	2		3, Tankard's Close	Green grocer	2 6
Wheeler Ann, widow and child		26	1		Johnny Ball lane	Shoebinder	1 6
Williams, Ann		65			Church lane	Servant	2 6
Williams Step. wife Mary & 2 chil.			2	6, 11	Horfield road		3 0
Winns Mary, and 2 children		28	2		Upper Maudlin lane		4 6

WORKING CASES.

NAMES OF PAUPERS.	Ages of Men	Ages of Women	No. of Children	Age of Children receiving pay	RESIDENCE	OCCUPATION	Weekly Pay
Batt, Samuel	18				St. Michael's-hill	Laborer	3 4
Clarke, Joseph	53				Church lane	Baker	4 2
Fitzpatrick, Peter	39		2	7, 5	Host-street	Laborer	5 10
Harris, Mary		47			Ditto		2 0
Herne, Jane		32			Lower church lane	Servant	2 0
Jarret John, and 2 children	28		2	4, 2	Ditto	Laborer	5 5
Merrick, Edmund	44				Host-street	Ditto	3 4
Morgan, John		70			Church lane	Plasterer	6 0
Onion Charles, and wife	70	66			Maudlin lane	Mason	4 2
Owen, James	44				Alfred buildings	Ditto	3 4

John Wright, Printer, 14, Bridge-street, Bristol.

The list of persons in the parish of St Michael, Bristol, who were receiving relief from the Corporation of the Poor, 1834

Bristol Record Office: 39875/2

Andover Union Workhouse, 1846. The cruciform structure was typical of many post-1834 workhouses, giving separate exercise yards for the different classes of pauper

The parish workhouse, St James's, London, before 1834. This was the 'luxurious' type of 'unreformed' workhouse. The 1834 reformers objected to its air of ease and spaciousness

The New Starvation Law examined,

And some Description of the Food, Dress, Labour, and Regulations, imposed upon the poor and unfortunate Sufferers in the New British Bastiles.

Come you men and women unto me attend,
And listen and see what for you I have penn'd;
And if you do buy it, and carefully read.
'T will make your hearts within you to bleed.

The lions at London, with their cruel paw,
You know they have pass'd a Starvation Law;
These tigers and wolves should be chained in a den,
Without power to worry poor women and men.

Like the fox in the farm-yard they shly do creep;
These hard-hearted wretches, O, how dare they sleep,
To think they should pass such a law in our day,
To hate and to stop the poor widow's pay.

And if they don't like their pay to be stopp'd,
'Gainst their own will into th' Bastile they're popp'd;
Their homes must break up, and never return,
But leave their relations and children to mourn.

The three pension'd paupers in grandeur do live,
Poor riches that they from the taxes receive;
Which poor people pay from their scanty week's wage,
Though pinch'd, and confin'd like a bird in a cage.

But if they'd to work before they were fed,
They'd not go a tolling the poor children's bread,
Which fathers do earn very hard every day,
While they in carriages are dashing away.

There's many poor children go ragged and torn,
While they and their horses are pamper'd with corn;
Now is not this world quite unequally dealt?
The Starvation Law by some few is felt.

When a man and his wife for sixty long years
Have toiled together through troubles and fears,
And brought up a family with prudence and care,
To be sent to the Bastile it's very unfair.

And in the Bastile each woman and man
Is parted asunder,—is this a good plan ?
A word of sweet comfort they cannot express,
For unto each other they ne'er have access.

Of their uniform, too, you something shall hear,—
In strong Fearnaught jackets the men do appear;
In coarse Grogram gowns the women do shine,
And a ninepenny cap,—now won't they be fine?

On fifteenpence halfpenny they keep them a week;
' ad Commissioners this we should have them to seek.
They'd not come to Yorkshire to visit us here,
And of such vile vermin we soon should be clear.

To give them hard labour, it is understood,
In handmills the grain they must grind for their food,
Like men in a prison they work them in gangs,
With turning and tui ing it fills them with pangs.

I'll give you an insight of their regulations,
Which they put in force in these situations,
They've school, chapel, and prison all under a roof,
And the governor's house stands a little aloof.

The master instructs them the law to obey,
The governor minds it's all work and no play,
And as for religion the parson doth teach
That he knows the gospel,—no other must preach.

Ye hard-working men, wherever you be,
I'd have you watch closely these men, d'ye see;
I think they're contriving, the country all o'er,
To see what's the worst they can do to the poor.

But if that their incomes you wish for to touch,
They'll vapour, and grumble, and talk very much,
The Corn Laws uphold, the poor will oppress,
And send them to th' Bastile in th' day of distress.

R. H.

'The New Starvation Law Examined', by Reuben Holder, c. 1837. A reference to
the hardship caused by the Poor Law Reform Act of 1834

West Yorkshire Archives

The female ward at a refuge for the destitute, 1843

Mansell Collection

The Houseless Poor Asylum, Cripplegate, London, 1846. The people in the picture are probably waiting to ensure a place when the doors open. In bad weather such institutions tended to become very overcrowded

The Working Class Movement Library

Verses on the Bradford Riot.

Oh! how shall I begin to write,
Or tell you about Bradford fight,
 On th' twentieth of November,
Concerning of the dreadful deeds,
When soldiers were fetched from Leeds,
 Which some will long remember.

Now, while I'm writing these few lines,
Perhaps 'twill trouble some their minds,
 I can't please every one,
Betwixt three bands I thus am tied,
Soldiers, guardians, folks besides,
 About the deed that's done.

On Monday, about nine o'clock,
To the Bowling Green some scores did flock,
 Thinking t' soldiers would parade,
But they who o'er them had command,
Within their quarters caus'd to stand,
 Lest quarrels should be made.

The guardians at the Court-house met,
To keep the peace constables set,
 The law for to fulfil;
The Poor Law Bill is made, you know,
To it there will be friend and foe,
 And some do blame it ill.

Unto the Court-house people came,
And to get inside they did aim,
 But entrance could not get;
This vex'd them sore within their mind,
Disturbance then began we find,
 The building was beset.

Then stones like hail did fly about,
Some windows they were knocked out,
 And angry passions led;
Then soldiers were called out to guard,
Their patience long was tried hard,
 The riot act was read.

The stones continued flying still,
The people were against the bill,
 "No Poor Law," they do cry!
Both men and women are enrag'd,
Are not easy to be assuag'd,
 To stop it they do try.

Dear friends, I think it not a joke,
 And you may think the same,
Five young men are committed to York,
 I'll tell you what's their blame.

For throwing stones as I am told,
 Breaking the windows too,
And more they yet have not got hold,
 To them will have to go.

But all their trying is in vain,
Though it may give them grief and pain,
 Disturbance does no good;
The soldiers they did sadly wound,
But still they kept upon the ground,
 Their faces stain'd with blood.

Near three o'clock, as I suppose,
Each soldier to his quarters goes,
 But was call'd out again,
Some of the crowd were not content,
To break the windows they were bent,
 With all their might and main.

The soldiers then did ride about,
With sword in hand and pistol out;
 How dreadful was the sight!
To clear the streets, and alleys too,
And for to let the people know,
 Their orders were to fight.

But still the people did not heed,
Till some of them were made to bleed,
 Cut by the soldiers sore;
Some shots were fir'd, their swords did gleam,
And some were struck who will be lame,
 I'm told almost a score.

The shops were clos'd, bus'ness was o'er,
And Bradford was in an uproar,
 For a great length of time;
I tell to you as I did hear,
The public-houses were all clear,
 That night at half-past nine

But now, my friends, the riot's o'er,
Such work I hope to see no more,
 As long as I do live;
And if you do consider right,
No more in it you'll take delight,
 You'll shun it, I believe.

So now, my friends, do one and all
Take my advice, both great and small,
 I'd have it understood,
To back the poor it's my intent,
On peace and quietness I'm bent,
 It will do the most good.

Joseph Tillotson, a fine young man,
 And William Wheater too,
Have gone to York to take their trial,
 To their parents' grief and woe.

Joseph Greensmith and Joseph Swaine,
 And William Brooke, likewise,
Are going to York, there to remain
 Until the next assize.

For the satisfaction of my readers, I give the residences of the misguided and unfortunate young men who have been committed to York, charged with being concerned in the Riot of Monday : Joseph Tillotson, Churchbank; William Wheater, Silsbridge Lane; Joseph Greensmith, Undercliffe ; William Brooke, George-Street; Joseph Swaine, Cheapside.

Reuben Holder, Licensed Hawker, No. 5405. A.

E. KEIGHLEY, PRINTER, BRADFORD.

'Verses on the Bradford Riot', by Reuben Holder c. 1837. This and the pamphlet 'The New Starvation Law Examined' are examples of the fierce hostility to the New Poor Law in the northern textile districts

West Yorkshire Archives

The interior of the occupational workshop in Barnhill Poorhouse. Built in 1849, by the early twentieth century it housed 2,000 inmates with a staff of sixty-one

Heatherbank Museum of Social Work

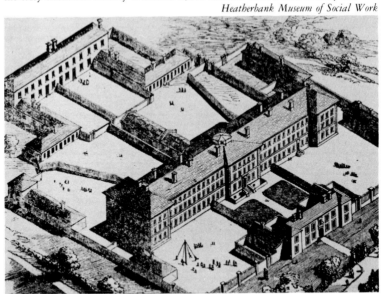

Fulham and Hammersmith Union Workhouse, London, 1849. This vast, well-planned establishment, with walls strictly separating the various categories of inmate, represented the ideal for which the 1834 Act aimed

Heatherbank Museum of Social Work

BIRDSEYE VIEW OF SCARBOROUGH NEW WORKHOUSE.

Scarborough New Workhouse, 1860. A good example of the second wave of workhouse-building, when new accommodation was often located on the outskirts of urban communities

Mansell Collection

DIETARY FOR THE ABLE-BODIED.

DIETARY FOR CHILDREN FROM 2 TO 5.

DIETARY FOR THE AGED AND INFIRM.

DIETARY FOR CHILDREN FROM 5 TO 9.

The Sick and Infants under 2 years of age, to be dieted under the direction of the Medical Officer.

TOBACCO AND SNUFF.

Male Paupers in the Workhouse over 6o years are allowed 1 oz Tobacco each per week, and the Master has power to allow Male Imbecile Paupers 1 oz of Tobacco per week each, and to Females 1 oz of snuff each per week ; also such quantity of Tobacco or Snuff as he thinks necessary to pauper inmates employed on work of a disagreeable character.—26 M.B., 113 41 M.H. 175.

Dietary published in Barton Regis Union Annual Book, May 1897. This records
the exact amount of foodstuffs required per inmate

Bristol Record Office: 10900

The shoemaking department of the boys' refuge at
Great Queen Street, Lincoln's Inn Fields, 1859; providing both for the obvious needs of the poor and the
industrial training of the boys

Mansell Collection

The communal bath in a casual
ward. The rule that all newly-
admitted casuals must have a bath
was strictly enforced for deterrent
as well as hygienic reasons.
Drawing by Gustave Doré dated
1872

*The Working Class
Movement Library*

The men's casual ward of the West London Union *c.* 1860

The Working Class Movement Library

Surrey.

IMPORTANT TO
PARENTS AND EMPLOYERS OF CHILDREN.

Act to Regulate the Employment of Children in Agriculture (5th August, 1873).

This Act came into full operation on the 1st January, 1875.

No employer, or his agent, may employ **any child under 8** in agricultural labour, unless he be its parent or guardian, and then only on land in his own occupation.

No employer, or his agent, may employ any child **over 8 and under 12**, unless the parent or guardian can produce a certificate [which will be in force for 12 months from its date] to the following effect:—

If the child be **over 8 and under 10**, he must have completed 250 school attendances (that is, **25 weeks at least**,) within the 12 months immediately preceding the issue of the certificate.

If he be **over 10 and under 12**, he must have completed 150 school attendances (that is, **15 weeks at least**) within the same period. N.B.—**No children, whether boys or girls, can be excepted** from these rules but those who have reached the 4th Standard.)

No child under the age of ten years shall be employed in any agricultural gang.

Morning school and afternoon school each, count as **one attendance**.

The school must be a school recognised by Government as efficient, if there be one within 2 miles of the parent's home.

Every employer (that is, any person occupying not less than one acre of land), or **agent of an employer**, guilty of an offence against the Act shall be liable to a **penalty of £5.**

Any other person committing an offence against the Act shall be liable to a **penalty of £1.**

But no penalty shall be inflicted for employing children above 8 years of age during School Holidays, or temporary Closing of the School—

Or in **Hay Harvest, Corn Harvest**, or **gathering of Hops**; and the Magistrates have the power to entirely suspend the Act during a few weeks in the busy seasons of the year.

The County Constabulary have been instructed to take proceedings under the Act on and after 1st August, 1875.

By Order,

H. C. HASTINGS,
Chief Constable of Surrey.

Act to Regulate the Employment of Children in Agriculture, 5 August 1873

The eviction of members of Joseph Arch's union from their cottage in Dorset, 1874
Museum of English Rural Life

Villagers watching the evictions of agricultural labourers who were members of the National Union of Agricultural Workers, at Milborne St Andrew, Dorset, April 1874

Museum of English Rural Life

ST. JAMES TURNING ST. GILES OUT OF HIS PARKS.
DEDICATED TO THE COMMISSIONERS OF WOODS AND FORESTS

Cartoon by Leech, 1850, depicting
the order issued by the Commissioners
of Woods and Forests barring certain
classes of the population from the
parks

Mansell Collection

'Couleur de Rose' by M. Mongau, 1867

Mansell Collection

Applying for relief, Windmill Street, Manchester

The labour yard of the Bethnal Green Employment Association, 1868, an area of considerable poverty and overcrowding, with heavy pressure on its poor rates. Labour yards provided men with food in return for work, but they had to find somewhere else to sleep

Cartoon 'A Court for King Cholera' depicting slum housing, 1852. Due to the associated dangers to health and morals, public health problems initially gained more publicity than the plight of the poor

Mansell Collection

A BANQVET SHOWINGE ye FARMERS FRIEND IMPRESSYNGE ON ye AGRYCVLTVRAL INTEREST THAT IT IS RVINED

A cartoon (No. 38) lampooning the Corn Law. 'Manners of ye Englyshe' from Rich and Doyle, London, 1849

Museum of English Rural Life

supervision of those on outdoor relief. In the eighteenth century intermittent use was made of the law ordering that the pauper be made to wear a distinctive badge, although this may have proved superfluous in small parishes and impossible to enforce in those which were more densely populated. By the time the law was repealed in 1810 the system was being replaced by the circulation of lists of those in receipt of relief in order that ratepayers could report any misuse of parochial funds. Both of these practices appear as cheaper alternatives to workhouse supervision.[11]

Contemporary debate from the middle of the eighteenth century was less concerned with the plight of the impotent poor than the burden of the able-bodied poor. The problem was largely viewed in terms of the southern agricultural labourer. Here earnings were being reduced below subsistence level by the fact that population was growing at a faster rate than the expanding agrarian economy could absorb. At the same time competition from the industrializing north was destroying the main sources of secondary income. The position worsened with the rise in food prices during the Napoleonic Wars and the issue continued with the depression in agricultural prices following the ending of the war. To cope with this problem the Poor Law intervened in a variety of ways. That which received most attention was the decision of the Speenhamland magistrates in 1795 to subsidize wages by an allowance system, calculated on the price of bread and the number in the family. Speenhamland became a convenient shorthand term to describe a complexity of arrangements.[12]

Not only did the allowance schemes adopted show a considerable degree of local variation, but the later years of the war and the subsequent depression saw the introduction of a variety of work-sharing schemes designed to cope with the problem of excess labour. Although differing in detail there were broadly four schemes in use. Some represented the expansion or re-introduction of long-standing practices, but many parishes appeared to be entering the area of work creation for the first time. The Roundsman System involved the sending round the parish of unemployed labourers to seek work, with their wages being subsidized by parochial allowances. A second method was to hold a weekly auction of pauper labourers with the wage offered being raised to subsistence level by the rates. Both of these schemes were seen as detrimental to the lesser ratepayer who used less labour and, in some areas, support grew for the use of a third system, the Labour Rate. In this case a separate rate was assessed for the purpose of maintaining labourers. Employers either paid the rate to the parish or employed the number of labourers equivalent to their assessment. Finally parishes could adopt a more traditional method of entering the labour market themselves, the most common form being the use of labour to maintain parish roads. [13]

During the Napoleonic Wars the cost of Poor Relief appears to have almost trebled and it was this aspect which caught the attention of contemporaries. However, with the threat of revolution spreading from across the Channel and with the incomes of landowners and farmers showing considerable gains, such costs could be accepted. However, the continuing high cost of relief at a time of falling wheat prices in the post-war period caused opinion to harden against the pauper. This unfortunate state of affairs was largely the result of the exceptional increase in population growth for, in per capita terms, the cost of Poor Relief decreased considerably between its peak in 1816 and 1832. However, it was the high total expenditure figures and especially the level in counties believed to be most involved in the use of Speenhamland type allowances and wage subsidies which caught the attention of contemporaries. [14]

Critics found support in the arguments being advanced by the leading traditional economists. It was no longer a question of settlement laws restricting the mobility of labour but of the administration of the Poor Law presenting such a threat to both economy and society that the future could best be served by their abolition. Critics saw the over generous Poor Law as diminishing the necessary practice of self-help. The strongest influence was to be found in the views of Malthus who is said to have; 'Formulated the terms of the discourse on the subject of poverty for half a century . . . It was Malthus who defined the problem, gave it a centrality it had not had before, made it dramatically, urgently, insistently problematic.'[15] For Malthus 'no person has any right on society for subsistence, if his labour will not purchase it.' He was convinced that mankind preferred indolence to work and therefore it was important that institutions such as the Poor Law should not encourage this tendency. His best known argument related to his belief that food production could not keep pace with population growth and that unless the mass of the people showed moral restraint and refrained from entering into improvident early marriages the result could only be more poverty. The Poor Law by its use of family allowances was therefore encouraging the evil it was supposed to relieve. For Ricardo the growing expenditure on the Poor Law was such that it would place a burden on the national revenue of such a size as would lead to the deterioration of rich and poor alike. It was a short step from this type of argument to the later belief that any expansion of Poor Relief must be at the direct expense of the fund of wages available for worker. Arguments in favour of the abolition were widely advanced in the period following the Napoleonic Wars, reaching their peak at the time of the Select Committee on Labourers' Wages in 1824. Total abolition was never a viable proposition, particularly at a time of serious distress. However, the abolitionists had established a theoretical justification for a more deterrent approach. For the reformer, Benthamite proposals for a stricter and more efficient administration appeared to bridge the gap between the theoretical claims of the abolitionists and the political necessity of maintaing social control.[16]

In the growing discussions of the Poor Law problem it was the reforms promising economy which captured the attention. The period of debate was accompanied by reductions in allowances, while progressive parishes accepted the recommendations of the Sturges–Bourne Act of 1819 and established select vestries to enable ratepayers to exercise greater control of expenditure. In concerned parishes, paid assistant overseers were appointed to conduct day-to-day management; some parishes experimented with outdoor labour tests as a condition of relief to the able-bodied, while others introduced deterrent workhouses. It has been concluded that, 'Practically all the key components of the new system had been developed within and outside Parliament during the last fifty years or so of the Old Poor Law – the problem was to integrate them into a national pattern.'[17]

Increasingly the blueprint for reform was to be found in the propaganda of the Nottinghamshire reformers, their enthusiasm for their system of relief being matched only by the vigour with which they claimed to be its originators.[18] Although as advanced by the Revd J.T. Becher in *The Anti-Pauper System* of 1828 the proposals included a range of positive features such as parochial development of schools, allotments and self-help agencies, as well as support for the administrative improvements suggested by Sturges–Bourne, it was the use of a deterrent workhouse for the able-bodied which was to receive most attention:

However, before we can enforce discipline, so as to control the vicious and refractory, we must provide a place of refuge as well as restraint. For this purpose commence your measures for the reformation of the poor by the establishment of a parochial workhouse, affording the means of distributing males, femals and children both by day and by night into separate classes; and of subdividing these classes into distinct wards, according to the conduct and character of the paupers . . . Let the system of management ensure every tenderness towards the infirm, the aged and the guiltless, while it imposes wholesome restraint upon the idle, the profligate and the refractory. . . Let it however be remembered that the advantages resulting from a workhouse must arise, not from keeping the poor in the house, but from keeping them out of it; by constraining the inferior classes to know and feel how degrading is the compulsory relief drawn from the parish to silence the clamour, and to satisfy the cravings of wilful and woeful indigence; but how sweet and wholesome is that food and how honourable is that independence, which is earned by perservering and honest industry. [19]

The support for a deterrent, carefully supervised, workhouse had an obvious appeal to reformers. On the one hand it countered the demands of abolitionists, while at the same time answering complaints that workhouses were both expensive and subject to malpractice. Hence, J.R. Poynter's conclusion, 'If the workhouse test became a dogma, it did so because thirty years of debate and doubt had created the need for one.'[20]

The rising expenditure on Poor Relief in the late 1820s encouraged a greater interest in the proposals for reform. However, the timing of remedial action was influenced by the impact of the Captain Swing Riots in 1830–1 and by the election of a Whig ministry in 1832. The riots seemed to prove the degradation to which farm labourers were sinking under the existing system of relief and the new government's immediate response was the establishment of a Royal Commission to investigate the question of Poor Relief.

The Royal Commission consisting of nine members was dominated by Nassau Senior, a *laissez-faire* professor of economics, with a known hostility to the allowance system, and by Edwin Chadwick, the young, active and ambitious, former secretary to Jeremy Bentham. Initially information was sought by questionnaires sent to all parishes in England and Wales, to which approximately 10 per cent of parishes, covering around 20 per cent of the total population replied. This stage was followed by the despatch of twenty-six assistant commissioners, including Chadwick. In total they visited approximately one-fifth of the parishes. The evidence gathered by these two exercises is massive, but, either because of the selectivity of the amateur enthusiasts who acted as assistant commissioners, or the preconceptions of Senior and Chadwick, the final report is generally regarded as lacking in objectivity.[21]

The Report set itself the double task of assessing the defects in the existing system of Poor Relief, including disposing of what it regarded as the false remedies being currently discussed, and of proposing effective remedial measures as a basis for legislation. The common feature of both aspects of the Report was the acceptance of the 43rd of Elizabeth as the guiding principle. In this way it was hoped to restore the Poor Law to its proper limited field of activity, namely the relief of the destitute.

In the first part of the Report Nassau Senior sought to prove the inadequacies of the existing system of relief, and in revealing the abuses the Report reflected prevailing critical opinion. The major problem was seen as the allowance system. Relief to the able-bodied in the form of allowances in aid of wages or towards the upkeep of the family were apparently regarded as equally dangerous. Condemnation also applied to 'outdoor relief in kind' such as relief from the payment of rates or assistance with rents. Allowances in any form were held to be an interference with the free play of market forces. The result would be the depression of wage levels as it was felt that employers would rely on the parish to raise earnings to subsistence levels. The resulting abuses were amply, if occasionally inconsistently, illustrated by examples drawn from the replies to the questionnaires and the reports of the assistant commissioners and local dignitaries.

It was believed that the allowance system resulted in high rates which encouraged such false economies as allowances and uneconomic work sharing schemes. High rates were detrimental to landowners, farmers and the respectable labouring classes. For the landowner in a pauperized district the burden of the Poor Rate was held to so discourage tenants that rents were reduced 'to half or less than half'. For the small farmer, unable to take advantage of cheap labour, high rates threatened destitution. 'The overseers sometimes called upon little farmers for their rates and found they had no provisions of any kind in the house, nor money to buy any.' For the larger farmers allowances produced poor quality labour which was 'dear whatever the price'. However the Report also found areas where rents were rising as farmers sought to take advantage of subsidized labour and in industrial areas it commented that such labour was being used to 'undersell other masters'. Finally, high rates were held to be encouraging the growth of 'close' parishes as 'economy was sought by pulling down cottages . . . to keep down the number of persons having settlement.'[22]

Allowances were equally damaging to the labourer, especially those who sought to be self-reliant. Those with savings were denied Poor Relief and, in a pauperized area, single men who had prudently sought to defer marriage could find themselves denied work. Despite the unfairness of their treatment the evidence cited invariably stressed the superiority of the independent worker. For the labourer in receipt of an allowance witnesses found the effect was degrading. It was found that such workers spent their parish allowances 'in two nights at the beer shop'. Their families were lowered with them. 'The wives of paupers are dirty and nasty and indolent: and the children generally neglected and dirty and vagrants and immoral'. The disease of pauperism could become hereditary. 'When once a family have applied for relief, they are pressed down for ever'. Astute paupers 'so understood the law, and also the practices of magistrates . . . that they claimed relief not as a favour but as a matter of right.' Allowances were destructive to family life as 'mothers and children will not nurse each other in sickness unless paid for it', and parents were held to have threatened to abandon their children unless paid an allowance. Finally, women with illegitimate childrn were placed 'in a better position than many married women'.[23]

Schemes for providing or sharing work were subject to similar complaints. The Roundsman System left the labourer 'half employed and half paid, and the parish imposed upon'. Such parish work as road repairs was so badly supervised that 'everybody complained of petty thefts, pilfering, poaching, etc., as the natural consequences. Whatever the previous character of a man may have been he is seldom able to withstand the corruption of the roads.'[24]

The belief that the main problem lay in the provision of outdoor relief to the able-bodied resulted in only the most superficial consideration of other aspects of relief. The Report admitted that it had found the granting of outdoor relief to the impotent subject to less abuse. 'Even in places distinguished in general by the most wanton parochial profusion the allowances to the aged and infirm are moderate.' Nevertheless, such was the belief that paupers in general were of a debased nature that all outdoor relief contained massive potentialities to defraud. Hence, there was need for eternal vigilance. 'It is an aphorism amongst parish officers that cases which are good today are bad tomorrow, unless they are incessantly watched.' There were general warnings that families should be placed under pressure to support their impotent members and against the giving of more generous relief to those regarded as of good character as this led to more general increases or to 'discontent and disorder'.[25]

In view of their later support for the workhouse test the limited space given to the examination of existing workhouse provision is surprisingly small. Outdoor relief provided around 90 per cent of the discussion of existing abuses and this was almost entirely devoted to the able-bodied. In view of the contemporary fears of the severity of some existing workhouses the absence of adverse criticism on this point has been seen as a major omission.[26] The Report considered that there were a few good workhouses such as those controlled by the Nottinghamshire reformers but their overall conclusion referred to the laxity with which existing workhouses were administered. It suggested that most resembled:

> . . . a large almshouse, in which the young are trained in idleness,
> ignorance and vice; the able-bodied maintained in sluggish, sensual
> indolence; the aged and more respectable exposed to all the misery of
> dwelling in such a society, without government or classification; and the
> whole body of inmates subsisted on food far exceeding both in kind and
> amount, not merely the diet of the independent labourer, but that of the
> majority of persons who contribute to their support.[27]

Having suggested widespread problems in the existing mode of relief it followed that little could be said in favour of the existing system of administration. Amateur administrators were presented as usually unwilling agents, who normally served for only a few months before relinquishing their posts just as they were beginning to understand the duties involved. Serious complaints were made on the subject of embezzlement and 'jobbing, partiality and favourtism' were presented as widespread. These evils were encouraged by the absence of effective supervision, and the fears of violence against the overseers' person or property made them court popularity. Paid assistant overseers were found to be more effective but were rarely appointed to the parishes regarded as most in need of their services. The self-appointed vestry was by its nature corrupt, the smaller open vestries were subject to undue pressure by the employers of labour, while in larger parishes the time consumed in accommodating 'petty and conflicting interests' caused the respectable ratepayer to opt out. The select vestries, although not without fault, were regarded as providing the most effective administration, but unfortunately their numbers were found to be in decline. Magistrates, unpopular as the originators of the allowance scales, were held to interfere with the overseers; usually to authorize more relief than was justified.[28]

Despite criticism of the recommendations of the Report, its attack on the allowance system was largely unchallenged until the 1960s. The belief that the lesser ratepayer was ruined by the burden of relief and that wages were being forced downwards was accepted by J.H. Clapham, the leading economic historian of the inter-war period. Among social historians the belief that the labourer was demoralized and enslaved by the system was commonplace. Finally J.T. Krause, a notable demographic historian of the 1950s, supported the view of Malthus on the impact of family allowances on the birth rate.[29]

The renewed interest in the survival of contemporary poverty from the 1960s has coincided with a reconsideration of the Old Poor Law. The initial and most acute revision was produced by Mark Blaug, who concluded:

> The Old Poor Law with its use of outdoor relief to assist the underpaid
> and to relieve the unemployed was, in essence, a device for dealing with
> the problem of surplus labour in the lagging rural sector of a rapidly
> expanding but still underdeveloped economy. And considering the quality
> of social administration in the day, it was by no means an unenlightened
> policy.[30]

Blaug believes that the Poor Law Commissioners' doctrinaire opposition to outdoor relief to the unemployed caused them to ignore the problem of structural unemployment in the southern counties and to place the blame on the administration of relief. This view they supported not by an analysis of their evidence, but by 'the endless recital of ills from the mouths of squires, magistrates, overseers and clergymen.' For Blaug, the statistics show that they had exaggerated the extent of able-bodied pauperism and that the allowance system, rather than increasing was in decline. Low wages and high poor rates were the result of a rising population in an area of limited economic opportunity. The Malthusian link between allowances and fertility rates was not borne out by the national picture. Indeed, if there was a link it was by lowering infant mortality rather than increasing the birth rate. Finally, the decline in the numbers of small farmers had commenced much earlier than the introduction of the allowance system, and the decline after Waterloo was the outcome of a complex mixture of factors.[31]

Blaug's main contention that the allowance system developed in response to the problem of the rural unemployed has been generally accepted. Later research would suggest that rather than allowances declining, they had never been as significant as the contemporary critics alleged. The impact of the Old Poor Law on wages is more problematic. McCloskey has pointed out the inconsistency of the Report in alleging that allowances both decreased the amount of labour that was supplied and at the same time lowered wages. Under normal conditions of supply and demand these statements were clearly contradictory. In practice he regards allowances, intended to provide an income subsidy, as raising wages to a maximum fixed at the minimum level of subsistence. With such a ceiling on earnings, allowances would tend to limit the amount of labour supplied and therefore increase wages. However, work creation schemes, such as the Roundsman System and the Labour Rate, by increasing labour supply would have the opposite effect. E.H. Hunt also argues that on balance the withdrawal of labour from the market, resulting from the payment of poor relief, would have the effect of raising wage levels. However, he is less sanguine than other critics in that he believes the main influence of the Old Poor Law on wage rates was 'by discouraging labour mobility not by wage subsidies'.[32]

In respect of the connection between allowances and population growth Blaug's views have been further supported by the research of J.P. Huzel. Family allowances were a response to population growth rather than its cause. Indeed their minimal subsistence level of payment and the fact that they were often not paid until the fourth child seems a fairly conclusive argument. Finally agricultural historians seem to confirm Blaug's views on the decline of the small farmer.[33]

Historians of the Old Poor Law owe a great debt to Blaug. However, there are many who would query his conclusion that the range of allowances and work sharing exercises carried out by the

Old Poor Law made it a 'welfare state in miniature'. For the Checklands: 'It can hardly be denied that the abuses described in the Report existed: no-one has accused the Commissioners or their Assistants of making up the cases they presented'. Finally, Henriques notes the gap between theory and practice:

> It now looks as though Blaug's claims may stand up when applied to family allowances in isolation. But when the allowances are considered in conjunction with their accompaniments, the roundsman and the Labour Rate, and the laws of settlement, a rather different picture emerges. The Old Poor Law's work-spreading devices, once intended as a means of mitigating the hardships of unemployment, had almost imperceptibly turned into a means by which farmers dominated and oppressed their workforce.[34]

It is almost certain that the inadequacies of contemporary administration produced policies which often strayed from their original intention. However, this is not to deny Blaug's main assertion that the policy of allowances and work creation was a civilized reaction to the problem of rural unemployment and rapidly rising population rather than their cause. Generalizations concerning the Old Poor Law are difficult to sustain as parishes varied not only in comparison with other parishes but individually varied over time. To the critic of the Old Poor Law this represents an unacceptable lack of uniformity while to its friend it may illustrate its flexibility. The complexity of the existing system makes any analysis difficult. However, this did not deter the Commissioners from recommending a clear policy for reform. On this aspect of the Report most historians would agree that an inadequate diagnosis produced controversial 'remedial measures', so that the cure was possibly worse than the disease.

However, before presenting their proposals the Commissioners sought to deal with what they regarded as their main potential rivals. First was the belief that Poor Relief should be made a national charge. Such proposals were being advanced in part to secure greater uniformity of burden, but were also seen as a means of overcoming the problems associated with the Law of Settlement. The Commissioners believed that any proposal of this type was impractical. In view of the limited nature of current administration, the lack of communication and the degree of variation between localities such a view appears to be justified. Nevertheless, the arguments advanced have been found 'not altogether persuasive'. Their case rested in part on the drastic nature of the change and the fact that local control could prevent abuse, arguments which could also have been used against their own later proposals for a central supervisory body.[35] The second proposal being advanced was for the poor to be supplied with a plot of land to earn their own keep. While this proposal was accepted as likely to promote independence it was also rejected as impractical. In this case it was felt that the units would be too small to be efficient and would leave the poor unable to survive the hazards of a bad winter. Such arguments were also not without merit although the Report was ignoring the fact that favourable comments on such schemes had been provided by five of its assistant commissioners.[36] The Labour Rate was regarded as the strongest rival and received more considered attention. Here the main argument against the scheme appeared to be that it penalized the smaller arable farmer and the grassland farmers, who were forced to employ labour they did not need with only the larger arable farmers gaining benefit. This objection was more an indictment of the mode of assessment than an attack on the principle of the Labour Rate, but the Commissioners had found what they regarded as a fatal flaw: 'The ultimate effect of a labour-rate, or, in other words, of a measure which forces individuals to employ labour at a given rate of wages, must be to destroy the distinction between pauperism and independence.'[37] For the Commissioners the only acceptable solution was one which separated the pauper from the mass of the poor. It was only by ensuring this division that the Poor Law could be accepted as performing its true function, and it was to this end that the Report presented its 'remedial measures'. Here Chadwick set out the principles on which legislation for reform should be based. The section began by pointing out that:

> The most pressing of the evils which we have described are those connected with the relief of the able-bodied. They are the evils, therefore, for which we shall first propose remedies . . . If we believed the evils stated . . . to be necessarily incidental to the compulsory relief of the able-bodied, we should not hesitate in recommending its entire abolition. But we do not believe these evils to be its necessary consequences. We believe that, under strict regulations, adequately enforced, such relief may be afforded safely and even beneficially.[38]

Having thus disposed of the abolitionist case the Report laid down the guide-lines by which relief to the indigent could be successfully provided. In Benthamite tone it pointed out that the good of either the individual or the public justified the imposition of conditions on those receiving relief. The main method by which the indigent could be separated from the working poor was by following the principle of less eligibility:

> The first and most essential of all conditions, a principle which we find universally admitted, even by those whose practice is at variance with it, is that his situation on the whole shall not be made really or apparently so eligible as the situation of the independent labourer of the lowest class. Throughout the evidence it is shown that as the creation of any pauper class it elevated above the condition of independent labourers, the condition of the independent class is depressed; their industry is impaired, their employment becomes unsteady, and its remuneration in wages is diminished. Such persons therefore are under the strongest inducements to quit the less eligible classes of labourers and enter the more eligible class of paupers. The converse is the effect when the pauper class is placed in its proper position, below the independent labourer. Every penny bestowed that tends to render the condition of the pauper more eligible than that of the independent worker, is a bounty on indolence and vice. We have found that as the poor rates are at present administered, they operate as bounties of this description, to the amount of several millions annually.[39]

The Report continued with examples showing how the application of this principle had proved beneficial in a wide variety of instances. The principle was not new but the Commission's conclusion that the principle could only be effectively applied in a well regulated workhouse was a stronger statement than any previous recommendation for a similar course of action. The element of compulsion was justified by the good which could be expected to follow both for the labourer and the ratepayer.

It was held that the workhouse test would improve the industry and habits of the labourer. In his turn he would find an increased demand for his labour which would result in more permanent employment and rising wages. Improvident marriages would diminish amid a general improvement in both their moral and social conditions. For the ratepayer the Report provided examples of dramatic reductions in pauper numbers and expenditure as found at Southwell; while at Welwyn, even those who had been a permanent charge on the parish over a number of years because of sickness had

68

made a partial recovery and were making some effort to contribute to the family income. The use of the workhouse test could also assist the administrator in practical ways. Checking the truth of pauper statements, a major problem for large urban parishes, would become unnecessary. The workhouse would restore the stigma of pauperism and the uniform test would remove the dangerous discretionary elements in outdoor relief which laid officials open to partiality or intimidation. Thus, the first measure proposed for legislation was that, except for medical relief, the able-bodied and their families could only be relieved in the workhouse.[40]

The first task of a well regulated workhouse was to provide closely supervised work for all able-bodied inmates. While such work was to be 'more irksome than ordinary labour', it should be such that the destitute would not refuse to carry it out, although they would not be tempted to continue it longer than absolutely necessary. Examples of task work mentioned being carried out in workhouses and presumably regarded favourably by the Commissioners included stone-breaking, bone-crushing and the digging of previously untilled ground. In providing work it was felt that a mistake of past schemes had been to expect to profit from the exercise. This it was believed was both impractical and wrong in principle, as it threatened the jobs of existing workers.[41]

Irksome labour was to be reinforced by strict discipline. However, this did not imply that:

> . . . the food or comforts of the pauper should approach the lowest point at which existence may be maintained. Although the workhouse food be more ample in quantity and better in quality than that of which the labourer's family partakes and the house in other respects superior to the cottage, yet the strict discipline of well-regulated workhouses, and in particular the restrictions to which the inmates are subject in respect to the use of acknowledged luxuries, such as fermented liquers and tobacco, are intolerable to the indolent and disorderly, while to the aged, the feeble and other proper objects of relief, the regularity and discipline render the workhouse a place of comparative comfort.[42]

The model of a well regulated workhouse as presented by that of Southwell would have classification of inmates by sex and character, regularity of hours, and the prevention of access to the outside world or the receiving of visitors and provision for the solitary confinement of those guilty of gross misconduct.[43]

With the foundations of 'less eligibility' and the 'workhouse test' established as guiding principles, the Commission proceeded to make recommendations concerning the administration of relief which were designed to ensure that these principles were universally applied. The most radical proposal was for the creation of a central supervisory body to ensure uniformity. Such a body was justified on the grounds that the past record of parochial cooperation with government legislation was unsatisfactory, and that the majority of parishes were ignoring the successful experiments in their own neighbourhood. This sorry state of affairs, which they felt they had proved, was the result of a combination of apathy and inefficiency, reinforced by corrupt vested interests and intimidation. The Report therefore recommended that 'the legislature should divest the local authorities of all discretionary power in the administration of relief'. The central board with the aid of 'such assistant commissioners as may be found requisite' was to draw up regulations for the administration of workhouses which should 'as far as may be practicable, be uniform throughout the country'.[44]

On the basis of the evidence they argued that classification would require separate buildings for the four main classes of pauper; the aged and impotent, the children, the able-bodied females and the able-bodied males. This would enable more appropriate treatment to be provided for each group: care for the impotent, education for the children and closer supervision of the able-bodied. To cover the expense of this arrangement they recommended that the central board be 'empowered to cause any number of parishes which they may think convenient to be incorporated for the purpose of workhouse management and for providing new workhouses where necessary.' They argued that classification in separate buildings would often be cheaper, as it would be possible to make use of existing buildings, although where additional expense had to be incurred they felt it 'would ultimately be found to be economical'. In general they believed that larger parishes had proved to be more economical than smaller parishes and that the new unions, effectively supervised by the proposed central authority, would produce significant economies of scale in staffing and the provision of work for paupers. It appeared to follow, therefore, that the central authority should have the right to state general qualifications for appointments, to make recommendations on specific appointments and to have the right to remove officials found to be unsuitable for office.[45]

By concentrating on solving the problem of the able-bodied pauper and wanting to produce recommendations capable of speedy legislative action, the Report left many issues unsettled. Hence, other categories of pauper were virtually ignored and although problems of rating and settlement were recognized only minor modifications were suggested. In addition the Report did not present any suggestions for the local direction of the new unions of parishes. Historians have seen a complex range of political factors governing both the wording of the Report and the legislation which followed.

The clarity of the Report's main recommendations allowed legislation to follow quickly. Although clearly based upon the Report, the Act carried the imprint of the compromises necessary to further speedy progress. A central commission, independent of parliament, was accepted, as was the appointment of assistant commissioners to help in the formation of local unions of parishes. The central body could issue rules for the conduct of relief as well as laying down qualifications for local officials, whom it had the power to dismiss in the event of misconduct. However, the commissioners were to produce an annual report to parliament and were only sanctioned for an initial period of five years. The central body could only order the building of workhouses where it had the support of either the local board of guardians or the majority of the local electorate. The local board of guardians was based on the model of the select vestry. Guardians were to be elected on a property qualification which allocated votes in accordance with property. To further reinforce the strength of such local boards, or to buy off opposition, local county magistrates were to be *ex-officio* members. The potential power vested in such a local body was a limit on the power of the central authority, but the board of guardians was curtailed in its turn by the retention of the individual parish as both the unit of settlement and of finance; parochial contribution to union finances being based upon the burden of paupers they provided to be maintained.[46]

The New Poor Law was born out of the belief that the Old Poor Law was causing a degeneration of the working classes by encouraging idleness and overpopulation at great expense to the ratepayer. The debate on the New Poor Law was initially based on the principles by which it sought to introduce reform. In particular the use of the workhouse test and the need for a supervisory central authority were strongly contested. While it is now agreed that in the case of the workhouse test the wrong diagnosis had produced a totally inadequate remedy, recent discussion has been concerned with the extent to which the principles represented the practice. As with the Old Poor Law there is a need to distinguish myth from reality and perhaps also to decide which was the more significant.

NOTES

1. D. Fraser, *The Evolution of the British Welfare State,* (2nd edn., 1984), 34.
2. J.D. Marshall, *The Old Poor Law,* (1968), 12.
3. U. Henriques, *Before The Welfare State,* (1979), 13–16; G.W. Oxley, *Poor Relief in England and Wales 1601–1834,* (1974), 18–21; J.S. Taylor, 'The Impact of Pauper Settlement 1691–1834', in *Past and Present,* 73, (November, 1976).
4. Oxley, *ibid.,* 40–42.
5. B.A. Holderness, '"Open" and "close" parishes in England in the Eighteenth and Nineteenth centuries', *Agricultural History Review,* xx, pt. 2, (1972), 126–39.
6. A. Digby, *The Poor Law in Nineteenth-century England and Wales,* (1982), 6; J.S. Taylor, 'The Unreformed Workhouse 1776–1834', in E.W. Martin (ed.), *Comparative Development in Social Welfare,* (1972), 62; J.R. Poynter, *Society and Pauperism. English Ideas on Poor Relief 1795–1834,* (1969), 189.
7. S. and B. Webb, *English Poor Law History,* pt. 1; *The Old Poor Law,* (1927), 102. Documentary coverage is to be found in A.E. Bland, P.A. Brown and R.H. Tawney, *English Economic History Select Documents,* (1914), 650–4; and M.E. Rose, *The English Poor Law 1780–1930,* (1971), 26, 28.
8. For contractors see Oxley, *op. cit.,* 96. For a contemporary hostile comment see R.M. Eden, *The State of the Poor,* vol. 2, (1797), 168.
9. Oxley, *ibid.,* ch. 4. Supplement on medical relief by H. Marland, *Medicine and Society in Wakefield and Huddersfield 1780–1870,* (1987), 57–65.
10. On lunatics the references in note 9 should be supplemented by K. Jones, *Lunacy, Law and Conscience 1744–1845,* (1955), also R. Porter, *Mind-Forg'd Manacles,* (1987), 118–20.
11. Oxley, *op. cit.,* 74–7. U. Henriques, 'Bastardy and the New Poor Law', *Past and Present,* 37, (July, 1967).
12. M. Neumann, 'Speenhamland in Berkshire', in E.W. Martin (ed.), *op. cit.,* describes the development of this generalization. G. R. Boyer, *An Economic History of the English Poor Law 1750–1850,* (1990) argues that the major problem was seasonal unemployment.
13. For documents illustrating these practices see M.E. Rose, (1971), *op. cit.,* 56–9.
14. J.D. Marshall, *op. cit.,* 26–7 gives the statistics in a convenient form.
15. G. Himmelfarb, *The Idea of Poverty. England in the Early Industrial Age,* (1984), 126.

16. *Ibid.*, 133–5, 78–85. For fuller discussion see R.G. Cowherd, *Political Economists and the English Poor Laws*, (1978).

17. A. Brundage, *The Making of the New Poor Law*, (1967), 14, 60–1.

18. J.D. Marshall, 'The Nottinghamshire Reformers and their contribution to the Old Poor Law', *Economic History Review*, xiii, (1961).

19. J.T. Becher, *The Anti Pauper System*, (1828), 17–21. See also; M.E. Rose (1971), *op. cit.*, 73–4; Poynter, *op. cit.*, 313–4.

20. Poynter, *ibid.*, 316.

21. See e.g. notes 30–2 below.

22. There have been a number of editions of the Report on the Royal Commission on the Poor Laws, 1834'. For the student S.G. and E.O.A. Checkland (eds.), *The Poor Law Report of 1834* (1974), is the most convenient and references cited as Report are to this edition. For the impact on proprietors and employers of agricultural labour see Report, 141–55.

23. On the demoralization of the labour force see *ibid.*, 155–61, 167–9 and 264.

24. *Ibid.*, roundsmen, 102–4; roadworks, 110–12.

25. *Ibid.*, out-relief in general, 115–23.

26. B. Inglis, *Poverty and the Industrial Revolution* (1971), 344–5.

27. Report, *op. cit.*, criticism of existing workhouses, 124–7.

28. *Ibid.*, criticism of existing administration; overseers, 180–90; vestries, 190–203; magistrates, 203–41.

29. Sir J. Clapham, *An Economic History of Modern Britain*, (1949), vol. 1, 364; for the classic statement of enslavement see J.L. and B. Hammond, *The Village Labourer*, (1966 edn.), 158 *et seq.*; J.T. Krause, 'Changes in English Fertility and Mortality, 1781–1850', *Economic History Review*, xi, (1958).

30. M. Blaug, 'The Myth of the Old Poor Law and the Making of the New', *Journal of Economic History*, (1963), 184.

31. *Ibid.*, and 'The Poor Law Report Re-examined', *ibid.*, (1964).

32. D.A. Baugh, 'The Cost of Poor Relief in South-East England, 1790–1830', *Economic History Review*, xxviii, (Feb, 1975); D. McCloskey, 'New Perspectives on the Old Poor Law', *Explorations in Economic History*, x, (1973); E.H. Hunt, *British Labour History 1815–1914*, (1981), fn. 135; G. R. Boyer, *op. cit.*, 191, suggests the Poor Law had little effect on rural-urban migration.

33. J.P. Huzel, 'The Demographic Impact of the Old Poor Law', *Economic History Review*, xxxiii, (1980); However, G. R. Boyer, *ibid*, ch. 5 argues against Huzel: G.E. Mingay, *Enclosure and the Small Farmer in the Age of the Industrial Revolution*, (1968).

34. The introduction to S.G. and E.O.A. Checkland (eds.), (1974), 39. U. Henriques (1979), *op. cit.*, 32–3. See also J.S. Taylor, 'The Mythology of the Old Poor Law', *Journal of Economic History*, (1969).

35. Report, *op. cit.*, 275–8. Himmelfarb, *op. cit.*, 166.

36. *Ibid.*, 278–94. D.C. Barnett, 'Allotments and the Problem of Rural Poverty', in E.L. Jones and G.E. Mingay, *Land, Labour and Population in the Industrial Revolution*, (1967).

37. *Ibid.*, 325. Discussion of Labour Rate, 295–333.
38. *Ibid.*, 334–5.
39. *Ibid.*, 335.
40. *Ibid.*, 339, 343, 347, 374, 377–8, 375.
41. *Ibid.*, e.g. 359, 379–81, 386.
42. *Ibid.*, 338.
43. *Ibid.*, 339.
44. *Ibid.*, 418–9, 471.
45. *Ibid.*, Classification, 429–30; unions of parishes, 438, 442; staffing, 456, 471.
46. A. Brundage, *The Making of the New Poor Law 1832–9*, (1978), especially ch. 3 and 33–9.

CHAPTER THREE

TEETHING TROUBLES AND GROWING PAINS
c. 1834–64

Discussions concerning the New Poor Law have focussed most strongly on its formative years with the greatest attention being paid to the new administrative machine and the pattern of relief. In considering the administration attention has been concentrated on the novel feature of a central body seeking to impose its will on the new unit of local government. In the matter of relief it has been the problems of applying the concept to less eligibility through the workhouse test which has provoked discussion.

To some extent the course of both administration and relief are reflected in the official statistics. As might be expected of an administration pledged to the production of a more economical regime, the most reliable figures appear to be those concerned with expenditure. During this entire period spending seems to have been remarkably restrained. An initial fall in expenditure was followed by a slow overall rise, punctuated by somewhat sharper increases in the depression of the early 1840s and the impact of bad harvests, cholera and Irish immigration in the latter part of the decade. Overall this period shows an annual increase in expenditure of only 0.5 per cent per annum.[1]

In the context of a rising population and the associated problems of increasing urbanization, the low level of expenditure is surprising. This is even more so when it is considered that the new regime was founded upon the application of the workhouse test with its consequent expectation of an initially increased expenditure on officials and buildings. For the supporter of the new system economy could be seen as the reward for a strong and efficient administration, a view fostered by the central authority. For the opponent of the new regime these apparent savings could be represented as resulting from cruelly enforced economies. The favourable view was the one which predominated in the nineteenth century, whereas the pessimistic critics have provided the orthodox view for much of this century. However, in the writings of the last two decades, economy has been seen as partially the result of the limitations of the system of administration.

From Bumbledom to Bureaucracy: Administrative Evolution or Revolution

From 1834–47 central supervision was carried out by a three-man Poor Law Commission with Edwin Chadwick acting as its secretary. From 1847–71 the central authority was the Poor Law Board, a government department under the control of a minister. To assist in the task of creating and supervising the new units of local administration the central authority had the services of a number of visiting officials of whom the assistant commissioners, termed inspectors after 1847, were by far the most important. The officials were supported by a massive correspondence between the central authority and the local unions in which orders and advice were given to the local authorities and in return evidence was gathered on a wide range of topics. Finally, the central authority slowly obtained some limited financial inducements in the form of cheap loans and grants to assist them in gaining the cooperation of the local authorities.

To a small but active minority of contemporary critics the establishment of a supervisory central authority, and in particular one with such a degree of independence from parliament, was an unconstitutional interference in the traditional rights of local government. In general nineteenth-century comment was to become increasingly favourable to the New Poor Law's system of administration. It was seen as setting the pattern for future central and local government relationships, partly because it could be used for a wide variety of additional services, but more significantly by acting as the prototype for an increasing range of central and local authority initiatives producing general bureaucratic improvement. This favourable impression was often based on the claims of the central authority and was aided by the fact that the first history of the new administration was the work of George Nicholls, a member of the original Poor Law Commission. The emphasis in nineteenth-century works was upon the growth of a sound administration with improved services being targeted to favoured sections of the destitute such as the sick, children and later the aged.[2]

For much of the twentieth century historians have taken a much more pessimistic view of the New Poor Law. In this case the leading initial work of the Webbs, represented not only the most substantial work available, but had been produced by activists leading the campaign to end the New Poor Law. For the Webbs, the new regime was 'revolutionary' giving 'a dogmatically uniform direction to English Poor Law policy'. In the 1920s the popular social history of G.M. Trevelyan echoed the Webbs, describing the New Poor Law as 'ruthless and doctrinaire', and in the 1930s, reflecting the fears of the time, H.L. Beales referred to the regime as 'social fascism'.[3]

In the period following the Second World War the consensus view that social and economic prosperity was attainable through the intervention of the State and the continued advance of the welfare state was paralleled by the greater interest taken by historians in the nineteenth-century origins of the bureaucratic machine and its contribution to the social services of the future. At first the most important work was in the traditional form of biographies of leading figures such as Chadwick. However, from the late 1950s discussion was concerned with explaining the mechanism of administrative growth. Debate was largely over the respective roles of the pressure of intolerable evils and the collectivist possibilities of Benthamism as the originators of State intervention in the early Victorian period. The protagonists did not dispute the significance of intervention and both sides recognized the importance of the momentum supplied by the administrator. For Oliver MacDonagh it was the appointment of executive officers 'we might almost say . . . which brought the process to life'. More specifically Jennifer Hart saw the 1834 Act establish 'an autocratic authority in the Poor Law Commission with the widest powers of controlling poor law authorities in the minutest details of their work.'[4]

The 1960s were to provide something of a water shed in the historiography of the New Poor Law. In the early years of the decade Roberts highlighted the work of Poor Law inspectors and Lambert saw the adminitration's supervision of vaccination as 'A Victorian National Health Service'. However, by the end of the decade Ruth Hodgkinson saw new ideas in medical relief, '. . . infiltrated into orders and regulations very slowly and often painfully, and developments came not from the small "expert" administration as it had been hoped, but through the pressure from below'.[5]

By the late 1960s attention was also being drawn to the wide range of local experience. Since this time the orthodox view of a powerful central authority has been increasingly modified by the publication of Poor Law studies based on local records and, in particular, the impressive but daunting Ministry of Health records detailing correspondence between central and local authorities and the reports of visiting officials such as inspectors and auditors. This evidence has tended to show the difficulties faced by the central authority in dealing with the local boards of guardians, the complexity of political, social and economic factors which dictated the pace of change and finally the resulting variety of experience.[6]

In 1971 Dr Lubenow attempted to reconcile the views of a powerful central authority facing increased local resistance by introducing the concept of incrementalism. Here local authority intransigence was not subjected to direct attack but rather cunningly encouraged to follow the line of an increasingly able bureaucracy which advanced its values according to the local situation.[7] However, although the existence of rising bureaucratic skills is largely accepted the weight of current opinion continues to emphasize the limitations of the central authority.

The Central Authority and its Agents

The Poor Law Commission was the subject of considerable attack from a wide range of opponents. The popular image of the 'three bashaws of Somerset House' dictatorially interfering with the traditional dispensers of Poor Relief was to some extent supported by their own propaganda which may well have strengthened the vigour of their opposition. However, to the administration it was the limitations to their powers which increasingly controlled the progress of their policy. In parliament the lack of an adequate spokesman made them appear a soft target, and the Commission was subjected to continual sniping. Moreover, there appeared to be a lack of overall government support. Their initial limited authorization for five years, was replaced by an annual authorization from 1839–42, followed by a further extension for five years. The feeling of impermanence was no doubt heightened by the refusal of the governments of this period to improve their accommodation although Somerset House became increasingly cramped and unhealthy. They were refused assistance in overcoming the opposition of the Gilbert Unions to central control and, of greater significance, they were not permitted to force reluctant unions to provide workhouses. The sense of insecurity was probably heightened by troubles within the central administration.[8]

Chadwick, disappointed at not being made a Commissioner can be seen as a man held back by a dislike of his humble origins, or as a dangerous doctrinaire intriguer whose loyalties could never be relied upon. Chadwick was undoubtedly usually prepared to test central authority powers to their limits, as is indicated by his frequent interventions in union affairs. However, of the Commissioners, only Nichol could be regarded as an ally. Both Shaw Lefevre and Frankland Lewis were more cautious, regarding Chadwick as a man always likely to overplay his hand. When Frankland Lewis was succeeded by his son, George Cornewall Lewis, in 1839, internal dissensions appear to have seriously disrupted the work of the central authority.[9]

The initial task of the Commission was to establish the local administrative machinery. Aided by good harvests and the building of railways, the Commissioners quickly got into their stride in establishing unions in the rural south. With the support of local ratepayers they were able to overcome sporadic local resistance and their annual reports of 1835 and 1836 support the confident claims which had been voiced in the report of the Royal Commission. They were able to boast of lower rates, rising wages and the moral regeneration of the labourer.[10]

The Commissioners appear to have been optimistic in expecting swift progress in the unionization of the north of England. Their success in the south and the absence of any ingrained allowance system encouraged their belief that all would be complete in time for the unions to undertake local responsibility for the registration of births, marriages and deaths in 1837. However, there were many in the north who saw little reason to change their existing administration, and the use of the workhouse test against large-scale unemployment seemed to fly in the face of commonsense. In bad years workhouses could never be large enough to accommodate the unemployed and their families, while in good years they would prove a needless expense. Against such views the assistant commissioners argued that the new regime would introduce further economies by reducing outdoor relief to the able-bodied, by ending the payment of rents, by curbing unnecessary legal costs and extravagent expenses charged by overseers in settlement matters and by reducing payments to the mothers of illegitimate children.

While northern ratepayers were not averse to a more economical administration, the success of the central authority was determined by local conditions of which the state of the local economy and its immediate prospects appear to have been of special significance. It was unfortunate for the Commissioners that they sought to apply the new regime in the West Riding and Lancashire at a time when the dominant textile industry was entering a period of depression. While the prospect of rising rates and a dislike of London super-vision encouraged ratepayer opposition, the threat of outdoor relief being withdrawn from the able-bodied at a time of crisis aroused working-class fears. Previous agitation for factory reform provided the organization necessary to mobilize protest which the doctrinaire Assistant Commissioner Power obviously underestimated. Opposition was strongest in those urban communities which were dependent on a single industry. Major towns around which unions were to be formed such as Huddersfield and Rochdale became centres for confrontation. This could take the form of refusing to elect guardians, electing opponents onto boards of guardians and threatening supporters and officials with violence.[11] Serious opposition, occurring at a time when the central authority was itself facing parliamentary investigation concerning its future, produced a more cautious approach. Caution was made easier by Chadwick's diminishing influence. Eventually, a less aggressive approach and the distractions of Chartism saved the day in the textile districts, but in

80

the grey area of central and local authority relations the advantage had veered towards the unions. [12]

Thus, although the combination of local prosperity and an accommodating assistant commissioner was able to secure an apparently easy passage in the north-east, the depression of 1842 and the replacement of the popular Walsham by the doctrinaire Assistant Commissioner Hawley turned cooperation to obstruction. The New Poor Law was designed to tackle the problems of an overabundance of labour in rural southern England and it is difficult to imagine any scenario in the industrial north where the onset of economic difficulties would not place strain on central and local government relationships. Disaffection was to be even more wide-spread, however. As the mid-1840s approached the honeymoon period had ended in rural Norfolk and, in Wales, Assistant Commissioner Day was sacrificed as the scapegoat for the Rebecca riots. [13]

The Poor Law Commission was replaced in 1847. Local independence combined with a divided and understaffed central authority to permit many departures from the model envisaged in 1834. The exposure of the resulting abuses provided ammunition for the enemies of the New Poor Law. The revelation of the Andover Scandal, where workhouse inmates had been on a diet so limited that they had been forced to eat the rotten scraps of meat attached to old bones provided for bone-crushing, had resulted in a parliamentary enquiry. The report which followed was critical not only of the local authority but of the inadequacies and divisions within the central authority. The result was the replacement of the Poor Law Commission by the Poor Law Board, whose president was a member of the government of the day. [14] While this may have assisted in dealing with parliamentary criticism, the basic problems of exercising control over reluctant local authorities remained. The continuing limitations of central authority powers meant that advance could only be achieved by a mixture of tact and persistence and this was slow to produce results.

The channels of communication between the central authority and the localities were initially centred on a considerable volume of correspondence and the use of the assistant commissioners. The correspondence was often concerned with the most trivial of details, giving the appearance of a considerable degree of influence being exercised by the central authority. However, time-consuming correspondence on such minor issues as individual medical fees for minor operations, and routine enquiries into every new appointment, weighed heavily on the inadequate clerical services available to both central and local authorities. At times important issues were seriously delayed, neglected and on occasion even lost for years. In practice much depended upon the willingness of the individual union to cooperate. Some boards of guardians became masters of constructive inaction. Such authorities did not challenge the central authority directly but rather presented alternative schemes, or, raised different priorities, in an effort to delay and possibly evade action by exploiting the inefficiencies inherent in the process of correspondence. The central authority sought to rationalize proceedings by an increasing use of forms and statistical returns. However, the records frequently refer to delays and inaccuracies in the presentation of such returns and matters were not assisted by the failure of the central authority's civil servants to develop a satisfactory filing system. The routine was also found wanting in that the returns were designed to reflect what the bureaucracy thought should be happening 'rather than the main functions which were actually being fulfilled'.[15]

Eventually such information was to assist progress towards a more uniform service, the Poor Law Commission making regional comparisons on such matters as workhouse diets, the size of medical districts and the salaries of relieving officers. Returns could give early warning of abuses in the case of workhouse overcrowding or failure to implement the public vaccination policy. However, as the volume of correspondence increased over time, greater skills were being continually cancelled by the inadequacies of expenditure on administrative staff.

To further their regional aims the central authority relied on the activities of a number of visiting officials. The assistant commissioners/inspectors were assisted by the work of district auditors, by the appointment of specialist inspectors in areas such as medical relief and the education and care of children, and by representatives of the Commissioners of Lunacy. Two things marred progress in this area. Firstly, there was a marked reluctance to finance an adequate inspectorate and, equally important, the central authority showed throughout 'a smug layman's arrogance' in dealing with expert opinion.[16]

The central authority was essentially dependent on the powers of persuasion of its regional inspectors. However, the most common generalization concerning this body is that they were seriously overworked. Central government economies meant that their districts were too large for effective supervision. Initially this was exacerbated by the inadequacies of the transport system, by the payment of only limited expenses and the lack of clerical assistance. To be successful the inspector needed to understand the vagaries of the local economy and to be able to exploit the local political situation to his advantage. Yet in practice many found that even the minimum twice yearly visits were impossible to maintain and by the end of the century these had often been replaced by an annual visit.

Initial appointments appear to have been the product of a mixture of patronage and expertise. The inspectorate was largely drawn from county squires and ambitious young barristers, and in addition to legal knowledge some appeared to have made some study of political economy. In the early years, as the administration struggled to establish itself, the inspectorate appears to have had considerable freedom of action, but in the second half of the century they have been seen as 'administrative beasts of burden; their role reduced to an endless form filling which stultified any individual initiative or interest.'[17]

Although the inspectorate accepted the principles of 1834 as the road which all should follow there were considerable differences in their methods, the doctrinaire rigidities of those of Power's or Hawley's persuasion contrasting with those who followed the more flexible methods of Kay or Walsham. To some extent such differences persisted in the more regimented second half of the century, the more humanitarian Knollys, who acted as a chief inspector in the 1890s, contrasting with the articulate but reactionary J.S. Davy, who presented such an unfortunate image at the Royal Commission of 1905–9.

The early inspectors suffered because of the divisions within the central authority and things were little better when this was replaced by the excessive caution of its successor. In cases of dispute, with either boards of guardians or other inspectors, they could normally expect to receive little support from their superiors. Pressure on their time, the timidity of the central authority, and the reluctance of individual unions to engage in expenditure caused inspectors to place most attention on the eradication of major abuses which might produce scandal, and sometimes, establishing their own priorities regarding particular aspects of workhouse provision or categories of pauper. Although the appointment of specialist inspectors in education and visits from the representatives of Commissioners of Lunacy assisted in the reduction of the workload, they also led to occasions where priorities were in conflict, a situation eagerly exploited by economizing boards of guardians.

The most important visitor to a union after the inspector was the district auditor. The district auditor by the nature of his position, was a more negative influence, but effective audit was crucial if acceptable bureaucratic standards were to be obtained. In this respect it is generally accepted that, 'in matters of audit the Poor Law provided the model for others to follow.'[18] The appointment of district auditors was not undertaken until 1844 and it was not until the 1860s that the central authority had effective control over appointments. Until 1866 auditors were only allowed to inspect completed accounts, and this after a week's notice. While auditors complained regularly of overwork, boards of guardians protested at the long intervals between their visits. Effective audit undoubtedly made a considerable impact on the honesty and efficiency of local officials, and while defalcation was a major problem in the early years of the New Poor Law it had virtually disappeared by the end of the century. As with the inspectorate, progress was delayed by the size of the workload of the individual auditor and the fact that in any area of doubt the central authority was reluctant to become involved. Discrepancies in accounts were always initially regarded as a matter for the board of guardians. While technically an auditor could not permit any illegal expenditure, surcharges were normally remitted by the central authority with a warning as to future conduct. In view of the overall caution exercised by the central authority the individual unions were to have a greater role in Poor Law policy than the report of 1834 had intended, and consequently frustrated the aim of a more uniform regime.

The Local Foundation

The rapid formation of the unions was the most obvious sign of the success of the central administration. By 1839 90 per cent of the parishes of England and Wales had been unionized. The ideal of a market town surrounded by a group of rural parishes would have been impractical in many cases, but what was achieved bore little resemblance to any form of plan. Speed was purchased at the price of making concessions to powerful local influences and bypassing areas of opposition. The result was the formation of unions of a bewildering variety of shapes, acreages, population and wealth. In achieving the propaganda victory of a speedy unionization the prospect for a uniform system of administration had been severely handicapped.[19]

The control of the unions by elected boards of guardians was intended to favour a more economical administration. During the early years the *ex-officio* county magistrates often played an active role, but the long-term trend was for the majority to attend infrequently, leaving administration in the hands of the representatives of the ratepayers. The result was that in rural unions decisions were reached by local farmers and in urban unions by small businessmen and shopkeepers. Although attendance seems to have varied between unions the overall impression is of limited interest. Guardians representing outlying parishes were, as might be expected, infrequent attenders. Indeed in such parishes it was often difficult to find candidates to stand for election, and where an individual guardian had a long record of representing a particular parish this had often been achieved without any contested election. In central urban parishes elections were sometimes contested with considerable vigour but inevitably they often became an extension of the broader, local political battlefield.[20] In view of the general level of low attendance, control of a union could pass into the hands of small groups of activists who varied in their support for the policy of the central authority. With such small attendance the introduction of an effective committee system, essential to achieve effective supervision, was often delayed, and in day-to-day administration the chairman and vice-chairman of most boards exerted a significant influence. However, at moments of crisis, which frequently involved discussion of increased expenditure, attendance would generally improve and at such times most boards of guardians showed themselves to be economizers. Even in times of prosperity boards of guardians were concerned with the interests of the lesser ratepayer. Attempts to increase expenditure were carefully scrutinized and where it proved impossible to avoid expenditure the second line of defence was to seek a cheaper alternative.

Even where a board of guardians had decided to support higher expenditure to pay salaries and erect suitable workhouses they faced what was often an insuperable burden. The new system of administration had retained the parish as the basis of union finance. It could be argued that the retention of the parish would ensure a more careful supervision of finance as the smaller unit would show a greater interest in economy. No doubt also there were those who saw the retention of the parish as helpful in lessening opposition to the new unions. However, it is also possible that the belief in the efficacy of the principle of less eligibility, when reinforced by the workhouse test was sufficiently strong to allow the issue of financial reform to be set aside in the interests of a more rapid introduction of legislation.

It is never difficult in any period to find contemporary criticism of the rating system. However, the exceptional level of criticism which accompanied the latter years of the Old Poor Law and the early years of its successor was not without foundation. A major area of adverse comment concerned the retention of the parish as the unit of finance. The new unions were to inherit the defects of the previous administration which the Report of 1834 had denounced as 'inconsistent and capricious'. Problems were now increased by the fact that the unit of resource was smaller than that authorising the expenditure.[21]

That the individual parish was a unit of limited potential had long been recognized with regard to workhouse provision. The method of apportioning expenditure in the new local authority made each parish responsible not only for the cost of relieving its own poor, but used this expenditure as a basis for calculating its contribution to the common fund of the union. The result was that the cost of expenditure on such vital matters as staffing and the cost of providing adequate workhouse buildings fell most heavily on the poorest parishes. In practice, therefore, a union was effectively limited to what its poorest parishes could afford and, in times of exceptional demand, the rate burden often became too exacting resulting in conflict between union and parish.

There was therefore a not unreasonable belief that union finances were not only inadequately based but were also extremely inequitable. That such views were held by the poorer parishes was easy to comprehend, but complaints were also voiced by many outlying parishes. Where a union had an urban core of parishes, the peripheral rural parishes often believed that they carried too heavy a burden. Certainly before the 1860s many unions had problems in valuing industrial and urban property and to some extent these claims were probably correct, although the heaviest burdens fell on the householders in the poorest parishes. However, the widespread complaints of unequal treatment certainly contributed to the reluctance to authorize expenditure on items related to the common fund.

Critics of the rating system were strengthened by evidence of widespread inefficiencies in its administration. Here also much was the result of the differing practices adopted by individual parishes. The Royal Commission had expressed its concern on the question of valuation, systems being 'inexplicable', 'outdated' and open to 'partiality and abuse'. The pace and unplanned nature of urban growth together with misplaced economies on officials meant that the situation often remained below any acceptable standard. Rating lists were not updated and the need for revaluation frequently ignored. Poorer parishes found that it paid to be inefficient, often maintaining rating lists which deliberately undervalued their property.

A more obvious concern for the general public was the system of rate collection. This important, but laborious, duty was often performed by lowly paid, part-time officials who were usually encouraged to take ill-defined but rapidly expanding duties by the offer of commission. The collector was probably the best known of a union's officials. It is unfortunate that the records suggest he was also its least honest. The initial weaknesses in the system of audit mentioned above encouraged sharp practice and, as the dishonest were exposed, it was not only their numbers, but the sums involved and the length of time which some had escaped detection which shocked the ratepayer. However, the dishonesty of the rate collectors was easier to correct than the more fundamental financial weaknesses.

Although the problems of finance received considerable discussion, the opposition of rural vested interests and the varied and complex schemes advanced for reform prevented any more than legislative tinkering in the period down to the 1860s. Indeed on balance alterations in the Law of Settlement may have worsened the position of the poorer parish in this period.[22]

The Law of Settlement was little altered in 1834 and the retention of the parish as the unit of settlement meant that in rural areas 'open' parishes remained critical of the financial burden thrust upon them by 'close' parishes. Although, B.A. Holderness has drawn attention to the fact that critics of the Law of Settlement may well have exaggerated the extent of 'close' parishes, there were areas where the problem was to remain of considerable importance. Thus Anne Digby quotes the considerable range of parish rates in Norfolk which in 1847 varied from ½d. to 12s. 4d. and which had only shown slight improvement by 1861. This wide difference she concluded was the result of 'close' parishes making use of the Law of Settlement at the expense of their 'open' neighbours.[23]

The problem of settlement was to have an increasing effect upon urban unions. The rapid growth of industrial towns in the first half of the nineteenth century was largely the result of migration. By 1851 many urban communities had more than half their population born outside of their boundaries. In addition there was massive movement within urban communities. Hence the range of bilateral arrangements developed under the Old Poor Law became more extensive, with the added complexity that movements were by this time often occurring between urban communities. Michael Rose has pointed out that approximately 20 per cent of those relieved in the West Riding in the period 1839–46 were non-resident.[24] Legislation passed in 1846 introduced a new concept whereby anyone resident in a parish for five years became irremovable. After an outcry from hard-pressed urban parishes the cost of these 'irremovable' poor was transferred to the common fund of the union. However, this was a doubtful blessing at this time as a major contemporary complaint among urban parishes was that the burden of the common fund fell most heavily on the poorer urban parishes. Thus problems of settlement remained a major cause for concern among both rural and urban unions. In 1861 when the Law of Settlement was in process of being reformed many industrial towns and cities were finding that from 30 to 60 per cent of their expenditure on Poor Relief was on the irremovable. Throughout the period 1847–61 proposals for the reform of the Law of Settlement were usually resisted on the grounds that further change might increase the financial burden of the irremovable poor. Hence reform of the Law of Settlement, as with many other issues, became associated with the need to introduce a radical reform of the system of local finance. Until this was achieved in the early 1860s the evils concerning both finance and settlement which had been exposed but not remedied by the Report of the Royal Commission of 1834 continued to cause problems for many unions and were a further factor frustrating the aims of the central authority.

The problems which resulted from a central authority of limited powers and displaying increasing caution in their use, working with economy-minded guardians operating within the constraints of an unreformed system of finance can best be judged by estimating progress in the essential areas of recruiting a professional staff and the provision of adequate workhouse facilities.

Staffing was one area where the central authority had clearly stated powers. They had the right to approve appointments and to dismiss those found unsuitable. In addition, from 1846, they obtained the power to make grants-in-aid of the salaries of medical officers and schoolteachers, an inducement which was later applied to a number of other officials.

Ideally, a union required a clerk to act as its legal officer, relieving officers to advise the guardians on the appropriate treatment for applicants for relief, a workhouse master and matron, and medical officers for both outdoor and workhouse sick. In addition the workhouse needed a number of subordinate officials such as a porter to control entry and exit, schoolteachers, and a variety of nurses and attendants to supervise other categories of inmate and assist in the running of the institution. As the only uniform unit of local government under central direction additional duties were placed on unions, such as the registration of births, marriages and deaths in 1837 and nuisance removals in 1847, each new duty requiring additional appointments. Initially, the desire of the central authority for economy and its failure to clearly define duties left considerable scope for local authority initiative. Unfortunately in many unions a pattern of low paid, underqualified and overworked staff resulted, which the central authority found difficult to change.[25]

In such key areas as relieving officers and workhouse masters the only experienced staff were those who had served under the Old Poor Law. In the early stages the central authority's powers of approval meant little since, apart from advanced age, they had little information on which to refuse to sanction an appointment. Large numbers of officials were to be dismissed for incompetence or dishonesty. It is difficult to decide how far this was the result of previous bad practices being continued and to what extent it was the result of low salaries leading to the recruitment of poor staff. Salaries in general were proportionate to duties, varying with the size, population and extent of poverty in relief districts and with the size of workhouse for indoor officials. In urban areas the rapid growth of population meant that relief districts which were often originally too large became unmanageable. Yet boards of guardians were always guided by the desire for economy in the appointment of officials. In the face of pressure due to increasing duties boards tended to offer a small-salary increase to an existing official rather than appoint an additional officer, and at times such increases took the form of temporary bonuses on the grounds that pauperism was expected to decrease. When the division of an overcrowded relief district could no longer be avoided and an additional officer was appointed this could be accompanied by a reduction in the salary of the existing official. Boards of guardians preferred to appoint part-time officials and where full-time officials were appointed they sought to consolidate several tasks into the work of a single official. Thus in the Nottingham Union one officer initially fulfilled the duties of clerk, relieving officer and workhouse master.[26] Increasingly the central authority objected to such consolidation and unions, interested in economy, responded by making a greater use of part-time appointments, naming the same officer for several posts. Thus clerks could also operate as registrars; rate collectors as nuisance removal officers and district medical officers were often also acting as the workhouse medical officer and sometimes monopolizing the position of public vaccinator. The widespread complaints of the forbidding demeanour of relieving officers and the limited attention provided by medical officers were to some extent the result of overwork and inadequate recompense.

The workhouse master was ideally recruited from ex-soldiers or policemen. In practice often the only suitable applicants had gained experience in the maligned workhouses of the Old Poor Law or as prison officers. The position improved over time as those with experience under the New Poor Law sought promotion within the service. Whereas outdoor officials were invariably local, workhouse masters and sometimes schoolteachers, being provided with accommodation, were more mobile and sought to increase their income by moving to larger establishments. However, there were many cases where boards of guardians, interested only in economy, were rewarded with inefficiency and corruption. Where it was exposed, scandal involving a workhouse master or matron was sure to attract considerable publicity; although no doubt inadequate supervision meant much was not discovered and many instances would be hushed-up by boards of guardians anxious to avoid the attentions of either the press or central authority. Although the central authority had the power to veto appointments and to dismiss officials, the career of the notorious psychopath George Catch, who was able to blight the lives of the inmates of three workhouses, illustrates how ineffective such control could be.[27] The majority of workhouse masters and matrons were married couples, which was exploited by some guardians as an excuse to offer a lower salary. Where such couples had families they were normally expected to have them raised outside the workhouse as a safeguard to workhouse rations and demands on accommodation. The workhouse master and matron bore a heavy responsibility for staff and inmates, yet the more paid assistants they had the less many boards of guardians believed should be their salary. The smaller workhouses carried very low salaries and appear to have had a rapid turnover of staff and in this respect the smaller rural workhouses tended to be most affected.

Within the workhouse the majority of subordinate officials were initially paupers or former paupers recruited from the outdoor pauper list as a measure of economy. Payments ranged from additional rations, such as an extra meat dinner in the case of paupers, to little more than board and lodgings plus pocket money in the case of those appointed from pauper lists. Drunkeness, petty theft and ill-health were partnered by incompetence in the charges brought against such officials. Even the provision of a parliamentary grant towards the schoolteacher's salary made only a slow impact on the quality of appointment, the workhouse life having as little appeal for the trained teacher as it will be shown to have had for the trained nurse. Thus in 1874 the Inspector of Schools for the northern district commented, 'On looking through the list of workhouse schoolteachers in my district I cannot help thinking that an undue proportion of them are dissatisfied with their position or are much less use to it than they might be.'[28]

The central authority was concerned to encourage the replacement of pauper labour by paid appointments. However, the combination of low pay and residence in the workhouse made recruitment of skilled staff difficult. The trained nurse was a rarity in workhouses before the 1870s, and even by that date was only to be found in the larger urban unions. In many cases the only progress to be noted was the purely cosmetic change of name from pauper nurse to pro-bationer nurse.[29]

Medical officers were the only appointments with recognizable professional qualifications for much of this period and they have tended to receive more attention from the historian. Here economy was introduced in some cases by making applicants tender for appointments, by making them supply drugs prescribed from their salaries·and by giving too high a patient load. In addition patients could only see the district medical officer with the consent of the relieving officer and in the workhouse the medical officer was regarded as subordinate to the master, who even had the power to decide whether the medical officer should be called out on the occasion of childbirth, for which the medical officer was entitled to an additional fee. The central authority made efforts to insist on high qualifications and to control the size of medical districts, although boards of guardians in offering inadequate salaries were often able to avoid such controls by claiming that no alternative could be found. There is some discussion as to why medical officers were prepared to undertake such poorly remunerated duties. One reason advanced is that it was a way to build up a practice for a newly-qualified doctor. Alternatively, it was sometimes seen that established practitioners undertook such work as a means of keeping out competition. In practice low pay meant that duties were often delegated to unqualified assistants, a fact which often came to light when an enquiry was held into a death or following a dispute between a workhouse master and the medical officer. Although, Ruth Hodgkinson shows that the growing professionalism of doctors in the nineteenth century produced many excellent Poor Law medical officers, who were a major source for improved workhouse conditions and, intermittently, the profession as a whole sought to improve pay and conditions, the position has also been seen as remaining unsatisfactory throughout the nineteenth century, with Poor Law medical officers being regarded as of second-rate status at all times.[30]

Adverse comment upon staffing was probably the most common complaint from the central authority to the unions. The combination of detailed returns on duties, the visits of inspectors and auditors and the payments of grants-in-aid of salaries did ensure slow progress. Often change was governed by local factors. Exposure of scandals caused boards of guardians to tighten arrangements and give a greater definition to duties. Supply and demand were often more potent forces for change than central authority pressure, and in the case of minor appointments the shortage of pauper labour in the workhouse was probably at least as significant as the central authority in governing the change from pauper to paid appointments. Thus, although staffing improved in this period it was often more apparent in numbers than quality.

Although the provision of an effective workhouse was a central feature of the new regime, the central authority's powers were confined to demanding a limited expenditure on the improvement of an existing workhouse and to ordering the closure of buildings which were regarded as seriously defective. In order to obtain expenditure on new buildings the central authority had to rely on the persuasive powers of its inspectorate, which could be reinforced by the offer of a cheap loan to cover some of the building costs.

The Royal Commission's belief in the possibility of paupers being placed in separate buildings quickly evaporated before demands for economy. It began to be argued that the single large workhouse would have the greater impact and should also be cheaper to administer. It was claimed it would be easier to inspect, more able to cater for the simultaneous admission and release of families, cost less to staff and be more adaptable to changes in the composition of the inmates. In practice necessity was paraded as a virtue. However, even to take the cheaper alternative, a board of guardians needed convincing that the erection of a workhouse was worth the expense. Boards of guardians were more amenable where it was felt that the result would be a reduction in the rates in the not too distant future. Only where this view was accepted was it possible to overcome parochial resistance to such a large burden being placed upon the common fund of the union.[31]

The ideal workhouse of the 1830s as suggested by the model plans advanced by the central authority was to be separated into male and female sections. Within each section there would be subdivisions for the three main classes; aged and infirm, able-bodied, and boys and girls aged between two and fifteen. Children under two should be in a nursery attached to the female section. Each class would have its separate day rooms, exercise yards and dormitories. The workhouse also needed an entrance which was controllable by the porter, with a reception area where new arrivals could be classified, cleansed and fitted with uniforms. The work-house also need a kitchen, bakery, dining hall, laundry, workshop area, stores and bathing and toilet facilities. In addition there would have to be accommodation for the master and matron and perhaps facilities for the holding of meetings of boards of guardians or their committees. By the 1850s demands had risen to include sick wards, with separate accommodation for the infectious and the insane, schoolrooms for the children and separate accommodation for vagrants.[32]

The extent to which these ideals were met varied with the locality. In much of the rural south and east anticipated savings from the ending of the allowance system and the belief that the workhouse would assist in disciplining the labour force ensured considerable cooperation. In its First Annual Report the Poor Law Commissioners recorded the approval of 127 new workhouses, the majority of which could be classed as large, 69 holding between three and five hundred beds. In addition a number of existing workhouses were being substantially altered to comply more closely with the system of classification laid down by the central authority.

Acceptance of the need to spend ratepayers money on workhouse provision was never universally popular even in the south and east, but it became more difficult to justify in other areas. That remote areas such as Cornwall and much of Wales should remain wedded to the unsuitable poor-houses of the old regime was disappointing but not a major disaster. However, the failure of the central authority to obtain adequate support in the metropolitan area and in the Midland towns, particularly in Nottinghamshire, which many saw as the cradle of reform, was much more dangerous. In view of their opposition to the whole idea of the New Poor Law the northern textile area produced the major examples of resistance. In the extreme case, Todmorden, the union sold off its existing workhouses and survived without any institution. Only four new workhouses had been built in the textile area by 1846, although many of the old poor-houses were difficult to convert to even a pretence of compliance with the wishes of the central authority. The absence of classification meant that children shared beds with adults in the Bolton workhouse and in Leeds, 'copulating in the privies which was the great public scandal of the old regime continued under the new'. Although the four northernmost counties appeared more amenable to the pressures of the central authority, spending on workhouse accommodation was limited. Where new workhouses were built they tended to be inexpensive and many unions relied on the updating of existing buildings. Thus Sunderland with an expenditure of just over £4,000 was a high spender by north-eastern standards but this would have been very modest by the standards of the south-east.[33]

Objections to the building of workhouses were often an extension of the more general opposition to central authority supervision. For those professing sympathy to the new regime there was the argument that the existing administration was a sufficient deterrent. When evils were exposed they were countered by arguments that conditions in urban slums or poorer rural parishes were even less eligible. Those unsympathetic to the new regime often posed as the defenders of the poor, particularly in the case of those unemployed as the result of problems in local industry. All boards of guardians claimed to be acting in the defence of the interests of the ratepayer.

The rapid population growth in many urban unions and the growing demand by the central authority for more specialized accommodation for the sick, children and vagrants made many workhouses appear increasingly unsuitable. However, the 1840s were hardly a propitious time for urging increased expenditure on workhouses. The depression of the early 1840s often produced localized drives for economy in all aspects of administration and relief. At such times the influence of the central authority was at its lowest when urging increased expenditure. Thus in good years unions eager for economy would urge that additional expenditure was unnecessary, while in bad times they had the more cogent defence that the ratepayers could not afford additional expense.

Unions rarely admitted that additional expenditure on work-houses was necessary. Rather it was usually urged upon them by the inspectorate sometimes with the assistance of local medical officers. When faced with evidence of serious defects which could not be ignored many boards of guardians proposed cheap alternatives as opposed to expensive building projects, and the central authority often had to approve temporary measures rather than be faced with no action at all. Thus the Sunderland workhouse was opened in 1838 after expenditure on altering the best of the available parochial workhouses. Yet this building was accepted as inadequate within a year. A committee of guardians proposed the addition of a new three-storey wing, but this ambitious proposal was shelved in favour of a decision to make fuller use of the workhouse attics and basement. Thus the attics became dormitories and the basement became day-rooms; increasing the workhouse capacity from 200 to

300 beds. Continued pressure on the workhouse was met by continual re-allocation of the existing space. Thus the mangle room became a day-room and the day-rooms were converted into sick wards, with the female sick being housed in the reception area. This workhouse was never to have an infectious ward, a bakery or adequate work space. Although the need for additional hospital accommodation was accepted in 1846 it had to await the opening of a new workhouse in 1855 and even then matters remained unsatisfactory. Within five years of the new workhouse opening the process of readaptation had recommenced. Pressure on the accommodation for both sick and children had been met by turning the washroom into an infectious ward and the male insane ward into a children's sick ward, with the insane being housed in what had been the workhouse mortuary.[34]

Expenditure could be forced on guardians with the revelation of serious defects as at Coventry where the guardians were finally forced into action after an epidemic had resulted in the death of one-quarter of the inmates.[35] However, at times the acceptance of the need for expenditure by a board of guardians could arouse fierce ratepayer opposition. Thus the entire political complexion of Nottingham changed in 1840–1 following a decision by the board of guardians to build a new workhouse. The town council, board of guardians and a parliamentary by-election were affected. Similarly a close vote in favour of building a new workhouse in Sheffield in 1855 aroused passions reminiscent of the 1830s opposition. Thus the best the central authority could obtain, and this after closing down part of the existing workhouse because of its unsuitability, were alterations to the existing workhouse. Although the Sheffield workhouse was to be the cause of repeated complaints throughout the 1860s, being plagued with dampness and still having uncovered stone floors, the guardians refused to take action on the grounds that the ratepayers would oppose central government intervention.[36]

By the early 1850s most unions had a workhouse but many were 'very imperfect'.[37] However, the 1850s saw greater interest in workhouse-building especially in the north of England. In part this was made possible by better economic conditions, but the change in policy reflected a change in the case presented by the central authority. Workhouses were no longer urged for the treatment of the able-bodied, but improvements were now suggested for the better care of sick and children or the deterrence of the vagrant. It was a sign of this new emphasis that when the new Sunderland workhouse was opened in 1855, of its total accommodation of 500 inmates, only 37 beds were allocated for the able-bodied of both sexes. The central authority had not forgotten its principles, rather it hoped that by expanding facilities for other groups it would indirectly create space for the able-bodied. However, even after three decades of support for workhouse expansion the principle of the workhouse test remained a largely untried solution in urban areas and the demand for specialist accommodation for other classes of pauper was making the workhouse an ever more expensive institution.

In matters of administration the supervising central authority had shown a diminishing zeal for revolutionary change, rather there had taken place a slow bureaucratic evolution. By 1860 it had succeeded in establishing a new unit of local administration in the unions, normally with a nucleus of paid officials and a workhouse. However, the central authority had proved itself better at checking abuses rather than in initiating change. In many areas continuity with the former regime was only slowly changed. Indeed as knowledge and skills increased so also did bureaucratic caution. The resulting lack of uniformity in both staffing and workhouse provision would suggest that in practice the pace of change was controlled in the last resort by the local authority.

In considering the impact of the locality on the role of the central authority a number of complementary explanations have been advanced. First it can be seen that when faced by serious local opposition the central authority was forced to seek uniformity by attacking outstanding abuses and restraining local experiment. Thus Anne Digby concludes her thorough investigation of the rural county of Norfolk with a largely negative verdict on the role of the central authority:

> The unpopularity and political weakness of the Poor Law Commission and the bureaucratisation of the Poor Law Board, resulted in a blanket condemnation of local initiative as harmful abuse. In mid-century the central administration attempted to stultify progressive developments made by the Norfolk administration . . . and tried to impose a uniform mediocrity on poor law practice.[38]

Secondly, there is the view that the increasing skills of the central authority were countered by the emergence of suitable defensive techniques by the local authorities. Thus Norman McCord, summarizing a considerable amount of largely urban research in north-east England, found that the New Poor Law had little impact before 1850, and although noting the emergence of a more sophisticated system of administration from the centre he concludes that even after 1850: 'Boards of guradians in practice retained a high degree of local autonomy in the ways in which they were able to handle local affairs and a high degree of dexterity in frustrating attempts by central authorities to impose uniformity in relief attitudes and practices.[39] Derek Fraser has sought to solve the conundrum of a more efficient central bureaucracy faced by local opposition in a third way. At the 'macro scale of major policy issues' he finds the central authority was forced to compromise 'to accommodate local practice'. However, at 'the micro level of petty regulations the central authority was much more successful'. The result was that 'in time the poor law had the appearance of a unified and uniform social service'.[40] Finally there is the view that the role of the parish, particularly in the field of finance and settlement, acted as a major limiting factor. Taking these views together the revolutionary image of the new administration is difficult to sustain, although for the relief of the poor this could be something of a mixed blessing.

The Pattern of Relief

The feature of the New Poor Law which caught the attention of contemporary opinion was not the system of administration but the threat of seeking relief, with special emphasis being paid to the workhouse test. Official records are unfortunately stronger on administration than relief, but they do give more attention to the inmates of the workhouse than to those on domiciliary or outdoor relief. In some ways this is unfortunate as the majority of paupers were normally recipients of outdoor relief. The statistics of this period suggest that over 80 per cent of paupers were on outdoor relief, subsisting on very small weekly allowances which often appear to have lacked any apparent rationale even within an individual union. The continued reliance on outdoor relief was to a considerable extent the result of a desire for economy, and in unions facing pressure on their workhouse facilities it could be favoured as a means of postponing expenditure on additional facilities.

Although the workhouse test was designed to deter the able-bodied, the majority of workhouse inmates were normally the impotent; the physically and mentally disabled, the aged, the orphan and a wide variety of sick. The number of able-bodied inmates was often dependent on the space left after these categories had been housed. In dealing with the able-bodied the workhouse was invariably offered to those regarded as of bad character, such as aged or diseased prostitutes, ex-criminals, mothers with more than one illegitimate child, known alcoholics and vagrants. In addition the workhouse test was often applied in case of doubt; where it was believed that savings or casual earnings were being concealed, in dubious sickness claims and in the case of deserted wives and their children. It could also be used as a means of putting pressure on relatives to contribute towards the maintenance of an applicant for relief. Where space remained for other able-bodied it was the single of both sexes and widows with one child who were most likely to be offered the house. In practice one of the most feared characteristics of the workhouse was the supposed nature of its inmates. Regarded as a refuge for undesirables, the workhouse gave its inmates a greater stigma than applied to those in receipt of outdoor relief.

Even within the workhouse there were categories of pauper who were regarded with more sympathy than the rest. There was always a tendency to look upon the children as more deserving and after some initial confusion it began to appear that many of the sick were also regarded with more sympathy. The Victorian workhouse was faced with the impossible task of providing a refuge for the impotent while deterring the scrounger. In that the mass of poor regarded the workhouse with considerable dread the deterrent feature had been successfully conveyed, despite the fact that the majority of inmates were usually unsuited to such treatment. Thus although the principle of less eligibility was intended to apply only to the able-bodied in many cases there was 'a constant tendency to think of it as applicable to all applicants for relief' and this was certainly the case with all who entered the workhouse. Indeed for the Webbs, the workhouse became 'shocking to every principle of reason and every feeling of humanity'.[51]

This dismal view corresponds to that of contemporary critics of the 1830s and 1840s such as *The Times* and the novelist Charles Dickens. The picture of the workhouse presented by its early opponents suggested a life of horror. For even the mildly refractory there were savage beatings and solitary confinement in the most unsuitable of cells. For the majority, existence was endured on a starvation diet, families were ruthlessly separated in the interests of classification, accommodation was overcrowded and unhealthy, and daily life was a monotonous routine supervised by unsympathetic officials. Finally, for those unfortunate enough to die in the workhouse, the end was a burial without dignity or respect.

For the modern historian the picture is no longer entirely a study in black. There was much variation between workhouses, and those which paid most attention to the directives of the central authority probably provided better food and accommodation than was available to many of the poor who struggled to survive outside. The central authority, while never encouraging anything remotely resembling rash expenditure, appeared at least to be trying to raise the standards of the worst institutions to the general standard of other workhouses in their area. In the case of the children and the sick foundations were being laid for future progress, although developments were both slow and partial up to the mid-1860s.

Most historians accept the conclusions of David Roberts that the sensational stories of cruelties were either false or the result of survivals from the former regime. In a number of cases, such as the flogging of young girls at the Hoo Workhouse or the scandal at Andover, the local authority could be shown to have ignored the directives of the central authority. However, this did not entirely excuse the inadequacy of the supervision which allowed such happenings to take place.[42]

The best known image of the New Poor Law was presented by Charles Dickens in *Oliver Twist*. The account of the starving child who asked for more was almost certainly based on the earlier system, although the extent to which the old survived in the new does not entirely invalidate the criticism. However, there can be no doubt that in the report of 1834, and the subsequent regulations issued by the Poor Law Commissioners, there was no intention of starving the inmates. The official diets issued in 1836 gave six choices from which boards of guardians were to select that which appeared most suitable for their union. Manufacturing districts tended to choose diets with a more generous meat allowance while in rural unions cheese and bacon were more common. In making a selection unions were advised, 'especial reference must be had to the usual mode of living of the independent labourers of the district . . . and on no account must the diet be superior or equal to the ordinary mode of subsistence of the labouring classes of the neighbourhood.'[43] It is true that diets were intended to provide nourishment as cheaply as possible and largely consisted of cheap fillers, but so also did the diet of the poor generally. Yet for generations workhouses in north-east England were known as 'the grubber'. According to the popular view workhouse food was unattractive. There are several reasons why this was the case. In many instances food was bought in bulk from the lowest tender and was not always of good quality. Institutional cooking always presented problems and in the hands of untrained pauper cooks could be not only unattractive but actually dangerous. Food could often arrive from inconveniently placed kitchens to be served cold at the table. There were numerous complaints of food being wasted by children and outbreaks of stomach complaints were a feature of hot summers. Above all the sheer monotony of the diet for the long-term inmate was a major drawback. To some extent these complaints were the result of inadequate skills rather than deliberate cruelty. However, the rigidity of the diets and their limited range of ingredients were also the product of that combination of less eligibility and parsimony which was at the root of many other complaints regarding life in the workhouse. Workhouse problems can normally be traced to at least one of three interconnected problems; the survival of institutions and practices from the former regime, the belief in less eligibility and the desire for economy.

A major cause of complaint, in urban workhouses particularly, was the extent of overcrowding. Many of the most serious cases reflected the survival of former institutions often maintained, against the wishes of the central authority, in the interests of economy. However, many of the petty savings such as the lack of backs on benches and other deficiencies of furnishings and the inadequate lighting and heating appear to be a mixture of economy and less eligibility for which both central and local authorities should be blamed. A similar situation contributed to the psychological cruelties of the workhouse. It was the regulations of the · central authority which encouraged workhouse dress to be made in the workhouse. The result was hardwearing, badly fitting uniforms which survived generations of inmates. It was the central authority which ordered silence at meals, the strict daily timetable and visiting rights at the discretion of the master. Classification was a special problem where it involved the separation of aged married couples. However, at first such regulations could only be suspended with a resolution of the board of guardians approved by the central authority. With accommodation in short supply the answer was almost total separation. The workhouses were intended to provide heavy labour which was not in competition with private enterprise. For men the alternatives were stone-breaking, spade husbandry, oakum picking and corn grinding. Women could also be employed in oakum picking, although the majority were used in cooking, cleaning and laundry work. The shortage of able-bodied in the workhouse meant that many, however unsuitable, could expect to become pauper officials. Ursula Henriques gives an appropriate conclusion, 'The terror in which the workhouse was undoubtedly held throughout the nineteenth century must be at least partly accounted for by the frequent combination of the depersonalization of the new order and the surviving squalor and inefficiency of the old'.[44]

When Hippolyte Taine visited the model workhouse at Manchester, probably in the early 1860s, he felt obliged to explain why so many of the poor preferred to accept the poorer diet and harsher living and working conditions of the outside world. He believed that for some it was being deprived of drink and for others it was the loss of freedom and discipline. He concluded:

> The workhouse is regarded as a prison; the poor consider it a point of honour not to go there. Perhaps it must be admitted that the system of administration is foolishly despotic and worrying, that is the fault of every administrative system, the human being becomes a machine; he is treated as if he were devoid of feeling, and insulted quite unconsciously.[45]

Taine was correct in stressing the depersonalization of the workhouse. However, in view of the low ranking of workhouse inmates in the hierarchy of respectability, the insult was often quite deliberate.

The central authority was on uncertain ground when considering groups less suited to the principle of 'less eligible' treatment. Such groups provide a yardstick by which progress can be measured. Children were clearly such a category as they had fallen on the poor rate through no fault of their own. Little is known of the children in receipt of outdoor relief, although they appear to have formed approximately 80 per cent of the children in receipt of relief during this period. They exist in the records merely as small financial additions to the weekly payments allowed to their parents. Boards of guardians often required that children regarded as of working age should seek work before their parents could be assessed for any relief payment. Payment of school fees for children on outdoor relief was permitted by an Act of 1855, although by 1869 only 10 per cent of such children were having their fees paid by boards of guardians.[46]

The Poor Law authorities at both national and local levels had to be more concerned with children who became inmates of the workhouse. At times during this period children have been variously estimated as forming between one-third and one-half of the inmates in many workhouses. Of special concern were the large numbers of orphans who became the long-term responsibility of the system. It was regarded as essential that workhouse children should be raised to become independent of state relief by being taught the moral values of hard work and thrift. Hence strict classification was regarded as essential, so that the workhouse child should not become contaminated by the low moral values of the paupers who surrounded them. One method of furthering this end, while at the same time economizing on the rates, was to adopt the practice of the Old Poor Law and apprentice children to outside employers as soon as possible. In the early years of the New Poor Law this was often at nine or ten years of age, and later was normally as soon as the law allowed. Workhouse children could rarely expect to gain entry to the better positions. Girls were particularly vulnerable, many becoming domestic servants in return for little more than board and lodgings. Mrs Nassau Senior, the first woman inspector, commented in 1874 on these 'bargain basement workhouse girls' who were sought after by people 'whose incomes do not permit them to keep a superior servant and who often look on their little servant as a mere drudge'. Of people taking girls from Rochdale Workhouse in the period 1851–70 the occupations of ninety-seven have been identified, just over half being manual workers. From 1851 the Poor Law Board required boards of guardians to carry out checks on the situation of children apprenticed by their union, a practice already adopted in the best unions. In 1862 it was reported that approximately 20 per cent of children had been returned, 9 per cent on the grounds of misconduct.[47]

The area where the New Poor Law laid most claim to success in the care of children was in the development of an educational service for workhouse children. Assistant Commissioners Tufnell and Kay-Shuttleworth worked hard to convince the Poor Law Commission of the value of an educational programme aimed at inculcating the virtues of an independent lifestyle. The aim of Poor Law education was to provide both an intellectual and moral curriculum similar to that enjoyed by non-workhouse children attending state-aided schools, and also to provide the workhouse child with industrial training. This latter feature was intended to provide the pupil with work experience rather than training for a particular occupation. In view of the cost of providing an effective schooling in the individual union, Tufnell and Kay-Shuttleworth began to advocate the establishment of district schools serving several unions. It was hoped that these larger institutions, separated from the workhouse influence and employing professional staff, would produce an efficient educational programme. Although there were some unions prepared to adopt this solution, notably Swinton for the Manchester unions and Kirkdale for those of Liverpool, the idea did not receive general support. The schools were more expensive than their supporters had suggested and the associated transport and administrative problems provided further discouragement. From the 1850s the inspectorate of the Poor Law Board favoured district schools with decreasing ardour, largely because of the administrative problems involved. However, the Educational Committee of the Privy Council, which had Kay-Shuttleworth as its initial secretary, and which controlled the inspection of workhouse schools from 1847, continued to support the district school on educational grounds. The dispute was eventually to lead to the inspection of workhouse education returning to the inspectors of the Poor Law Board in 1863. Both poor law administrators and workhouse children probably benefitted in the long-term from the limited support given to district schools. By the 1870s critics were suggesting that these institutions left much to be desired. Descriptions such as 'barrack schools' and 'hothouse plants' indicate the main areas of criticism. Discipline in schools, containing as many as one thousand pupils, was necessarily more regimented and access to the open air, even for exercise, was a rare luxury. From the 1870s the acceptance of more imaginative schemes for removing children from the workhouse influence were to gain acceptance and any large investment in district schools would inevitably have handicapped this progress.[48]

For children residing in the workhouse fortunes varied with the institution. Where accommodation was overcrowded children faced the same pressure as other inmates, adaptation of rooms, increases in the number of beds per dormitory and in extreme cases of persons per bed. Normal diet was the same as for other inmates, except that portions were usually smaller, children below nine years being at the discretion of the individual union and those above nine being placed on the women's diet. The ideal of a separate building for children with its own staff was only economic in the larger unions and this use of the 'detached school' had made limited progress by 1870.[49]

In receiving any education the workhouse child was being placed in a more eligible position than many of the poorest labouring families could afford. This could be justified on the grounds that such children faced a more difficult start to life. The unique feature of the Poor Law educational system was intended to give assistance in overcoming this handicap by the provision of industrial training. Gardening, tailoring and shoemaking were the main occupations for the boys, and the girls were employed in cleaning, laundry and cooking. Inevitably at first many of the tasks were routine and poorly supervised. In some cases the children appeared to be making good the shortage of able-bodied inmates. On occasion the demand for child labour was such that it provoked dispute between workhouse master and schoolteachers who saw their certificates of proficiency being threatened by the inadequate time left for academic schooling. Where badly supervised there were also charges that classification was being threatened, although such charges appear to have diminished over time. As children were increasingly transferred from the workhouses in the latter part of the nineteenth century the gaps they left in the labour force could often lead to the employment of paupers from the outdoor lists for essential workhouse duties.

With regard to academic education, there was considerable variation in the facilities provided and in the quality of the teachers. Initially schoolteachers were appointed from inmates, the major criterion being the ability to read and write. From 1846 grants in aid of salaries encouraged the appointment of professional teachers. However, low salaries, the strain of having to live in the workhouse, often with additional duties being ordered by the master, made the work unattractive. In addition the pupils were often sickly, those with parents who were continually 'in and out' of the workhouse posed problems of continuity, and in many cases there was a battle with economy-minded guardians to obtain even the minimum of facilities.

Teachers were graded into categories of 'efficiency', 'competency', 'probation' and 'permission' and initially most teachers were graded in the two lowest categories, approximately equivalent to a pupil-teacher in a voluntary school. However, within a decade of the coming of grants the majority of teachers were being recognized as competent.[50] In general, workhouse teachers were rarely of the highest quality. Indeed, economy-minded guardians feared the impact of a teacher obtaining a high grant on the workhouse salary structure. The well qualified teacher could normally find more attractive posts outside of the workhouse and for those who remained the best prospect often lay in seeking promotion to a position as master or matron, providing a suitable marriage could be arranged.

Nevertheless, workhouse classes were normally smaller than those in other schools and this combined with the improvement in teaching made the Poor Law educational system appear to be at least a partial success, although the extent to which this was so remains open to discussion. Thus Francis Duke concludes that:

> A situation of chaos and neglect had been transformed within 20 years. That the district school movement failed so completely is, among other things, testimony to the progress made in the mass of union schools. From the 1830s Poor Law schools had pioneered important developments in educational practice, often providing a lead to the state-aided elementary schools, whose social and educational aims, though less pronounced, were similar. Prior to 1870 it was generally held that Poor Law schools provided a sounder basic education than comparable day schools, though they usually taught a narrower range of subjects.[51]

A more cautious verdict is provided by Anne Digby:

> In the early years of the New Poor Law, workhouse schools had aimed to give pauper children 'superior eligibility' so that their better education would permit them to compete in the labour market and not become the burden on the rates which their parents had been. Some unions had a limited success in this objective, but penny-pinching by many boards of guardians, and the difficulty of recruiting efficient teachers, eroded standards to such an extent that monotonous rote-learning in the schoolroom did little either to lighten a bleak workhouse-environment or to fit a child for the world beyond it.[52]

The sick, the other main deserving group among the applicants for Poor Relief, followed an equally unplanned approach to that

106

adopted for the children. It is difficult to make any accurate assessment of the size of this group in the early years of the New Poor Law. The limited statistics available adopt a variety of approaches when making distinctions between the able-bodied, the temporarily sick, the partially disabled and the feeble-minded. Such confusion could on occasion have been deliberate on the part of local unions seeking to hide the giving of outdoor relief to the able-bodied. It is also difficult to distinguish between those given medical relief only and those families relieved because of destitution following ill-health. Even when simple, standard classifications had been introduced into returns the grouping of the aged and infirm as one class makes any firm calculation difficult. Finally it is impossible before the late 1860s to make any accurate distinction between the indoor and outdoor sick. The official returns then suggest that nationally two-thirds of the sick were in receipt of outdoor relief and that the indoor sick formed around 30 per cent of the indoor poor. [53] There can be little doubt that these generalizations conceal considerable differences between unions, relating to the social problems of the area and the nature and extent of other medical provision. In addition unions varied in their desire to economize in the area of the sick and in the extent to which they regarded the sick pauper as 'less eligible'.

In dealing with the sick poor the central authority was itself torn between the desire to produce an efficient and humane service and the principle of less eligibility. In practice the central authority always recognized the danger of tempting the poor into becoming paupers via medical relief. However, the Poor Law was legally bound to care for the destitute sick and it was difficult for the central authority to frame directives in this matter. Confusion existed over those not normally classed as destitute but who were unable to afford the cost of medical treatment. In practice such difficult decisions were left to the individual board of guardians and this produced further examples of the diversity of the service.

A further area where uniformity was noticably absent was in the matter of domiciliary or workhouse provision for the sick. Initially it was believed that the sick would receive outdoor relief and only the inmates of the workhouse who became sick would require indoor treatment. Such a distinction was to prove impractical at a very early stage. Yet the central authority was never able to formulate any guidelines on whether outdoor relief or the workhouse should be offered to the sick. It was not until 1869 that enquiry was made of the individual unions as to their practice in this matter. However, the replies showed that the principles on which such decisions were made were so varied that it was impossible to draw any conclusions and the matter remained at the discretion of the individual board of guardians.[54] In practice a major determinant was the space available in the workhouse. This was a matter which could produce major problems when the demands of the sick coincided with the problem of the treatment of the able-bodied during periods of trade depression.

The problem for the Poor Law medical service was one familiar to students of twentieth-century provision; the needs of the sick always appeared to be out-running the resources available. The strong linkage between poverty and ill-health meant that the sick claimant was always likely to present the Poor Law administration with a major financial burden. In 1854 the medical reformer Dr Rumsey informed a parliamentary inquiry that half the population required free medical relief and that in any given year 25 to 45 per cent of this group would require medical attention.[55] Such figures are not unreasonable in view of what is known of the extent of poverty at this time. For the Poor Law administrator it was not only the extent of possible claimants which was worrying but the range of services which might be demanded. The Poor Law medical officer was not merely in demand as a general practitioner but was also required to cover a variety of surgical and highly contagious medical cases. Infections could vary from the severe discomfort of 'itch' and 'scald head' to life-threatening epidemics. This burden fell upon a medical service which was at first unaware of its potential responsibilities and one that was subsequently always struggling to find the resources to cope effectively.

In an attemtpt to secure some measure of uniformity in the field of outdoor relief the Poor Law Commission in 1842 placed a limit of 15,000 acres or 15,000 people on a medical relief district. Such a standard was not particularly generous, yet, in 1861, Dr Griffen, a leading figure in the campaign to improve the Poor Law medical service, reported that there were 583 districts with more than 15,000 acres, some reaching between 80,000 and 100,000 acres; and 120 districts with a population exceeding 15,000, some reaching 40,000.[56] The demands of economy were also partly responsible for the regulation that applicants for medical relief should approach the relieving officer before the medical officer. The intrusion of this unqualified official reinforced the pauper stigma, and could be used to curtail access to doctors regarded as over-generous. In rural areas the result was often long journeys by the sick to obtain treatment, always assuming both officers were available, so providing a futher deterrent. Where medical officers were expected to pay for drugs prescribed from their own salaries there were complaints that drugs were not supplied or were of inferior quality. Household rags were often used as dressings and bandages. Where a patient required expensive medication or frequent visits it was in the interest of the district medical officer to refer him to the workhouse, whereas in the case of a surgical case the medical officer would prefer to operate in the patient's home in order to obtain the fee. In cases involving malnutrition the medical officer could order medical extras, food and drink supplied from the union funds, and it is possible that doctors sought to make up for the supply of inadequate medication by making such demands. However, such a tendency could well lead to a restriction in the number of relief orders issued by the relieving officer.[57]

The necessary back-up facilities of district nurses and dispensaries were largely dependent on voluntary provision. These were not always available and where they existed they did not always accept those in receipt of outdoor relief. From the 1850s the best unions began to provide public dispensaries and others supported voluntary dispensaries with annual allowances from the rates as a cheaper alternative, although the overall provision remained haphazard and inadequate. The cooperation with the voluntary sector in this field, the acquisition of public health duties and the use of the Poor Law medical officers as public vaccinators were all examples of how the health services of the Poor Law began to expand beyond the field of destitution before the 1860s.[58]

The principle of less eligibility was held more strongly in the treatment of the indoor sick. However, even in this area the belief in the workhouse test was to prove difficult to maintain. Medical officers found it necessary to transfer patients to the workhouse sick wards where their domestic circumstances were such that they were likely to inhibit recovery. As with the children, more is known of the workhouse sick than those on outdoor relief, although information frequently followed the revelation of a scandal. As the area of the workhouse most likely to be visited by the public at large and often the only section under the control of a recognized professional, such revelations feature more strongly than on other aspects of workhouse life. Thus scandals were initially revealed by visitors, by medical officers and by coroners investigating suspicious deaths. They were rarely revealed by the visiting committees of boards of guardians or the overworked inspectorate of the central authority, who usually lacked the professional expertise to discover faults in this area. Indeed until the appointment of a specialist medical inspector in the mid-1860s the central authority was forced to bring in outside expertise to investigate difficult cases. It would normally be unwise to judge any institution on its failings and undoubtedly the workhouse sick could face a wide range of experience, but historians have generally found the service inadequate even when judged by the low standards of the period.[59]

While district medical officers often had little choice but to make use of the workhouse sick wards, the extent of the demand was unexpected. Moreover, the less eligible workhouse was ill-suited to the care of the sick. Adverse comments on stone floors, bare walls inadequate ventilation, lighting and heating were often accompanied by references to defective sanitation, primitive privies, insufficiencies in water supply, washing facilities and defective laundries. There were comments on the stench of the 'foul' or fever wards, where they existed, and of the infected sharing baths, towels and beds. Clean bedlinen was often in short supply as was night attire. Conditions became worse during epidemics and in urban unions the pressure of population when combined with economy-minded guardians produced longer-term problems. Overcrowding produced the inevitable unsuitable adaptations, including the breakdown of classification as the sick were mixed with the able-bodied and the children with the adults. The sheer range of illnesses posed special problems. For example, ideally the female sick area should have had separate accommodation for the lying in, the fever stricken, prostitutes with venereal disease and a place for the insane in addition to its general ward. Such sophistication developed slowly and was largely confined to the more progressive of the larger unions. After childbirth many women could find themselves transferred immediately to the able-bodied wards and in general the issue of convalescence appears to have been largely neglected in this period. Dirt and inadequate segregation brought problems of cross-infection and disease was often introduced by new admissions. Such was the fear of the workhouse that many of the poor only sought help as a last resort. Medical officers could only draw the attention of boards of guardians to the problems they faced, and in cases necessitating heavy expenditure long delays and repeated requests were commonplace. The only solution to the problem of the workhouse sick was usually to be the building of a separate hospital building, but this was a rare answer before the 1860s and in some rural unions was never undertaken.

The accommodation problems were accompanied by economies on staffing. The consolidation of duties of the district and work-house medical officer was gradually abandoned from the late 1840s, but workhouse medical officers remained largely part-time appointments. Yet he was expected to make regular attendance on the sick, to medically inspect all new admissions, to maintain patients' records, to supply drugs, to make recommendations on diet and to comment on the building and its equipment, all for a totally inadequate salary. While some doctors made heroic responses to these unfavourable conditions, there is also evidence of those who matched their efforts to the salaries provided. In the worst cases attendance was not even daily, new admissions were never examined, most of the work was performed by unqualified assistants and the keeping of records was largely ignored.

While the quality of medical officers appears to have varied there is little doubt that the nurses were normally well below any acceptable professional standard. Nurses showed the most dramatic increase in numbers of all categories of workhouse official, but in this period they were largely recruited from the able-bodied in the workhouse. As such they often provide illustration of the shortage of suitable inmates. They included many of advanced years, a number suffered physical or mental defects and there were frequent complaints of excessive drinking suggesting that a number were probably alcoholics. The use of alcohol, an unofficial currency in many workhouses, could well have been used as a bribe to secure nursing of such dangerous areas as the fever ward. The only initial requirement of the central authority was that nurses should be able to read the instructions given by the medical officer, though even this minimum was evaded on occasions. The central authority supplied no instructions concerning hours of work or accommodation for nurses, some appearing to have slept in the same ward as the patients, otherwise the provision of night nurses was largely ignored. Professional nurses were scarce in the workhouses and the central authority's attitude to expenditure was initially unhelpful. As late as 1850 the Poor Law Board discouraged Croydon Board of Guardians from employing too many paid nurses. Pointing out that major workhouse hospitals managed with one paid nurse and the majority of country unions had none, they could see no reason why the Croydon medical officer required five. Hence they ruled that, 'Three at least of the paid servants in the hospital must be discontinued.'[60]

From the late 1850s interest in the workhouse sick was advanced by the activities of such pressure groups as the Poor Law Medical Reform Association, founded in 1856 and the Workhouse Visiting Society established in 1858. Nevertheless, despite their publicity, the Select Committee on the Poor Law of 1861–4 appeared satisfied with the care given to the pauper sick. The following year disclosures in *The Lancet* concerning the condition of the sick wards of London workhouses revealed a state of affairs as shocking as the isolated scandals of the 1840s and 1850s, but on a much wider scale. The appointment of Dr Edward Smith as medical inspector in 1866 brought further exposures of inadequate facilities and treatment, and marked a turning point in official attitudes to the treatment of the sick. However, progress was disappointing in the first thirty years and has been seen to be somewhat tarnished throughout: 'The Victorian development was cheap, poor, grudging and wasteful: and the original brand of the broad arrow could never be altogether effaced.'[61]

A similar verdict could be applied to the treatment of the insane, many of whom ended up in the care of the Poor Law. Where possible the merely feeble-minded were left in the care of relatives on outdoor relief. However, a growing number needed institutional treatment. In practice the pauper-lunatic ranged from the congenital idiot to the severely depressed and from the dangerous to the amiable. The dangerous were supposed to be transferred to county asylums or other licensed institutions, but the shortage of facilities together with resentment of the cost meant that many remained in the workhouse. The reports of the Commissioners of Lunacy reveal that initially most workhouses lacked any specialized accommodation for the insane, though many were unsuited to mixing with the general body of inmates. When specialist accommodation was provided it was often very unsuitable and pauper attendants who looked after the insane received even more critical comment than did pauper nurses. In the worst cases there was a widespread use of manacles, straitjackets and other instruments of restraint, while at best the insane were largely neglected. Lack of medical attention meant that the diagnosis of this group left much to be desired, epileptics and alcoholics often being placed in the insane wards. The growing numbers of insane paupers increased the problem. The numbers of lunatic-paupers appear to have doubled during the 1850s and in 1861 out of a total of 33,000 pauper-lunatics over one-quarter remained in the workhouse. Despite the regular inspection by the representatives of the Lunacy Commissioners and their pressure on the Poor Law Board, expenditure on appropriate specialist facilities was a rarity before the late 1860s. Similarly, for the blind, the deaf and dumb and other handicapped the use of outside specialist facilities appears to have been totally inadequate in this period.[62]

The aged poor were barely recognized as a problem until late in the nineteenth century. Then the increased awareness of poverty as a problem and the longer life expectancy made the aged of greater significance and they joined the children and the sick as a more favoured group. Although the statistics suggest that the numbers of aged had increased dramatically as a proportion of the larger workhouse population by the end of the century, two generalizations occur throughout. The first is that, as with pauperism generally, the majority of aged paupers were in receipt of outdoor relief and the second is that at all times the aged formed the majority of long-term inmates of the workhouse. Those entering the workhouse were often those unable to care for themselves any longer, hence the classifying of aged and infirm as a group. Inevitably there were always more old men than old women in this category, as women were either more self-sufficient or more likely to be assisted by relatives. At times the aged were in the workhouse because they were regarded as being of bad character due to their failure to make provision for old age as a result of their wasteful lifestyle, or, because it was believed that relatives could be shocked into contributing to their support rather than face the disgrace of having a close relative in the workhouse. Arguments such as these were used to justify the aged suffering the deterrent accommodation and discipline of the workhouse.

As early as 1836 the Poor Law Commission had recognized that the aged could be supplied with extras and from 1847 the workhouse medical officer could recommend additions to their diet, although he was not allowed to order such until the 1880s. From 1847 boards of guardians could allow aged couples to have rooms rather than be separated into the male and female dormitories. In practice this relaxation of the rules was almost totally ignored. Few workhouses in urban areas possessed the space to provide such facilities, and increasing pressure made this become less likely with the passage of time. Rather the central authority provided a cheap justification alleging that many couples preferred to be separated. Descriptions of the aged in institutions often stress the apathy of the individual forced to spend long periods in an institution. In the deterrent workhouse of the nineteenth century there can be little doubt that the long-term inmate faced a depressing future.[63]

Much of the hardship inflicted on the impotent poor was justified on the grounds that the workhouse was meant to encourage the able-bodied to value the need to secure an independent lifestyle by the practice of self-help. Yet the official returns suggest that in the period of the Poor Law Commission over three-quarters of the able-bodied were in receipt of outdoor relief and that the percentage increased under the Poor Law Board. That such a situation should prevail was never the intention of the central authority, rather it was a further instance of local interests determining the nature of Poor Relief.

The Poor Law Commissioners began by issuing newly-formed unions with individual orders prohibiting outdoor relief to the able-bodied. However, the strength of the resistance in the northern textile districts caused them to retreat from this policy of outright prohibition. Opposition to the curtailment of outdoor relief to the able-bodied was strengthened by the impossibility of many unions applying the workhouse test during the major unemployment of the early 1840s. The result was that the Poor Law Commission produced two policies for dealing with relief to the able-bodied. A General Order prohibiting such relief was issued in 1841 and revised in a slightly stricter form in 1844. This order applied to both male and female able-bodied and their families, with exceptions being limited to urgent necessity, temporary sickness and infirmity affecting any member of the family of an applicant, for burials, for widows in the first six months following bereavement and for widows with a legitimate child. The alternative was a second General Order issued in 1842, replacing the insistence on indoor relief with a policy evolved to obtain the cooperation of obstinate boards of guardians, particularly in unions in industrial areas. By this order the workhouse test was replaced for males by a task of work with the proviso that at least half of the relief should be paid in kind, namely food and fuel. The unions permitted to operate under this order were mainly large urban unions where in time of chronic unemployment the workhouse would be unable to cope. In practice this also included unions which failed to provide adequate workhouse accommodation. In some cases the Outdoor Labour Test Order was issued to unions operating under the Prohibitory Order making it possible for such unions to adapt to the degree of severity of the situation. The Labour Test was intended to be as deterrent as possible, involving heavy and repellent work carefully supervised and thus encouraging those relieved 'to seek for independent employment'. Payments were to be related to need, i.e., number of dependents, not the amount of work performed, but as the workers were in the full employment of the board of guardians it was stressed that this did not mean any return to the practices of the Old Poor Law.[64]

The Poor Law Board attempted to restore some degree of uniformity into the situation by the issue of a General Order in August 1852, ordering that outdoor relief for all groups should be given partly in kind, at least half to the able-bodied and one-third to other classes, such relief was moreover only to be authorized for one week at a time. This interference with the discretion normally allowed to boards of guardians aroused such a general protest that the order was rapidly withdrawn and an amended order was issued in December 1852, whereby the restrictions only applied to the able-bodied, and the instructional letter accompanying the new order permitted the granting of outdoor relief to workers on short-time:

> The Board desire . . . to point out, that what it is intended actually to prohibit is the giving of relief at the same identical time as that at which the person receiving it is in actual employment, and in the receipt of wages, and that relief given in any other case, as, for instance, in that of a man working for wages on one day and being without the next, or working half the week and being unemployed during the remainder, and being then in need of relief, is not prohibited.[65]

In practice boards of guardians often appear to have resented the deterrent outdoor labour test as much as they did the workhouse test when applied to those normally in work. This was observable during the times of seasonal or cyclical unemployment and could be justified on the grounds of humanity or of lessening expense on ratepayers at times when the existing burden was already higher than normal. The test most likely to receive the support of the central authority was stone-breaking. In theory broken stone could be sold to the highways authorities for road building, but in the reality of a severe depression, more stone was being broken than was likely to be needed in any reasonable future period, making any possible sale a fiction and posing immediate problems of storage. The result was a search for economic alternatives to the test or, if this proved impossible, a means of reducing its cost.

Many boards of guardians contained members who served on other local authorities or who had connections with the administration of local charities. At times of heavy unemployment such bodies were encouraged to engage in public works or provide soup kitchens or other distribution of food, fuel and clothing. On such occasions the distinction between poverty and pauperism was seriously eroded despite the efforts of the central authority. Some unions were also to be found hiring out labour to public and private undertakings and exploiting the exceptions permitted in the regulations. Temporary sickness was used in both urban and rural unions on the most trivial of excuses to justify the payment of outdoor relief. The 1852 order allowed such payments to be made to women and the permission to make payments to those on short-time was used to hide the continuance of the allowance system. Many unions felt that payments in kind either from the workhouse stores or in the form of tickets to purchase groceries was a sufficient defence, although there can be little doubt that the latter practice was often abused. The granting of loans to be repaid when work was resumed was another method of postponing resort to the outdoor labour test. Even the Law of Settlement had its uses. Its retention was favoured by some northern guardians as a cheap method of discouraging Irish and Scots paupers from seeking relief.[66]

Where the outdoor labour test was operated it could prove a harsh task for the half-starved or aged workers. However, in many cases the test was less than effective largely as the result of the search for economies. At first a number of authorities failed to appoint supervisors and when the central authority protested at such inaction the answer was often to appoint a supervisor from among the able-bodied applicants. A number of unions also sought cheaper alternatives to stone-breaking. The chopping of firewood, a variety of forms of spade husbandry and oakum picking in bad weather were all proposed as cheaper alternatives. When stone-breaking was introduced boards of guardians sought to economize on the amount of stone to be used by complex scales limiting the amount of stone to be broken or the number of days work offered. Such schemes gave the man with dependents more work and higher payments, but they were clearly contrary to the central authority's directive that payments should not be related to work performed, but to need. Boards of guardians could often rely on the fact that by the time the central authority had corresponded on this issue, and received suitably vague initial replies, the stone yard would be closed before the issue had been resolved. At times the test could be made more deterrent by the insistence that the stone be collected by wheelbarrow and removed after breaking over a considerable distance and the increasing use of tight grilles to ensure the stone had been broken into sufficiently small pieces. The central authority always faced the problem of comparing the tests proposed by the individual unions. All stone was not equally difficult to break nor was all ground equally difficult to dig. If a quantity of work was set, the more able worker tended to finish earlier. If a time limit was set the test required strict and expensive supervision to ensure that all maintained their effort. Although tests of work were supposed to be uniform, the same test normally required two hours less to complete in winter than it did in summer in north-east unions. Indeed, the central authority found great difficulty in establishing a uniformity of standard and perservered with the test as a safeguard against the return to the malpractices of the Old Poor Law.[67]

There was always some confusion over the question of responsibility for the vagrant. The vagrant was ignored in the Report of 1834 and many felt that the Vagrancy Act of 1824 made this group a concern of the police. However, in 1839 the Poor Law Commission was to remind boards of guardians of their duty to care for the destitute, casual applicant for relief. Although the records show vagrants of both sexes and their children, the adult male vagrant predominated forming around 85 per cent of the total relieved.[68] As a group vagrants were regarded by both central and local authorities as the lowest of the undeserving poor; many being regarded as too close to the criminal classes and they were also widely believed to act as carriers of disease. At local level attitudes varied with the severity of the problem. Unions which faced heavy pressure from the movement of seasonal workers in agriculture, or those on the main migrant routes from Scotland and Ireland tended, in self-defence, to be harsher in their policy. A General Order in 1842 instructed boards of guardians to keep casuals in a separate ward and to set them a task of work. The Irish famine of the late 1840s brought a considerable increase in the number of vagrants and a tougher attitude, which received some support from the central authority:

> It was found necessary by the late Poor Law Commissioners to remind the various Unions and their officers of the responsibility which would be incurred by refusing relief where it was required. The present state of things renders it necessary that this Board should now impress on them the grievous mischiefs that must arise, and the responsibilities that may be incurred by a too ready distribution of relief to tramps and vagrants not entitled to it . . . . Those who are responsible to the Poor Law Board may feel assured that, while no instance of neglect or hardship to the poor will be tolerated, they may look to the board for a candid construction of their acts and motives.[69]

The reputation of individual unions for a hard or soft approach could determine the size of their vagrancy problem. At first many unions preferred to keep vagrants out of their workhouse by paying for a night's lodging in a common lodging house. In the longer-term this often proved a false economy as such a policy served to attract transients. However, although the central authority preferred separate accommodation and a work task many unions still sought economy by cheaper methods. Thus vagrants were deterred by being housed in the oldest and dirtiest accommodation, often lacking in bedding, heating, or sanitary arrangements. Some unions employed a member of the police as vagrant relieving officer, hoping that a preliminary visit to the police station would deter applications from undesirables. Since deterrent policies were usually adopted by neighbouring unions as a form of self-defence there was a tendency for treatment to become harsher over time. Where vagrants travelled together they could often prove disorderly, particularly in the smaller workhouses. The large urban institutions often appointed attendants on vagrant wards who in practice were little better than uniformed bullies. The insistence on a cold bath on entering the workhouse was for a time regarded as a cheap but effective deterrent.

However, the official solution required expenditure on specialized accommodation, test work and effective supervision and in view of the low priority given to the vagrant compared with more deserving groups, progress was very limited in this period.[70]

By the early 1860s the New Poor Law has been seen as entering a period of crisis.[71] The critics of its limited progress in the care of the destitute child and the pauper sick were now joined by the clamour of those worried about the impact of economic disaster. In London in 1860–1 trade depression and a severe winter combined so that, 'nearly the whole of the labourers in and about the London docks and the banks of the river were thrown out of work'.[72] In this instance and the fate of the Lancashire cotton workers thrown out of work by the disruption to imports of cotton during the American Civil War, the fate of the poor appeared to many observers to depend on private charity. Critics suggested that the Poor Law was unable to cope. In 1861 a Parliamentary Select Committee was established to review the administration of Poor Relief, and a three-year review of considerable thoroughness was published in 1864.

For the opponents of the New Poor Law the report was to prove disappointing. For the children they concluded: 'Whatever may have been the state of education previously to 1847, there can be little doubt that since that period it has made remarkable progress.' The improvement was seen as being the result of the parliamentary grant towards the salaries of teachers and the subsequent inspections. They believed that the academic training was better than for the 'same class out of the workhouse'. Industrial training, particularly for girls, was in advance of education generally and the influence of the workhouse teacher it concluded was more beneficial than that of their homes.[73]

The position with regard to the sick was rather less certain, for the committee heard much criticism. However, to some extent criticism was blunted by the fact that medical critics appeared more interested in their salaries than the plight of the sick and even on this issue opinion was divided as to how salaries should be calculated and on the inspection of the work of medical officers. The view of the Poor Law Board prevailed. Inspector Cane, who had given evidence to the Select Committee on Poor Law Medical Relief in 1854, stated that, 'the poor were never so well attended as they are at the present time', and the Select Committee concluded that there were no grounds for recommending any change in the system of medical relief.[74]

It was more difficult to deny the distress in London, although Farnell, the inspector for the metropolitan district sought to do so. In his view the distress 'scarcely ought to bear the name of a crisis'. Of over 15,000 applicants for relief, just over 1,000 had entered the workhouse and a further 4,230 had accepted the stoneyard, 'the rest were never heard of again'. Although there was much counter-evidence on the extent of the distress particularly among 'vast numbers of the most deserving people who would never go near the poor-house; they would sooner die', the weight of evidence from boards of guardians was that they could have coped without assistance from charity. Indeed the indiscriminate granting of charitable relief was widely condemned for its failure to distinguish between the deserving and the idler. Boards of guardians were also eager to show the good relations which existed with the Poor Law Board, although more stress was placed on the fact that unions had been allowed to tackle the problem without undue intervention than on any assistance given.[75]

The conclusion of the Select Commission was that the New Poor Law was functioning satisfactorily. It stressed the almost unanimous desire of local boards of guardians for the continuation of a supervisory central authority in order to prevent abuses creeping into the system and producing a return to the anarchy which had existed before 1834. However, the Select Committee saw no reason to increase the powers of the central authority, although they believed that existing powers were wisely used. Hence the Committee resolved: 'That the power of issuing General Orders now possessed by the Poor Law Board is salutary and useful, and should be continued.'[76]

The bland conclusions of the Select Committee were perhaps more a recognition of the absence of any alternative to the New Poor Law than a balanced judgement on its performance. After thirty years the administration of the Poor Law, whatever its defects, represented a powerful and experienced vested interest intent on defending the status quo. The pragmatic and rather colourless Poor Law Board survived with the blessing of the unions. Indeed, with the role of the State being confined to the destitute discussion was perhaps inevitably more concerned with administrative detail than the making of policy. Certainly, the central authority was a government department of lowly status which was unlikely to attract the appointment of an ambitious politician. With the Poor

'Woman in a turnip field.' Women were commonly used by farmers as cheap labour for the hard, dirty work of topping and tailing turnips. Photograph by Sir George Clausen *c*. 1883, it was one of the first unposed photographs of fieldworkers

Museum of English Rural Life

'The Labourer's Plight', from G. Mitchell's *The Skeleton at the Plough*, 1874. An attempt to highlight the low wages and awful living conditions of the rural poor

Museum of English Rural Life

At work in the smithy at Dr Barnardo's Home

The laundry at Dr Barnardo's Home. Evangelical Christianity was a major force in charitable provision for the poor

THE NEMESIS OF NEGLECT.

"THERE FLOATS A PHANTOM ON THE SLUM'S FOUL AIR,
SHAPING, TO EYES WHICH HAVE THE GIFT OF SEEING,
INTO THE SPECTRE OF THAT LOATHLY LAIR.
FACE IT—FOR VAIN IS FLEEING!
RED-HANDED, RUTHLESS, FURTIVE, UNERECT,
'TIS MURDEROUS CRIME—THE NEMESIS OF NEGLECT!"

A *Punch* cartoon of 1883, reflecting the increasing awareness of the problems of poverty from the 1880s
Mansell Collection

STRANGERS.

FATHER CHRISTMAS. "WHAT! NOT KNOW ME?—OH, THIS MUST BE ALTERED!"

A *Punch* cartoon of 1888
Mansell Collection

Catherine Booth. The Salvation Army was one of the first organizations to regard men and women as being of equal status

Heatherbank Museum of Social Work

William Booth, founder of the Salvation Army, with the aim of converting the urban poor. From the 1880s the movement came to emphasize social work as necessary to saving souls

Heatherbank Museum of Social Work

Inmates of the Salvation Army's
Eventide Home at Clapton
Heatherbank Museum of Social Work

A Slum Sister from the Salvation Army visiting her parish
Heatherbank Museum of Social Work

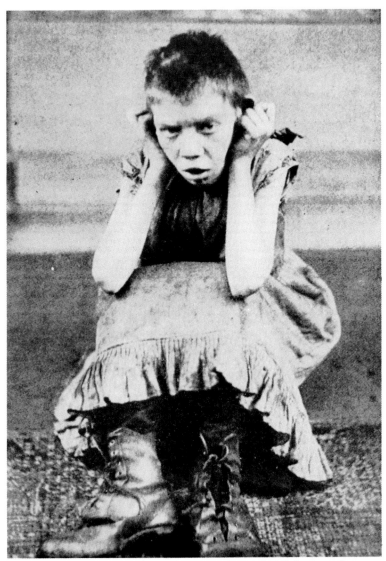

Found in a garret in an appalling state, this child gained 10 lb in eleven days once taken into care by the NSPCC. A copy of an original photograph by the NSPCC c. 1900

Heatherbank Museum of Social Work

Those admitted to the workhouse were made to wear workhouse uniforms, and their own clothes were put into the de-lousing machine to be disinfected by steaming

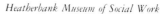

Heatherbank Museum of Social Work

A day room in a workhouse. An obviously posed photograph with the inmates on their 'best behaviour' for the camera

Heatherbank Museum of Social Work

Slum visitation by the Salvation Army nurse. These nurses worked in communities where poverty meant that medical care was almost totally non-exsistent

Heatherbank Museum of Social Work

A newly-opened casual ward at Marylebone Workhouse, London, probably late nineteenth century. The ubiquitous texts are typical of the period

These children have been brought before the Glasgow Juvenile Delinquency Board, possibly for petty theft, to be placed in an Industrial School, 1886

Heatherbank Museum of Social Work

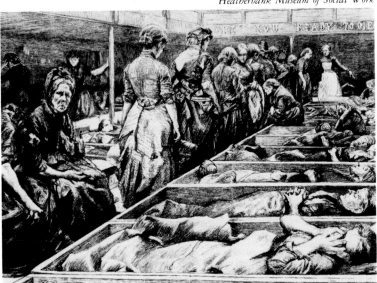

A Salvation Army shelter for women in Whitechapel, drawn by Paul Renouard. Considering the coffin-like sleeping accommodation the inmates must have pondered on the quotation on the upper gallery supports, 'Are you ready to die?'

Communist Party Picture Library

Homeless and destitute, a photograph from the Salvation Army

Heatherbank Museum of Social Work

Farm workers 'flitting' to avoid payment of rent

Museum of English Rural Life

The dining room at Cambridge Workhouse *c.* 1910. The scales on the table are a reminder of the 1834 Act, which established the right of any workhouse inmate to have their rations weighed in front of them.

Heatherbank Museum of Social Work

Dinnertime at St Pancras Workhouse, London, 1900

Heatherbank Museum of Social Work

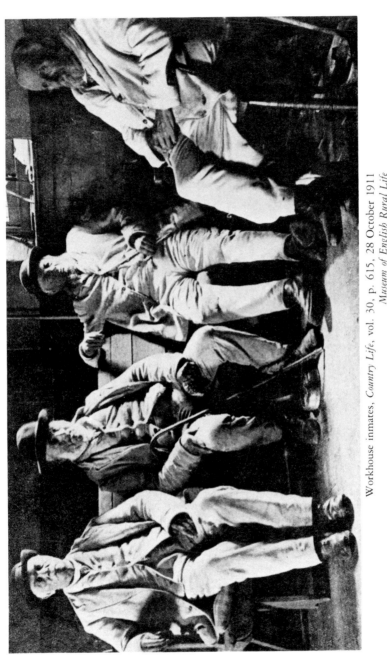

Workhouse inmates, *Country Life*, vol. 30, p. 615, 28 October 1911
Museum of English Rural Life

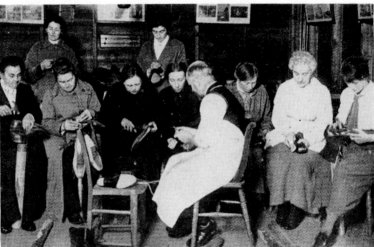

Tinkering class (top) and a shoe mending class at Scaynes Hill Institute, Sussex. Some institutions did make some effort to provide their inmates with skills, but despite Victorian views on self-help, it was not normal practice for adults

Heatherbank Museum of Social Work

Sidney and Beatrice Webb, married in 1892. As leading members of the Fabian movement they were major supporters of social reform and especially critical of the Poor Law

Heatherbank Museum of Social Work

The women's day-room and men's sick ward at Cambridge Workhouse *c*. 1910. A showpiece rather than a typical example of the 'improved' provision for old people introduced in the 1890s, as indicated by the flowers and pictures. The old ladies, however, are still in uniform and married couples remain separated

Law Board more intent on restraining abuses than seeking additional powers much depended on the individual union.

The dominance of the unions makes it difficult to pass judgement on the progress of the New Poor Law in this first thirty-year period. Unions reflected local economic and political considerations to an extent which makes generalization difficult.[77] It is certainly true that many were so mindful of economy that efficiency suffered. However, even where a union was disposed to follow the advice of the central authority in matters of staffing and workhouse accommodation, the retention of parochial control of finance could limit progress. Indeed, as with the Old Poor Law financial defects contributed considerably to the diversity of administrative pattern. The result was that in many areas traditional practices survived even in the matter of allowances to the able-bodied.[78]

If the seeds of the welfare state were sown in the period before the mid-1860s the central authorities had proved themselves rather ineffective husbandmen and the unions had provided an infertile soil. Progress in this period lay in the achievement of superficial administrative uniformity, and in limited achievements in the care of children and the sick. Advance was also claimed in the reduction of the percentage of paupers to the total population. This was a claim based on insubstantial foundations. To some extent the expanding role of self-help could be represented as the outcome of the fear of the workhouse test, but in practice this could often produce the destruction of independence. At times of hardship such as during depression, the number of unredeemed pledges at pawnbrokers increased substantially.[79] When essential items disappeared from the home the possibility of any return to sturdy independence was diminished. Fortunately, in practice the full rigours of less eligibility and the workhouse test were as rarely on offer as less fortunately were the best features of education or care of the sick. Judgement on the New Poor Law, for better or for worse, awaited an improvement in financial resources. As the Select Committee was discussing the future of the Poor Law significant progress in this area was being introduced. The financial reforms of the 1860s were to usher in a new and more robust phase of Poor Law history.

NOTES

1. Calculated from the returns for expenditure given in the Annual Reports of the Poor Law Commission, and the Poor Law Board.

2. E.g. J. Redlich, *Local Government in England,* (1903) and G. Nicholls, *History of the English Poor Law,* (1854), completed by T. MacKay, *History of the English Poor Law,* (1896).

3. For these and similar examples see D. Roberts, 'How Cruel was the Victorian Poor Law?', *Historical Journal,* (1963), 100. Also H.L. Beales, 'The New Poor Law', *History,* xv, (1931).

4. S.E. Finer, *The Life and Times of Edwin Chadwick,* (1952) and R.A. Lewis, *Edwin Chadwick and the Public Health Movement 1832–1854,* (1952). For the early stages of this debate see: O.O.G.M. MacDonagh, 'The Nineteenth-Century Revolution in Government: A Reappraisal', *Historical Journal,* 1,(1958); H. Parris, 'The Nineteenth-Century Revolution in Government: A Reappraisal Reappraised', *ibid.,* 3, (1960); J. Hart, 'Nineteenth-Century Social Reform: A Tory Interpretation of History', *Past and Present,* xxxi, (1965).

5. D. Roberts, *Victorian Origins of the British Welfare State,* (1960), 179–81, 216–18. R.J. Lambert, 'A Victorian National Health Service', *Historical Journal,* v, (1962). R.G. Hodgkinson, *The Origins of the National Health Service,* (1967), 680.

6. E.g. see M.E. Rose, 'The Allowance System under the New Poor Law', *Economic History Review,* xix, (1966); N. McCord, 'The 1834 Poor Law Amendment Act on Tyneside', *International Review of Social History,* xiv, (1969); and A. Digby, *Pauper Palaces,* (1978).

7. W.C. Lubenow, *The Politics of Government Growth,* (1971), ch. 2.

8. A. Brundage, *The Making of the New Poor Law,* (1977), 171–2.

9. D. Roberts, (1960), *op. cit.,* 238–42.

10. *Ibid.,* 221–2.

11. N.C. Edsall, *The Anti-Poor Law Movement 1833–44,* (1971). M.E. Rose, 'The Anti-Poor Law Movement in the North of England', *Northern History,* 1, (1966).

12. Supplement the references in note 11 above by S.E. Finer, *The Life and Times of Sir Edwin Chadwick,* (1952), 181–92.

13. P. Dunkley, 'The "hungry forties" and the New Poor Law; a case study', *Historical Journal,* xvii, (1974). A. Digby, *op. cit.,* (1978) 230. For Day see M.E. Rose, *The English Poor Law 1780–1830,* (1971), 123–6.

14. M.E. Rose, *ibid.,* 127–32.

15. R. Pinker, *Social Theory and Social Policy,* (1971), 62.

16. R.J. Lambert, *Sir John Simon 1816–1904,* (1963), 152–4.

17. D. Roberts, *op. cit.,* (1960) 152–4. A. Digby, *op. cit.,* (1978), 77.

18. On audit see R. Jones, *Local Government Audit Law,* (1981), ch. 1.

19. On union formation see: A. Brundage, 'The landed interest and the New Poor Law', *English Historical Review.* lxxxvii, (1972); and P. Dunkley, 'The landed interest and the new Poor Law: a critical note', *ibid.,* lxxxviii, (1973). On the textile areas see E.C. Edsall, *op. cit.,* (1971) 263, App A.

For Norfolk A. Digby, *op. cit.*, (1978) 56.

20. D. Fraser (ed.), *The New Poor Law in the Nineteenth Century*, (1976), 111–27.
21. On rating see: J.V. Becket, *Local Taxation*, (1980); A. Digby, *op. cit.*, (1978), ch. 5; P.A. Wood, 'Finance and the Urban Poor law', in M.E. Rose, *The Poor and the City: The English poor law in its urban context, 1834–1914*, (1985).
22. D. Ashforth, 'Settlement and Removal in Urban Areas', in M.E. Rose, *ibid.*, (1985), 62–80.
23. B.A. Holderness, '"Open" and "close" parishes in England in the Eighteenth and Nineteenth centuries', *Agricultural History Review*, xx, pt. 2, (1972). A. Digby, *op. cit.*, (1978), 89–96.
24. M.E. Rose in D. Fraser (ed.), *op. cit.*, (1976), 36.
25. On staffing in this period see M.A. Crowther, *The Workhouse System 1834–1929*, (1983), ch. 5.
26. N.C. Edsall, *op. cit.*, 46.
27. For Catch see N. Longmate, *The Workhouse*, (1974), 102–4.
28. Local Government Board, Third Annual Report, (1873–4), 261.
29. See B. Abel Smith, *The Hospitals, 1800–1948*, (1964), 55–7 and 97–100.
30. On medical officers see R.G. Hodgkinson, *The Origins of the National Health Service*, (1967), ch. 2, 12 and 13. M.A. Crowther, *op. cit.*, 156–65; M. Flinn, 'Medical Services under the New Poor Law', in D. Fraser (ed.), *op. cit.*, (1976), 49–52; F.B. Smith, *The People's Health 1830–1910*, (1979), 382, 386–7.
31. M.A. Crowther, *ibid.*, 38–40.
32. Model plans were included in the early *Annual Reports*. For the 1850s the ideal is based on the correspondence between the inspectorate and the central authority in the MH/32 series.
33. The early *Annual Reports* present an optimistic picture. See e.g. N. Longmate, *op. cit.*, 88. For later difficulties see: N.C. Edsall (1971), *op. cit.*, 43–4, 222; M.A. Crowther, *op. cit.*, 47–8, and 50; the Leeds quotation is from D. Fraser, *The Evolution of the British Welfare State*, (2nd edn. 1984), 53. The *Annual Reports* show tenders approved for workhouse building which probably underestimate final cost.
34. P. Wood in M.E. Rose (ed.), *op. cit.*, (1985), 31–2.
35. P. Searby, 'The Relief of the Poor in Coventry', *Historical Journal*, 20, (1977), 351.
36. D. Fraser, 'The Poor Law as a Political Institution', in D. Fraser (ed.), *op. cit.*, (1976), 117–22; also on Sheffield F.B. Smith, *op. cit.*, (1979), 393.
37. G. Nicholls, *op. cit.*, (1854), vol. 2, 427.
38. A. Digby, *op. cit.*, (1978), 229–30.
39. N. McCord, *North-East England*, (1979), 93–4.
40. D. Fraser, *op. cit.*, (2nd edn. 1984), 53–4.
41. S. and B. Webb, *English Poor Law History*, (1929), pt. 11, vol. 1, 316, 138.
42. D. Roberts, *op. cit.*, (1963).
43. Poor Law Commission, Second Annual Report, (1836), App. A.
44. For workhouse regulations see *ibid.*, First Annual Report, (1835).

U. Henriques, 'How cruel was the Victorian Poor Law', *Historical Journal*, xi, (1968), 366.

45. H. Taine, *Notes on England*, (1957 edn.), 241.
46. A. Digby, *op. cit.*, (1978), 194.
47. J. Greenwood, *The Seven Curses of London*, (1869) found the idea of less eligible treatment for pauper children still being advanced at the close of the 1860s. F. Prochiska, 'Female Philanthropy and Domestic Service in Victorian England, 1800–1914', *British Institute of Historical Research*, (May, 1987) quoted in A.V. John (ed.), *Unequal Opportunities. Womens' Employment in England 1800–1914*, (1986), 13; E. Higgs, 'Domestic Service and Household production', in A.V. John (ed.), *ibid.*, 133; A. Digby, *op. cit.*, (1978), 192.
48. On the education of workhouse children see: F. Duke, 'Pauper Education', in D. Fraser (ed.), *op. cit.*, (1976), 67–86; M.A. Crowther, *op. cit.*, 201–7; and R. Johnson, 'Educational Policy and Social Control in Early Victorian England', *Past and Present*, November, (1970). I have also used R. Thompson, 'The Education of Pauper Children with special reference to Cumberland and Westmorland', Diss., Dip.Ed. Newcastle, (1973).
49. F. Duke, *ibid.*, 74.
50. *Ibid.*, 75.
51. *Ibid.*, 86.
52. A. Digby, *The Poor Law in Nineteenth-century England and Wales*, (1982), 34.
53. R. Pinker, *English Hospital Statistics, 1861–1938*, (1966), 91–5.
54. R.G. Hodgkinson, *op. cit.*, 303.
55. *Ibid.*, 323.
56. M. Flinn, in D. Fraser (ed.), *op. cit.*, 54–5.
57. On district medical officers see: R.G. Hodgkinson, *op. cit.*, ch. 2 and 11; M.A. Crowther, *op. cit.*, 136, 158; M. Flinn, *ibid.*, 49–52.
58. On expansion and cooperation with other bodies see: N. McCord, 'The Poor Law and Philanthropy', in D. Fraser (ed.), *op. cit.*, 100. On dispensaries see R.G. Hodgkinson, *ibid.*, ch. 7.
59. On the workhouse sick and their treatment see: R.G. Hodgkinson, *ibid.*, ch. 3; M.A Crowther, *op. cit.*, 160–7; B. Abel-Smith, *The Hospitals, 1800–1948*, (1964); F.B. Smith, *op. cit.*, 382–401; N. Longmate, *op. cit.*, 194–209; H. Marland, *Medicine and Society in Wakefield and Huddersfield 1780–1870*, (1987), 71–4.
60. G.M. Ayres, *England's First State Hospitals, 1867–1930*, (1971), 4.
61. O. MacDonagh, *Early Victorian Government*, (1977), 128.
62. On lunatics see: R.G. Hodgkinson, *ibid.*, ch. 4 and 15; K. Jones, *Lunacy Law and Conscience, 1744–1845*, (1955) and *Mental Health and Social Policy, 1845–1959*, (1961); J.K. Walton, 'The Treatment of Pauper Lunatics in Victorian England', in A. Sculled.), *Madhouses, Mad-Doctors and Madmen*, (1981)
63. For a good contemporary description see Charles Dickens, 'A Walk in the Workhouse', *Household Words*, 25 May 1850.
64. General Outdoor Relief Prohibitory Order, 2 August 1841; Outdoor Relief Prohibitory Order, December 1844; Outdoor Labour Test Order,

30 April 1842. The full text of these orders can be consulted in W.C. Glen, *General Orders of the Poor Law Commissioners,* (1852).

65. Poor Law Board, Fifth Annual Report, (1852), App. 3.

66. A. Digby, *op. cit.,* (1978), 109–14. J.H. Treble, *Urban Poverty in Britain 1830–1914,* (1979), 140–8. For Scots and Irish see M. Flinn in D. Fraser (ed.), *op. cit.,* 30 and M.E. Rose, *op. cit.,* (1971), 205–6.

67. On failure to appoint supervisors see D. Ashforth, 'The Urban Poor Law', in D. Fraser (ed.), *ibid.,* 136. For a contemporary discussion on the labour test see J. Greenwood, *op. cit.,* (1869), 281–6.

68. Poor Law Commission, Fifth Annual Report, (1839), 52–3; R. Vorspan, 'Vagrancy and the New Poor Law in late-Victorian and Edwardian England', *English Historical Review,* (1977), 59.

69. Poor Law Board, First Annual Report, (1848), App. A, No. 1.

70. For vagrants in addition to R. Vorspan, n. 68 above, see M.A. Crowther, *op. cit.,* ch. 10; and M.E. Rose, *op. cit.,* (1971), 208–13.

71. M.E. Rose, 'The Crisis of the Poor Relief in England, 1860–1890', in W.J. Mommsen (ed.), *The Emergence of the Welfare State in Britain and Germany,* (1981).

72. Select Committee, Final Report . . . on Poor Relief, ix, (1864), 189.

73. *Ibid.,* 216–8.

74. *Ibid.,* 45.

75. *Ibid.,* 189–92.

76. *Ibid.,* 197–8.

77. Hence the continuing debate over the acceptance of the New Poor Law by the gentry. See *Past and Present,* (May, 1990).

78. M.E. Rose, 'The allowance system under the New Poor Law', *Economic History Review,* xix, (1966); A. Digby, 'The Labour Market and the Continuity of Social Policy after 1834', *Economic History Review,* xxviii, (1975).

79. M. Tebbut, *Making Ends Meet. Pawnbroking and Working Class Credit,* (1983), 24–7.

CHAPTER FOUR

THE POOR LAW COMES OF AGE
c. 1865–94

The doubts which had threatened the New Poor Law in the early 1860s had largely disappeared by the end of the decade. The Poor Law Board had been made a permanent department of government and, when it was merged with the two sections which had administered public health to form the Local Government Board in 1871, it was the officials of the Poor Law Board who dominated the new department. In 1869 Goschen, as President of the Poor Law Board, had felt sufficiently confident to issue his famous minute complaining of the laxity in the administration of outdoor relief and reminding boards of guardians of the advantages to be obtained from a greater use of the workhouse test. This reassertion of the principles of 1834 was to be supported with considerable vigour by the Local Government Board which pursued what has became known as the 'crusade against outdoor relief'. The 1860s therefore are beginning to be regarded as a watershed in the history of the New Poor Law. Michael Rose has concluded: 'Thus by the mid-1870s the English Poor Law had come through its decade of crisis and had been so reconstructed as to be within sight of realising the Chadwickian ideal of 1834.'[1]

The new approach was reflected in the statistics of relief. The low

126

pattern of expenditure which had characterized the first three decades of the New Poor Law was followed by a decade of relatively high expenditure. A comparison of the annual average expenditure on Poor Relief for the quinquennium 1859–63 with that of 1869–73 shows spending had increased by 35 per cent with the rate of expansion increasing over the period. This represented a rate of expenditure seven times higher than the average for the three previous decades. This short spurt of high spending was followed by a return to the traditional pattern of severe economy. The decade 1869–73 to 1879–83 showing only a 3 per cent increase overall, while in the following decade, despite the severe depression of 1884–7 the rate of increase in expenditure was almost at a standstill. While the major problem for the historian is to explain the ability to curtail expenditure in the face of a rapidly rising population and demands for higher standards, the increased expenditure which introduced this period is worthy of special attention.[2]

During the period 1865–71 the statistics of the Poor Law Board show an increase in all major items of union expenditure, with the most significant increases occuring in the related areas of relief to the indoor pauper, salaries and borrowing to improve and extend workhouse facilities. For the central authority the explanation lay partly in 'a growing number of the more costly classes of pauper' and partly in 'a higher standard of efficiency'.[3] The more costly groups were the sick and the children. In the period 1864–5 to 1870–1 authorized borrowing for the creation of workhouse hospitals and schools alone was at twice the total annual rate of investment of the previous thirty years, and grants-in-aid of the salaries of medical officers showed a 20 per cent increase in the period 1867–8 to 1873–4. The borrowing was largely by urban unions, with London unions accounting for approximately 50 per cent of the total and Lancashire unions a further 25 per cent.[4] Although the causes of the crusade against outdoor relief were complex, it was undoubtedly aided by the associated expansion of specialist facilities for the more favoured groups. The more the children and the sick were removed from the existing workhouse buildings the greater the space for other pauper groups, particularly the able-bodied. Moreover, as these more deserving groups were removed it became possible to justify a more deterrent treatment for those who remained. An important prerequisite for the increased expenditure on buildings was a significant change in the administration of union finances.

The economies of the first three decades were in part the result of the financial limitations of the new regime and in particular the retention of the parish as the unit of settlement and finance. During the 1860s these restrictions were largely removed at a time when the overall financial environment was becoming more favourable. In the early 1860s three pieces of legislation transformed the rating system. First the Irremovable Poor Act of 1861 significantly altered the Law of Settlement by reducing the period required to claim irremovability from five years to three years. More significantly the area of residence was changed from the individual parish to the union. This change considerably increased the significance of the common fund and, in order to counter the objections of poorer parishes, the act also introduced its most significant change. In future contributions to the common fund were to be calculated on the rateable value of the various parishes, not their expenditure on Poor Relief.

At this time rateable value was to be based on existing county or borough valuations, but such was the variation in such valuations that additional legislation was produced in the following year. The Union Assessment Committee Act of 1862 ordered unions to establish committees to supervise new valuations with the aim of securing a more uniform standard. In 1865 the third piece of legislation completed the process. The Union Chargeability Act transferred the total cost of Poor Relief from the parish to the union, while at the same time reducing the period for claiming irremovability to one year.[5]

For many urban unions the increased cost of the irremovable poor was probably more than compensated for by the removal of parochial influence and the use of rateable value as a means of apportioning the rates. Improved assessment also meant that the growing wealth of many urban unions was now available to their boards of guardians. The more progressive system of rating was not without its limitations, however, as significant differences in the rateable value of the various unions remained. Indeed rural unions were sometimes to find their rateable values declining as agriculture faced severe overseas competition. The position was rendered more complex by the movement of the urban wealthy to the suburbs and boundaries drawn up in the 1830s became outdated, although the central authority was, not without good cause, wary of demands for boundary changes.

The stronger financial base of many unions was assisted by the improved borrowing prospects of this period. The gap between the ending of railway construction and the rise of colonial investment left many financial institutions seeking safe domestic outlets. Friendly societies and building societies expanding with the growth of self-help were facing increasing competition in some of their regular investment outlēts from the banks. The latter gaining deposits from the growing use of cheques, and losing the easy commission with the decline in the use of the bill of exchange, sought new outlets. Although the banks rarely sought the long-term involvement of lending to local authorities, their competition in other areas appears to have made the main institutional lenders favour local authority mortgages as a safe and attractive outlet.[6]

The Poor Law Board also had its role in the expansion of borrowing. As a result of the Lancashire Cotton Famine the Public Works Loan Commissioners had been established in 1863. This provided a source of cheap loans within the public sector. At first such loans were for a more restricted period than many of those available on the open market. However, the Poor Law Loans Act of 1869 allowed unions to extend their borrowing period from twenty to thirty years, which significantly reduced the annual repayments, so that additional borrowing could be accommodated without any increase in rates. This act was clearly intended to encourage those unions which had already taken advantage of central authority provision to undertake further borrowing.[7]

The financial changes made possible new approaches to the problem of Poor Relief. However, the long-standing respect for economy which had always dominated local decisions required more positive support than the easing of financial restrictions. In the matter of improving the conditions of the sick and the children the central authority was rarely to be the originator of change, rather it reacted to external pressures. The Local Government Board had a reputation for taking a cautious approach to social problems which at least matches that of its predecessor. To some extent its bleak reputation results from the fact that it has tended to receive the most careful scrutiny during periods when it has been dominated by those most vociferous in defence of the principles of 1834. Thus the controversy surrounding the Royal Commission of 1905–9 gave considerable publicity to the extreme views of Davy, and more recent attention to the campaign against out-relief has highlighted

Lambert as the main force in the administration of the 1870s. The resignation in 1876 of Sir John Simon has given added weight to the critics of this period. Although, for much of the 1880s and 1890s the central authority presented a more humane image, it remains true that able political leaders such as Charles Dilke and Joseph Chamberlain had only brief periods in charge, and that the leading civil servants were usually internal appointments, so that even the most tolerant were steeped in the traditions of less eligibility and the workhouse test.[8]

Although the inspectorate showed some increase, and there was a limited appointment of specialist inspectors, the increasing workload meant that the inspectorate continued to be too small to be effective. Problems also continued in the matter of correspondence with the localities. Indeed, until the 1890s the records tended to become even more chaotic as no attempt was made to separate Poor Law business from that concerning the various authorities associated with public health. The failure to introduce rational procedure is best illustrated by the continuing failure to acquire reasonable statistical information until faced by the demands of the Royal Commission of 1905–9.[9] Overburdened by routine, the central authority attempted where possible to avoid any prolonged correspondence. Where a third party was involved the Local Government Board would initially merely act as a 'post office', forwarding complaints to the union concerned and sending copies of the reply to the originator of the correspondence. If discussion continued it would ease itself out of further contact by explaining its limited powers and suggesting further correspondence be conducted directly with the union concerned. To some extent this caution was partly conditioned by the central authority's desire to advance more easily in areas which they regarded as significant, such as the campaign against outdoor relief, or some particular workhouse expenditure. Here they were also assisted by the growth of regional meetings of boards of guardians which were always attended by the regional inspector. Reports of such meetings were published from the mid-1870s and served as a means· by which the central authority could indirectly disseminate its views and assisted progress to regional uniformity.[10]

In the larger unions boards of guardians often appear to be better organized in this period. Particularly noteworthy was the development of a more effective committee system sometimes with further delegation to standing sub-committees. This increased supervision, especially in the areas of finance and the workhouse, and the chairmen of such committees often became the most powerful figures on the boards of guardians, with the chairman and vice-chairman of the board becoming more of a figure-head, appointed as a reward for long service. Nevertheless, although boards of guardians were in a stronger position, politically the dominant view continued to be the support for economical administration, and the strongest recommendation for increased expenditure remained that it would produce early economies.

The Changing Frontiers of Relief

In view of the prevailing desire for economy it is not surprising that the initiative for providing a better service for the sick pauper should have arisen largely outside of the Poor Law. Any complacency resulting from the Select Committee Report of 1864 was quickly dispelled. Its disregard of the medical profession's demands for improved salaries and conditions of service had aroused a formidable opponent which was to be favoured with considerable public support following the revelations of scandals in workhouse hospitals in the metropolis and the fears of epidemic disease. The result was that 'every propaganda weapon in the reformers' armoury was trained on parliament and government from 1865'.[11] The inadequacies of hospital provision in the workhouses which had been revealed by such as Louisa Twining without any significant effect, became a national matter in 1865. The protest appears to have commenced with newspaper reports covering the deaths of two paupers in London workhouses. The central authority had weathered other such scandals, but in this case the leading medical journal, The Lancet, established its own enquiry into London workhouse infirmaries. This thorough investigation produced evidence of widespread defects, confirming earlier findings which had been largely ignored.

London workhouses were often badly sited having such unsuitable neighbours as bone-boilers and carpet-beaters. Buildings which were intended to deter the able-bodied had often proved difficult to adapt to the needs of more deserving inmates. Inadequacies of drainage and water supply were reflected in primitive toilet and washing facilities. 'Bedridden patients habitually washed their hands and faces in their toilet utensils'. The neglect of elementary cleanliness was also found in dirty bed linen and the sharing of towels; one ward for patients with syphilis having only one towel for the use of eight inmates. In some cases water closets were in wards in public view. Buildings were so overcrowded that sick wards could be scattered inconveniently throughout the building and at times classification was forgotten as the sick and aged and infirm were crowded into any available space. Lack of effective classification was observed most among the long-term aged and insane inmates. Attitudes to skin infections were often apathetic in such circumstances and in the more serious cases patients with highly contagious fevers were housed among non-infectious patients. Overcrowding encouraged too many beds per ward while in Lewisham beds were shared, with but 2 ft being available to each occupant because of a wooden separation down the centre of the bed. The report suggested that the Poor Law Board's standard of 500 cubic ft of space for each patient was woefully inadequate, although in five workhouses even this minimum was not being met. Overcrowding was made more uncomfortable by failings in heating, lighting and ventilation. Windows were often sited high in the walls and were limited in quantity, presumably to prevent easy exit by the able-bodied. For the long-term infirm and feeble-minded diet was often that provided for the able-bodied. From overworked medical staff such patients received a low priority and in the worst instances lack of space even prevented the use of day-rooms to provide a minimum of recreation. According to *The Lancet*, the majority of 'permanents' led a 'vegetable' existance.

Staffing was also widely condemned. Although paid nursing staff was developing there remained a widespread employment of paupers, unsuited on the grounds of age, handicap or alcoholism, to be termed nurses. Even using the inefficient, the number of nurses was frequently inadequate and control over patients in such cases was often maintained by fear. Night nursing appeared to be uniformly neglected. In the face of these difficulties *The Lancet* presented the medical officers as overworked and grossly underpaid, engaged in a ceaseless battle on behalf of the poor against tyrannical workhouse masters and economy-minded boards of guardians.

The Lancet concluded that no amount of patching-up could remedy the defects, yet the Poor Law provision was likely to remain the main source of hospital care for the London poor. 'The State hospitals are in the workhouse wards'. It saw little chance of improvement in a system which continued to house the sick with the able-bodied in the workhouse and where control lay with the ignorant and parsimonious. What was needed was the creation of specialist hospitals away from the workhouses. 'To perpetuate thrity-nine bad hospitals where half a dozen good ones will suffice will be an act of grave and dangerous misgovernment.'[12]

The Lancet enquiry had not found all hospitals to be equally bad. Indeed, approximately one-third of the infirmaries examined were capable of being developed to the standards of the voluntary hospitals. A larger number, however, even with considerable expenditure, would never be suited to taking care of more than the chronic and infirm, while the worst six buildings were regarded as unsuitable even to house the able-bodied. It was unfortunate that those buildings with the best prospects were generally in the more prosperous areas so that the majority of the poor faced the least adequate facilities.

The Lancet recommended that the central authority should appoint specialist medical and surgical inspectors. They were certain that the sick poor should be housed in separate institutions, with an allocation of space per bed at least twice the current minimum. They believed that effective classification required separate wards for imbeciles, acute cases and the aged and infirm, and that long-term patients should have day-rooms. On staffing they suggested that there should be a paid day and night nurse and one assistant nurse for every fifty patients. They felt resident medical officers should be appointed on the scale of one for every 250 patients and that these officers should not be concerned with the supply or dispensing of medicines.

Agitation from The Lancet was supported by pressure from the Poor Law Medical Officers' Association and a prestigious new foundation, the Association for the Improvement of Workhouse Infirmaries. The campaign was given added impetus by the findings of the Poor Law Board's own investigations. Its newly appointed medical inspector, Dr Smith and Inspectors Farnall and Cane produced reports which have been seen as broadly supporting the need for reform.[13] Although noting current improvement their conclusions suggested that any significant building programme would require financial help being given to the poorer unions. In 1867 the government responded by introducing the Metropolitan Poor Act. In recommending this legislation, Gathorne-Hardy gave the most quoted remark by any President of the Poor Law Board, apparently rejecting the doctrine of less eligibility regarding the treatment of the sick. He informed the House of Commons that the evils exposed were the result of applying the necessarily deterrent workhouse administration 'to the sick, who were not proper objects for such a system.'[14]

The legislation ordered the amalgamation of the medical services of the London unions to provide treament by larger units. The Metropolitan Asylums Board, consisting of forty-five representatives of boards of guardians and fifteen members appointed by the Poor Law Board, became the hospital authority for the whole of Greater London with respect to the treatment of typhus, smallpox and insanity, which, together with other items, the most important of which was the salaries of medical officers, were to be paid from a Common Poor Fund financed by the unions in proportion to their rateable value. Regarding other items of medical relief the unions were grouped into 'sick asylum districts' which were to provide separate hospitals for the pauper sick. The Act has been represented as a 'carefully balanced compromise between central direction and local autonomy with some measure of rate equalisation built into it'.[15]

The Act was followed by proposals for a substantial building programme by the London unions. In order to reduce expenditure the Poor Law Board made the 'sick asylum districts' into full unions, taking over all the property and duties of the member unions, thus enabling individual workhouses to be allocated special functions; such as acting as the union hospital. Successful pressure was meanwhile maintained on unions which stayed outside the amalgamations to make additional hospital provision. Any union which refused to establish separate infirmaries for the non-infectious sick was refused money from the common fund for the payment of its medical officers. As a result of the building programme, between 1868 and 1871 approximately 11,000 new places were created in London workhouses, although almost half of these were taken in relieving the overcrowding of existing institutions. Thus even this expansion appears to have been insufficient to keep pace with the rising numbers of paupers and the central authority's desire to increase numbers in receipt of indoor relief.[16]

The 1867 Act is widely regarded as important because of the building programme it instigated and for freeing hospitals from the influence of workhouse masters. London was to lead the way in provision for the sick poor. By 1882 six fever hospitals, four asylums and twenty infirmaries had been created in the metropolitan area.[17] In 1888 a Select Committee of the House of Lords was informed that the transfer of patients from the sick wards of London workhouses to separate infirmaries was almost completed. It was also alleged that the gap between Poor Law and voluntary hospitals in London had narrowed; paid nurses who in 1866 had only numbered 111 had increased to over 1,000 and in addition part-time medical officers, often supplying their own drugs, had been largely replaced by resident officers and their assistants with medicines supplied by boards of guardians.[18] This progress was the result of twenty years of considerable effort and was unfortunately not typical of Poor Law provision in other areas.

Events in London stimulated greater interest in the provincial workhouses. *The Lancet,* the popular press and the Poor Law Board's inspectorate all provided evidence of the need to improve both buildings and staffing. The hostile *Lancet* tended to publicize the sensational, but was able to provide a varied selection of horror stories well-suited to capturing the attention of a wider audience. Farnham in Hampshire, an old overcrowded workhouse, had an infirmary which held six times the number for which it had been built. In this institution all who were remotely able-bodied left the workhouse during the hop-picking season leaving it unclean for several weeks each year. Although, one-third of the inmates were sick there was only one paid nurse in what was termed 'a marvel of bad construction' with the patients usually as ill-cleansed as the building.[19] Even new buildings could be scandalously ineffective. Marland Workhouse, near Rochdale, a building opened in 1864 to house 210 inmates at two per bed was occupied in 1870 by 194 patients, none of whom were able-bodied. Here the infectious wandered indiscriminately, there were inadequate facilities for washing clothes or patients and medicines were administered by pauper nurses who couldn't read. Medicine bottles were kept in a box with blacking and firewood. Inmates urinated in a tub in a corner of their ward, the contents of which were sold for scouring cotton. Diets prescribed by the medical officer were rarely provided and the only vegetable appeared to be potatoes. The inmates suffered from itch and head sores and diarrhoea was endemic.[20]

The official inspectors were more cautious in their criticisms, although Cane, a belated convert to the cause of hospital reform, was severe on the continuing defects in the northern textile district. There was a lack of anything approaching classification of the sick in the Stockport Workhouse; in Preston the sharing of beds by those with different diseases was increasing, and in the grossly overcrowded Huddersfield Workhouse 'puddings were boiled in the same copper as the foul linen was washed and boiled in'. In general Cane found the majority of workhouses and their staffing very unsuited to the care of the sick. In 1867 the Poor Law Board ordered its medical inspector, Dr Smith, to prepare a report on forty-eight provincial workhouse infirmaries. His report is perhaps the most balanced, showing the widespread variation which existed between institutions. Nevertheless, the report contained much evidence of defective buildings and furnishings, of inadequacies in classification, especially for the infectious, and of the continued widespread employment of pauper nurses. Smith's report was circulated to all unions and was followed by a campaign to improve provincial standards. Some of the recommendations proposed by the Poor Law Board indicate how far less eligible standards had been applied to the sick. The provision of benches with backs and (for special cases) cushions, combs and hair-brushes, pottery urinals to each bed, lockers or bed tables and a small individual towel were among items detailed as suitable for sick patients. Even more basic were instructions on the size of bed and the filling of mattresses.[21] However, without the incentives of the London Common Poor Fund regional improvement was less marked and the statistics of union borrowing support the view that improvements were largely confined to large urban unions. Thus in Norfolk in 1896 only eight unions had 'separate infirmaries or infectious wards and these were administered as part of the workhouse, rather than, as was beginning to be the case in some urban areas, as a state hospital which provided free medicine.'[22]

Nevertheless, the improvement in terms of numbers was significant. Each year between 1861 and 1891 it has been calculated that 1,000 beds were added to public provision and by 1891 three out of four beds for the sick were in Poor Law institutions.[23] The expansion of Poor Law hospitals was in part the result of popular fear of infectious disease, however, even in this vital area progress was both slow and patchy. Thus in the 1890s Dewsbury Workhouse was found to be admitting smallpox cases.[24] When *The Lancet* had a further burst of interest in the workhouse sick in 1895 it was to find many provincial workhouses as bad as they had been in the 1860s.[25]

For the medical profession the Poor Law doctor remained part of a second class service, with the profession being normally more concerned with the fee paying sector. Rural guardians in particular continued to make part-time appointments, whose inadequate salaries were often matched by limited effort. Although the Local Government Board was to claim that all pauper nurses had been replaced by 1878–9 they were still ordering an end to their employment in 1897. In rural Norfolk any noticeable recruitment of paid nurses had to await the 1890s with the isolation of rural unions adding to the difficulties of obtaining professionals for the boring routine of caring for workhouse geriatrics in poor-quality facilities.[26]

Despite Gathorne-Hardy's declaration of 1867 the doctrinaire belief that the pauper sick were to some extent undeserving persisted, particularly among the officials of the Local Government Board. Thus Chief Inspector Langley believed that where the sick had obviously neglected opportunities for self-help their family should be made to enter the workhouse as a condition of obtaining treatment. Both the Local Government Board and the Charity Organization Society were anxious that improved medical relief should not deter self-help and voluntary provision. Thus the Charity Organization Society members of the Birmingham Board of Guardians were able to obtain a ruling that all sick should be brought into the infirmary by the workhouse gate and officially the term pauper or Poor Law was always used when reference was made to infirmaries or dispensaries provided by boards of guardians.[27]

The belief in a less eligible treatment for the sick poor continued to be expressed in the twentieth century, but by the Edwardian period they were increasingly unrepresentative. In practice there was an enormous variation of service as boards of guardians weighed the benefits of reform against the traditional prejudices and the desire for economy. Nevertheless, the evidence suggests that the tide was slowly flowing against the application of a deterrent policy for the sick. The campaign against outdoor relief when applied to the sick placed greater pressure on indoor facilities and, in widening the clientele, possibly added to the pressures for reform. Wherever standards were improved to approach the level of voluntary provision the impact of less eligibility was diminished. By 1891 almost 73,000 sick were in Poor Law accommodation compared with under 30,000 in voluntary hospitals. Slightly more than 12,000, or in excess of 16 per cent of Poor Law patients, were in separate infirmaries, and it seems fair to assume that here the change from pauper to patient was most noticeable. The change was always more obvious to the politician than to the civil servant of the Local Government Board. Hence, following the extension of the franchise in 1884–5, parliament gave legal recognition to the changes which were underway. The Medical Relief (Disqualifications Removal) Act of 1885 allowed those who received medical relief only, to retain their vote thus removing the legal stigma of pauperism.[28]

For the insane financial expediency continued to dictate progress. The Lunacy Commissioners consistently urged the removal of the insane from the workhouse. Under the 1867 Act London erected two very large asylums intended to house the harmless, chronic lunatics. However, the prospect of transferring the cost of their lunatics to the Common Poor Fund appealed to the unions to such an extent, that these institutions were soon 'filled up with patients of all ages suffering from every type of mental disorder, acute and chronic'.[29] In 1874 the weekly payment of 4s. from the Consolidated Fund towards the cost of each pauper lunatic transferred to an authorized asylum, resulted in the rapid increase in the movement of pauper lunatics from provincial workhouses as boards of guardians sought to make space in their workhouses while profiting from the grant. In 1875 the Lunacy Commissioners warned of the inevitable result as pressure became too great for existing establishments. Thus for many of the insane the use of unsatisfactory workhouse accommodation was to continue.[30] Nevertheless, the official statistics show that whereas pauper lunatics in institutions had absorbed 8 per cent of total expenditure on relief in 1861–5 they totalled almost 12½ per cent in 1876–80.

For children the principle of removing them from the corrupting influence of other workhouse inmates was already widely accepted. Although Inspector Tufnell continued to support District Schools until his resignation in 1874, the general trend of informed opinion was moving against the larger institution. In addition to the practical administrative problems which had first produced concern, there were increasing doubts being cast on the virtues of the education and morals being inculcated. Too strict a discipline was held to be producing 'a routine of duty which leaves open no temptation to wrong and annhilates the choice of right'.[31] It was held that many were being trained for nothing more than a life of pauperism. Indeed some girls it was noted had turned to prostitution quite soon after leaving the school, a widely recognized step on the road to pauperism. Health problems, in particular the prevalence of eye infections, and the special problems relating to transient workhouse inmates, known as the 'ins and outs' raised further complaints.

Discontent with the District School was heightened at local level by the belief that they were more expensive and that the individual union had limited control over expenditure. The result was a greater enthusiasm for the expansion of the detached school, with children being accommodated and taught in self-contained buildings separate from the workhouse. By 1870 all London Poor Law authorities maintained such schools and the larger provincial urban unions were moving in the same direction, with forty-nine separate schools having been established outside of the metropolitan area.[32] In 1873 the first woman inspector, appointed to inspect girls in workhouses and schools, Jane Senior, presented a survey of the educational situation. She had no hesitation in condemning the large District Schools: 'I was unfavourably impressed with the effect of thus massing children together in large numbers . . . considering the amount of money and labour bestowed, did I consider the physical condition of the girls in the schools and their moral condition on coming out of them, disappointing and unsatisfactory.'[33] For Mrs Senior the answer lay in alternative solutions currently being discussed.

The alternatives being discussed were based on the belief that pauper children should have some family foundation to their upbringing. Pauper children were regarded as being in greater need of physical and moral care. One answer was the cottage homes. The original idea is generally accepted as coming from the Continent, but by the 1870s there were many examples of such establishments being provided by charity in England and Wales. The idea was that by placing children into smaller groups they could be provided with close supervision while avoiding the excessive discipline of the district schools. For the Poor Law authorities they also had the attraction of requiring a lower capital investment.[34]

Between 1874 and 1878 six unions were to obtain permission to build such homes as an experiment. Their success led to the gradual wider adoption of the scheme. The nature of the cottage homes varied considerably. The ideal appeared to be a well situated group

139

of self-contained cottages providing a village atmosphere. Each cottage would be presided over by foster parents and the village would have its own school, industrial training and residential facilities.[35] However, in some rural areas economy was served by having a separate home in each parish, while for some urban unions, the cottage homes, like the detached schools, were built adjacent to the existing workhouse. In these cases the children usually attended the local elementary school.

The more advanced reformers of the period such as Louise Twining and Florence Hill tended to favour the boarding-out of children. By this system, its supporters held that the child was provided with a more settled and normal home. Successful experience in Scotland and Ireland preceded the commencement of experiments in English unions in 1869. The Local Government Board reported twenty-one such schemes in operation by 1870.[36] The central authority was initially less than enthusiastic in its support, being concerned with the problems of obtaining suitable foster parents and with the need for careful supervision of the future upbringing of the child. Progress was therefore at first rather slow, although the scheme was to be eventually widely adopted.

Effective supervision was the initial stumbling block, being at first an additional duty for overworked relieving officers. From 1885, the appointment of an inspector, Miss Mason, to report on children boarded-out and the establishment of boarding-out committees in individual unions began to make the system more acceptable. In 1889 the Local Government Board produced model rules to control boarding-out while Miss Mason's reports exposed the potential dangers of child abuse and the need for regular supervision.[37]

It is difficult to gauge the exact numbers boarded-out. Duke asserts that as early as 1877 9,248 children were boarded-out although only 374 were under the regulations of the Local Government Board. In practice many children were being placed with relatives, but supported by outdoor relief. Mrs Senior had recognized the danger of boarding-out being adopted by boards of guardians seeking 'to avoid the necessity of providing better accommodation for children in workhouse schools'. By the end of the century 9,000 children were officially boarded-out, approximately one-seventh of those in institutions. A major problem with boarding-out, particularly in rural areas, was that payments for the upkeep of the pauper child were higher than the amount spent by the labourer on his own children. However, this evasion of the spirit of less eligibility was accepted by many boards of guardians as boarding-out was cheaper than maintaining children in an institution.

A further method of moving children from the workhouse atmosphere was the use of certified schools. From the early 1860s some unions had paid for certain children's education in charitable institutions. Roman Catholics and Jews were usually anxious to remove the children of their respective faiths from the workhouse, a factor duly noted by boards of guardians interested in economy. Increasingly, the need to provide for the handicapped such as the blind and the deaf was recognized by individual unions. There was also the possibility of sending children to special training estab-lishments such as the Wellesley Training Ships for boys and domestic science training for girls. In a number of cases unions sought to remove their more troublesome children to such institu-tions. Some unions for a time also took advantage of organized emigration schemes, children from a number of unions being escorted to Canada to be indentured as servants and farm workers. However, revelations of scandals resulted in the central authority condemning such schemes on the grounds that they were incapable of responsible supervision. Finally, in 1893 Sheffield originated the 'scattered homes' experiment whereby children were placed in small family homes in rented or bought accommodation scattered throughout the city. Each home was controlled by a salaried foster mother, usually assisted by one of the elder children. Here the departure from the institutional spirit was a strong recom-mendation, but the scheme was delayed by central authority fears over supervision and by the dislike of local residents over the prospect of pauper children being housed in their district.

The coming of state schools in 1870 has been seen as a watershed in the history of pauper education. Before 1870 the sending of children to schools outside the Poor Law had been looked upon with disfavour because of the inability to secure effective industrial training. However, from the 1870s the emphasis was to place the pauper child as far as possible in a normal environment mixing with other children. Hence to the reformers of the period the state schools provided an ideal answer, while for boards of guardians it was increasingly cheaper than employing their own teachers and equip-ping their own schools. By 1898 only sixty-eight workhouse schools remained, 493 unions having their pauper children attend local elementary schools. However, it must not be forgotten that the uniformity of clothing and the regulated lifestyle of the pauper child often continued to distinguish them from their fellow pupils.[38]

The overall conclusion with regard to both the handling of the sick and the children in this period must be one of confusion. In these areas, although eager to restrain abuse, the central authority was to display only the most vaguely positive line of development. It accepted the need for separate treatment but its overall desire for economy and its limited powers of coercion usually left the final decision to the individual board of guardians.

The Crusade Against Outdoor Relief

The limited initiative shown by the central authority in securing the provision of better facilities for the sick and the children was in contrast to the increasing certainty with which they reasserted the principle of the workhouse test from the late 1860s. For those taking a Whiggish approach to the Poor Law, the improvements with regard to the sick and the children provide signs of a more humane treatment which prepared the ground for the improvements of the twentieth century. The picture becomes less clear when the crusade against outdoor relief is considered.

The failure of the Poor Law Board in its attempt to exercise control over outdoor relief in 1852 had resulted in many unions giving outdoor relief indiscriminately, even to the able-bodied. Although in some of the larger urban communities a growing population had resulted in overcrowding of workhouse facilities, in general most workhouses were only 50 to 70 per cent fully occupied in the 1850s.[39] In some cases boards of guardians regarded workhouses as suitable only for those of known bad character and they were reluctant to mix other applicants for relief with so contaminated a group. Many of the workhouses matched the supposed character of the inmates being of poor quality and this too may have deterred the more humane boards from making greater use of their facilities. Such boards frequently justified outdoor relief as necessary to maintain the family unit. However, there seems little doubt that for most unions the most significant factor was economy. The cost of maintaining a pauper in the workhouse in the 1860s was approximately 6s. per head, whereas many unions were offering out-relief at one-third of this amount or less.

Such miserly amounts were not calculated to maintain the pauper. They were often justified on the grounds that applicants had unrevealed resources, but the reality was that the boards were either subsidising inadequate earnings or expecting others to make up the difference. The expansion of out-relief was aided by the fact that there was no clear dividing line in the majority of cases which separated the applicant who was suitable for indoor relief from those suited to outdoor relief. In some unions 'revision' committees were established with the express purpose of examining lists of indoor paupers, the intention being to transfer as many inmates as possible to the outdoor relief lists. The limitations of central-authority guidance and the strength of local independence had produced a most unsystematic approach to outdoor relief with a wide range of policies. Thus the Royal Commission on Friendly Societies in 1871 was informed that in the matter of sickness benefit paid by societies some did not recognize such benefit as income in assessing outdoor relief, some took half into consideration while others took all sick pay into account.[40]

For the central authority the disturbing feature was that the 1860s had seen an increase in spending on outdoor relief approaching 25 per cent and the ratio of outdoor paupers to total population had risen from 1 in 27 in 1860 to 1 in 25 in 1870.[41] Official discontent was brought to a head by the recurrence of distress in London in the late 1860s. Trade depression, cholera, severe weather and higher food prices following bad harvests combined with the decline of the Thames shipbuilding industry to produce serious problems. The resulting disorders assisted in the passage of the Second Reform Bill, which can be seen as an attempt to separate the respectable working class from the undeserving. However, while political reform may have eased the tension it did nothing to relieve the problem of poverty among the unemployed casual workers in the East End of London. As in 1860–1 the threat of disorder produced a considerable increase in the distribution of charitable relief. This in its turn raised complaints from both the Poor Law and influential figures in the charity movement that indiscriminate charitable relief was discouraging the practice of self-help and so demoralizing the poor that many scroungers were obtaining relief in addition to earnings, and that charity and the Poor Law were often relieving the same individuals. In 1869 the establishment of the Charity Organization Society and the issuing of the Goschen Minute showed the determination of both charity and the Poor Law that these abuses should cease.[42]

Goschen, as President of the Poor Law Board, commented upon the recent events in the metropolis. He was especially concerned with the increase in outdoor relief and in particular stressed the need for boards of guardians to recognize that their legal obligation was to the relief of the destitute and, however harsh it might appear, relief could never be given in aid of wages. He was concerned that recent large sums expended by charities had 'tended to attract pauperism to districts where money flowed most freely'. He thought it of 'essential importance' that the Poor Law authorities and the administrators of charities should cooperate to 'avoid the double distribution of relief'. By limiting its provision to the destitute the Poor Law would minimize expenditure and encourage 'recognition of the necessity for self-reliance and thrift'. The role of charity was equally easy to define, their role lay 'in assisting those, who have some but insufficient means, and who though on the verge of pauperism are not actually paupers'.[43]

Goschen's belief was very much in accord with the ideals of the Charity Organization Society. Both believed that by careful enquiry into the individual case it would be possible to separate those deserving of charity from those destined for Poor Relief. The Poor Law unions by refusing to give relief to any but the destitute would finally eliminate the scrounger. The test of destitution was the workhouse and both the central authority of the Poor Law and the Charity Organization Society had as their objective the reduction, and if possible the elimination, of outdoor relief. Outdoor relief was regarded as weakening the spirit of self-help and destroying the recognition by families of their duty to provide for their impoverished members.

For London the crusade received early financial encouragement. The Metropolitan Poor Law Amendment Act of 1870 gave a supplement of 5d. a day towards the cost of indoor paupers, the charge falling upon the Metropolitan Common Poor Fund. The crusade was taken up with enthusiasm by the Local Government Board. With Lambert's energetic support Goschen's recommendations received a stricter and more detailed interpretation and were carried from London to the provinces. In this instance there can be little doubt that the central authority was providing a clear lead. However, the central authority did not repeat the error of 1852. No general prohibitory order was issued, the explanation being that what was needed was a stricter administration of existing regulations. In this way direct confrontation was avoided. The central authority used every effort to persuade the boards of guardians of the virtues and savings to be made by a stricter administration. The first step of the Local Government Board was a circular to the inspectorate urging them to stress 'the advantages which result not only to the ratepayers but to the poor themselves from the offer of indoor relief in preference to outdoor relief.'[44] The exhortations of the inspectorate were supported by the regular publication of regional tables comparing performance of individual unions with regard to reduction in outdoor relief and total expenditure. Thus, in addition to the basic aim of cost reduction, the Local Government Board sought to encourage greater uniformity of practice. Throughout the 1870s and 1880s the Annual Reports gave regular publicity to conferences and individual union administrations which supported the official policy. The early comments largely concern London but attention was paid later to what were regarded as successful provincial unions.[45]

The Charity Organization Society assisted the central authority in its campaign to propagate the advantages of following the crusade. COS activists addressed regional conferences and in the localities some were elected to boards of guardians where they could be relied upon to give support to the inspectorate. However, the success of the campaign did not depend on COS support as there were many unions which gave support where COS influence appeared negligible.[46]

Few unions could be expected to reach the ideal of the termination of outdoor relief and the inspectorate sought to advance by urging an increased use of the workhouse test and a stricter administration of out-relief. Indoor relief was urged for all single able-bodied applicants and it was encouraged for widows, including those with a single child. Married women who had been left as a charge on the rates by their husband for any reason were suspected of collusion, and the workhouse was also recommended for any whose family were felt to have the means to contribute towards their support. The campaign was particularly harsh on women, and as a result the number of women in receipt of outdoor relief fell from 166,407 in 1871 to 53,391 in 1891.[47] Increasingly unions who supported the crusade began to take legal action against relatives who had a liability to support relatives and some boards of guardians paid a percentage inducement to relieving officers who obtained contributions from relatives towards the maintenance of pauper claimants. Inspector Knollys reported that the Sunderland Union in 1890 had reclaimed 9 per cent of its total expenditure on relief from relatives.[48]

The use of the partial workhouse test could also be used as a means of deterring applicants as workhouses became overcrowded. Widows with large families could find themselves in the position whereby some of their children were offered the workhouse as a condition of relief, and in other cases the father of a family might be required to enter the workhouse before relief was given to his family. For outdoor relief generally the recommendation was for more regular checks on recipients by relieving officers. After meetings with the Poor Law authorities in Malvern, Reading and London, the COS reported that the agreed aim was to 'treat out-relief as an exceptional privilege to be allowed only to persons of good character under exceptional circumstances.'[49]

Accompanying the demands for stricter control of outdoor relief the central authority showed greater concern for the operation of the outdoor labour test. Although the test was in conflict with the emphasis on the workhouse it was retained as a safety valve in dealing with the industrial areas. Where outdoor relief was given the inspectorate began urging that it be adequate in amount. This had the double advantage of diminishing the need for claimants to obtain additional income from charitable sources and by making the item more costly served to diminish the reluctance to use the workhouse test.

It seems likely that the campaign against outdoor relief was aided by the nature of the financial reforms of the early 1860s and by the resulting greater expenditure on workhouse buildings. Although the financial reforms had improved the position of many unions it did not follow that there would be any drive to greater expenditure. Indeed the transfer of the financial burden from the poorer to the richer parishes meant that ratepayers in these areas would be more supportive of attempts to reduce spending. Moreover, the prevailing financial climate has been shown to favour capital expenditure financed by borrowing rather than immediate increase in rates thus causing some unions to rethink their policy. To some extent expenditure on buildings may have produced improvements which lessened ratepayer opposition to the use of the workhouse test.

146

Certainly the removal of the sick and the children from the workhouses made it possible to justify a more deterrent regime.[50] Although it is dangerous to generalize the main supporters of the campaign for ending outdoor relief among the unions often appear among the lists of major borrowers.

The outstanding example of a more deterrent approach was the use of the main Poplar Workhouse for the able-bodied only. The transfer of the aged and infirm to the Bromley Workhouse enabled the Poplar Workhouse to become a 'House of Industry'. Here men were to pick 5 lb of oakum per day and women were required to pick 3 lb. The harshness of this task can be seen in comparison with male convicts who were only expected to pick 3½ lb. Failure to complete the task could result in being placed on a bread and water diet or being charged before a magistrate. The Poplar test workhouse was used by neighbouring unions. In 1873 the workhouse had 788 places but only 166 inmates of whom never less than 100 were on the bread and water diet. Similar schemes were operated in Kensington and Birmingham, the latter substituting sloping wooden shelves for beds. Inevitably such schemes that were dependent on maintaining institutions which were largely empty came under pressure when rising urban populations produced demands for the expansion of other accommodation. Poplar Workhouse started re-admitting sick inmates in 1882.[51]

The belief that the greater use of the workhouse test would significantly reduce numbers was an essential part of the campaign which was emphasized by both the Poor Law and the COS. Indeed such a stress was essential to counteract the fact that indoor relief was more expensive per head. Initially the Local Government Board was to stress that only 10 per cent of those offered the workhouse normally accepted. Both central authority and COS always stressed that savings would follow any immediate increase in costs and both local and national statistics began to lend support to their view.

Local support appears to have varied considerably according to the official annual statistics. Exceptional support was to be found in Whitechapel, Stepney and St George's Unions in London's East End. Here outdoor relief virtually disappeared with deserving cases being handled by charity. In the provinces, Birmingham in the Midlands; Manchester, Liverpool and Preston in the north-west and Sunderland and West Hartlepool in the north-east were all to emerge as model unions.[52]

National statistics provide a picture of impressive progress. The early 1870s showed falls in expenditure on both indoor and outdoor relief, with the campaign being assisted by the economic prosperity of the period. In the long-term numbers on outdoor relief, which had always exceeded 700,000 in the 1860s, had been reduced by approximately 150,000 by the 1880s.[53] Whereas outdoor relief had comprised 53 per cent of expenditure on relief in the early 1860s it had been reduced to 35 per cent by 1876–80. In the same period indoor relief had risen as a percentage from less than 18 per cent to over 20 per cent and was to continue to rise. For the central authority the most impressive support for their campaign came in the figures for pauperism as a percentage of total population. In the late 1860s this had been 4.7 per cent, by 1880 it had been reduced to 3.2 per cent and by 1890 to a mere 2.7 per cent.[54] For the central authority and their supporters the campaign was being vindicated by both a reduction in pauperism and a lowering of expenditure.

Enthusiasm for the crusade waned at local level according to the circumstances of the individual union. Whereas in the 1860s the majority of workhouse inmates were sick, children and the aged and infirm, the crusade was accompanied by an increase in the proportion of the aged and the able-bodied males. By the close of this period attitudes to both of these groups were under considerable discussion. The most serious problems related to the able-bodied male.

In normal and good years the problem of the unemployed was largely the problem of the casually employed. However, bad weather and trade depression, especially when they occurred together, could extend the problem into the ranks of the better paid workers. The growing urbanization and the increased integration of the economy made such problems more obvious in this period. For the central authority it was usually held in the earliest stages of the severest distress that the workhouse test would be adequate. In the long-term they encouraged the use of the partial workhouse test to economize on workhouse space and in the final resort accepted the need for a well conducted outdoor labour test. For the more deserving applicants who were felt to be unsuited to the Poor Law, the answer lay in an appeal to charity. For the union, central authority remedies could be both expensive and politically unacceptable.

Both the central and the local authorities when in the initial stages of any severe economic distress would often deny its existence.

For the local authority further action depended on the local situation, although economy was often a common feature guiding response. Hard-pressed unions would seek to encourage charitable assistance, sometimes with the support of the COS and sometimes in forms of which it did not approve. In addition there was a long-standing tradition in urban areas of requesting the municipal authorities to undertake works of public utility at such times. When the burden was unavoidable an economy-minded authority could delay more expensive action by the offer of relief by loan. In the event of a depression continuing the deterrent use of the workhouse test might well be offered, but in view of the numbers involved such a threat was often neither practical nor effective, as the workhouse became overcrowded. Where test labour had to be introduced the union would have recourse to schemes whose main recommendation appeared to be economy of administration and cheapness of material. As in the previous period there were complaints that inadequate supervision was combined with ineffective tests such as cutting firewood or digging ground and when the stoneyard was opened there were often limits on the amount of stone to be broken or the number of days' work offered combined with lower payments. At times of considerable expense the test might also be limited to men with large families. It was actions such as these which made many of the inspectorate doubt the efficiency of the outdoor labour test.[55]

Although the combination of stricter administration of outdoor relief and the control of charity by the COS weathered the crisis of 1879, the depression of 1884–7 provided a more severe test. Distress, particularly in the heavy industries, was widespread covering both casual and skilled workers. The concurrence of the length of the depression, severe winters and a long-term downturn in the building cycle produced burdens beyond the capabilities of local charity and hard pressed ratepayers were faced with exceptional burdens. In London the situation was made more serious by the Trafalgar Square riots in February 1886. The result was a limited, but significant, departure by the central authority. In March 1886 Joseph Chamberlain, the President of the Local Government Board, issued a famous circular encouraging the provision of municipal public works in areas badly affected by the depression. The circular marked the first official recognition by the central authority that there was a class of the unemployed who were unsuited to deterrent treatment. While accepting that the returns of the numbers of paupers did not suggest a greater problem than in previous periods of distress, he asserted that the Local Government Board had on this occasion proceeded to investigate the condition of the working class in general, finding that: 'In the ranks of those who do not ordinarily seek Poor Law relief there is evidence of much and increasing privation and if the depression in trade continues it is to be feared that large numbers of persons usually in regular employment will be reduced to the greatest straits.' He recognized the need to keep these deserving poor separate from the pauper: 'It is not desirable that the working classes should be familiarized with Poor Law relief, and if once the honourable sentiment which now leads them to avoid it is broken down it is probable that recourse will be had to this provision on the slightest occasion.' What we needed was not a change in the traditional remedies of the workhouse test or the outdoor labour test, but the provision of an alternative method of relief for the deserving group. The principle on which this temporary assistance would be based was the provision of works by local authorities other than the unions. In this way the stigma of pauperism would be avoided, although in other respects the proposals appeared to resemble some aspects of the outdoor labour test. The work was to be that 'which all can perform whatever may have been their previous avocations' and was also to be 'work which does not compete with that of other labourers at present in employment'. Finally the work provided was not to be so attractive that it was 'likely to interfere with the resumption of regular employment in their own trades.'

The type of work suggested was that suited to unskilled labourers. Recommended tasks included work on sewage farms and water supply; the laying out of parks and cemeteries and street cleansing and paving. Workers were employed on the recommendations of the boards of guardians as being unsuited to Poor Relief and they were to be paid below the market rate to 'prevent imposture, and to leave the strongest temptations to those who avail themselves of this opportunity to return as soon as possible to their previous occupations.' Finally, for approved schemes the local authorities were informed that they would be supported by the Local Government Board in any request for a loan from the Public Works Loan Board.[56]

The significance of the Chamberlain circular is that it appears to be the first inkling of a change in attitude by the central authority.

The circular can be seen as establishing the principle of local relief work outside of the influence of the Poor Law. However, its theoretical possibilities exceeded its practical achievements. Although the circular was regularly re-issued at times of depression the responses were too small to be effective. During the 1892–3 depression the seventy-seven most active authorities were to employ fewer than 27,000 men at a time when the total unemployed was estimated at three-quarters of a million, and it is unfortunate that such experiments were to leave their mark in the belief that all public works schemes were necessarily uneconomic.[57]

The depression of 1884–7 was tackled, therefore, by a variety of institutions, the Poor Law, local authorities, charity and self-help. Inspector Knollys' report on the handling of the problem in the Sunderland Union was intended to show how such a range of responses could meet even the most exceptional distress. The union's male occupational structure was narrowly based on the building and sailing of ships. Knollys believed that the union had felt the depression 'more acutely' than any other in the north of England. In the first year of the depression the union estimated the total unemployed as between nine and ten thousand. Knollys commented upon the efforts made by all four main agencies of relief.

The union operated a stone-breaking yard, which in the final year of the depression was open from January to June relieving in that time '1,228 men and their families'. The union's returns to the central authority show a maximum of 405 relieved in any one week. Knollys commented upon the nature of those offered the outdoor labour test in this period. Just over 50 per cent of the number relieved were English, 37 per cent being Irish and 5 per cent Scots. Knollys' report illustrated the special problem of unions with large numbers of migrants. Clearly such groups had least reserves and probably also less security of tenure in their employment. More surprising, however, is the fact that over 20 per cent of those relieved were members of major friendly societies or trade unions offering friendly society benefits, a figure confirmed by the fact that around one-quarter of those relieved appear to have had skilled occupations. It is impossible to state how long such workers were in receipt of relief, but Knollys had made the point that even with the Chamberlain circular it was still possible for the deserving to be forced to seek Poor Relief in a long period of depression.

The Sunderland Corporation had obtained a loan of £7,000 from the Public Works Loans Board to introduce major improvements to the sea coast. Around 360 men were employed in two groups, each working three days a week, and another fifty had obtained employment via sub-contractors. In terms of numbers the most impressive effort was provided by charity. Here Knollys quoted figures relating to the winter of 1884–5, when charitable effort reached its peak in March 1885. At this time approximately 17,000 individuals, one in seven of the urban population, were in receipt of charitable relief; given in the form of a bread ration supplemented by a meal on six days a week for children. During this period local charities supplied almost 440,000 meals and distributed nearly 308 tons of bread. Knollys also stressed the assistance given to the unemployed by the major shipbuilding unions. The United Society of Boilermakers and Ironshipbuilders, with 2,300 branch members, had spent over £12,000 in the first two years of the depression.[58]

The optimism of the published report was in contrast to the record of correspondence during the course of the depression. The Sunderland Union supported the crusade against out-relief with some success. This involved a greater use of the workhouse and the enforcement of stricter discipline within the institution. From 1877 the union was urged to extend its hospital accommodation, but after heavy expenditure in the period 1866 to 1875 it was not prepared to engage in further expenditure. Consequently, by 1884 it was difficult to make use of the workhouse test.

The initial response of the union to the worsening economic situation in October 1884 was to employ sixty-six men in digging within the workhouse grounds, but within a fortnight they had opened a stoneyard with 253 men reported as on test labour. Knollys, who had visited the homes of the unemployed in the company of the relieving officers, urged the guardians to use the partial workhouse test, but this was angrily refused by the board of guardians on the grounds that it involved the splitting-up of families. Knollys also urged the Sunderland Corporation to engage in some public works and asked the Local Government Board to support any request for a loan. His anticipation of the Chamberlain circular was at this stage ignored by the borough council which had engaged in considerable and expensive public works schemes during the depression of 1879. The pressure on the stoneyard increased and the union was forced to engage extra supervisors and to request police protection for the relieving officers who paid out those relieved at the end of their test period. By the end of December 1884, with numbers close to 600, a second test yard had to be opened.

In 1885 despite organized trades union pressure to raise relief scales the union sought economies. Although in normal times it was the rule in this union that the single able-bodied were offered the workhouse test, this rule had been ignored with the opening of the stoneyard. Now under pressure from rising rates the guardians ordered that single men should not be offered the labour test. On a more positive note the board of guardians and the Sunderland Corporation prepared a joint highways scheme to share the cost of a public works programme. Knollys, however, condemned 'any attempt to mix relief with municipal action'. The union's initial reaction was to refuse outdoor relief to any able-bodied, but within a fortnight the guardians had introduced easier regulations for their labour test, hoping to secure savings on costs while improving discipline in the labour yards.

In 1886 the guardians continued to seek to operate the test more economically. Test labour was limited to men with at least two children, while the number of days' labour required and the payments offered were also reduced. The union also sought to economize by a proposal to contract labour to employers, only to be informed by a shocked Knollys that such schemes were illegal. Later the union proposed a scheme of spade husbandry which Knollys also rejected. He informed the union that as they had insisted on mixing payment by results with the relief of distress the increasing number of applicants in the previous year had been the result of their 'want of method and preparation' coupled with 'inadequate supervision'. He thought they should disabuse themselves of the notion 'that test labour was a farce'. He also condemned their unwillingness to separate the giving of charity from the receipt of relief. Knollys' admonitions appear to have had little effect on the Sunderland guardians. No changes in the running of the stoneyards were recorded and, in January 1887, the board of guardians ordered its district committees to act as distributors for the local unofficial charity committee.

For unions as badly hit by the depression as the Sunderland Union the depression exposed the limitations of the campaign against outdoor relief. It was not merely the difficulty of separating the deserving from the undeserving able-bodied. Families suffering because of the depression were often forced to allow aged relatives to seek Poor Relief and, once this had been accepted, there appears to have been some reluctance by such families to accept their burden when the depression ceased. Thus Knollys was to complain of the continuing high poor rates in the Sunderland Union late in 1888.[59]

One problem on which the campaign against outdoor relief could make little impact was the vagrant. Measurement of this group always posed special problems. There was considerable fluctuation between years and within the individual year. Numbers could vary with the state of the economy, vagrant numbers peaking in the period following the troughs of trade cycles. Figures were also affected by the severity of the weather and in any year numbers were always lowest in the summer months. Numbers also varied between unions, depending to some extent on the relative strictness of the local regime and the availability of cheap lodgings and charitable assistance. The overall conclusion is that the number of vagrants applying for relief showed a considerable increase in this period.[60]

Both central authority and the unions continued to support policies of deterrence as the solution to the vagrancy problem. By 1866 apparently around half of the unions were using a police officer as assistant relieving officer for vagrants. In the early 1870s the Local Government Board reported that almost 90 per cent of unions had separate accommodation for vagrants. In London, a mecca for vagrants, the Metropolitan Homeless Poor Act of 1864 had anticipated the sickness legislation of 1867 in requiring casual wards for vagrants to be maintained by a common charge on all metropolitan unions.[61]

Public interest and fears were kept alive by the work of such as the investigative journalist James Greenwood. In January 1866, disguised as a tramp, Greenwood spent the night in the casual ward of the Lambeth Workhouse.[62] His description contrasted the 'scrupulously clean workhouse' with the filthy conditions provided for the casual. Here he had to strip and take a bath 'in a liquid . . . disgustingly like weak mutton broth'. His sleeping quarters were in a 'far too airy shed . . . paved with stone, the flags so thickly encrusted with filth that I mistook it at first for natural earth'. The shed was around 30 ft sq, having three 'dingy whitewashed' walls, and the fourth consisting of a space roughly covered by boards and canvas, the whole covered by a roof of 'naked tiles'. Here forty men slept on narrow bags filled rather scantily with hay and covered by a rug. The food provided for both supper and breakfast was dry bread, and a thin porridge with water to drink. Throughout his account of a much disturbed night and the labour task which had to be performed before release Greenwood was at pains to distinguish between the dirty, idle blackguards who formed the majority of his companions and the handful of decent men who had fallen on hard times. Such publicity was reflected in future policy.

Legislation was used in support of a more deterrent policy. The Pauper Inmates Discharge and Regulations Act of 1871 and the Casual Poor Act of 1882 were both intended to make provision less attractive by allowing increased hours of work and longer periods of detention. Broadly, a night's lodging could be expected to provide three hours work and a day's detention nine hours. Male tasks were stone-breaking, oakum picking, digging, woodcutting and corn-grinding and for females, oakum picking, scrubbing and needlework. Meals consisted of 6 oz of bread with 1 pt of gruel or broth for supper and breakfast. For longer detainees the midday meal would be either 8 oz bread and 1½ oz of cheese or 6 oz bread and 1 pt of soup.[63]

Meanwhile the desire to assist the genuine traveller in search of work showed itself in two ways. Firstly, the introduction of a variety of 'way ticket systems' where a casual accepted as making a specific journey in search of work received a ticket which on presentation to workhouses en route was supposed to provide him with better food and accommodation than that given to the professional tramp. Secondly, in 1893 the Local Government Board ruled that vagrants seeking work could be allowed to leave the workhouse at 5.30 a.m. rather than the traditional discharge which could range from 9.30 to 11 a.m.[64]

High local numbers were used by the inspectorate to urge unions to adopt the separate cell system. Here the prison-like treatment was more strongly emphasized. Each vagrant was housed in an individual cell which was divided into two parts, one section containing the work area the other the bed. Thus the vagrant was denied contact with any but the tramp master, who was normally summoned by a bell. While this system had long been recommended by the inspectorate its expense meant that progress towards such a solution was slow. The fact that numbers of vagrants tended to be at their highest following periods of depression made solutions involving additional expenditure even more unattractive. Moreover, the continuing demands for better accommodation for more deserving classes meant that for many unions the answer remained in the encouragement of workhouse staff to be harsher in dealing with vagrants. Progress was probably fastest in London. When General Booth described the conditions in the casual wards of the metropolis in 1890 it was the cell system which he took as his example.[65]

In general there seems little doubt that the Poor Law authorities, whether central or local, tended to be unsympathetic to the casual poor throughout this period. In this view they were supported by the general body of public opinion. While General Booth sought greater public sympathy for these unfortunates a strong campaign was emerging to separate the professional vagrant from the casual ward and to place him in a labour colony for a longer period. In effect this was tantamount to an admission that the workhouse test itself had failed and that those regarded as the least deserving group of paupers required an even more deterrent treatment.[66]

Although there was no return of paupers by age until 1890 there is widespread agreement that the aged poor were placing a greater burden on the Poor Law during this period, and they also appear to have formed a growing proportion of workhouse inmates. In 1867 the aged formed approximately 37 per cent of the inmates of metropolitan workhouses, but by the mid-1890s, when interest in the aged poor was much stronger, many workhouses had over half their inmates in this category.[67] By this latter date Charles Booth had shown old age to be the largest single cause of pauperism and that with increasing age the prospect of having to depend on the Poor Law increased markedly. Approximately 20 per cent of those aged sixty-five to sixty-nine were paupers, whereas 40 per cent of those over seventy-five were in receipt of Poor Relief. The majority of these were on outdoor relief and Booth observed that in most unions such relief carried no stigma but was 'often claimed very much as a right'. However, he found that the aged were united in their opposition to the workhouse, and that they were prepared to accept considerable suffering rather than become inmates:

> Loss of liberty is the most general reason assigned to this aversion, but the dislike of decent people to be compelled to mix with those whose past life and present habits are the reverse of respectable is also strongly felt. There is no doubt, too, that there is a widespread dread of the separation of man and wife. This is not easily accounted for, as such separation, unless at the desire of the old people themselves is illegal.

There seems no doubt that in effect they are separated. It may be,
however, that married quarters are not often demanded, and that where
none are provided it would hardly occur to an old couple, probably
ignorant of the law, to make such an application.[68]

It is possible that the stricter regime introduced with the
campaign against outdoor relief had made the position of the aged
worse in workhouses where they were simply classed with the
able-bodied. The customary discomfort was supported by the
uniformity of the standard diet and rigid timetable which were
ill-suited to the needs of the aged. In such institutions the
grievances listed by Charles Booth were increased by the feeling of
being rejected by family and friends which served to underline the
stigma.

Discussion of the problem of the aged poor was encouraged by the
increasing interest in old-age pensions which appears to have
commenced in the late 1870s. Charles Booth stated that his interest
was aroused from this time, although at this stage Canon Blackley's
scheme of social insurance against sickness and old age was
dominating discussion. Blackley's analysis was to shock many by its
stress on complusion, although in some respects it was firmly based
in prevailing Victorian values. His concern was to give support to
the deserving members of the working class when sickness and old
age pressed heavily upon their income. However, he also sought to
protect the ratepayer from those who preyed upon the Poor Law by
forcing them to provide for these problems. In 1891 both Joseph
Chamberlain and Charles Booth introduced schemes for old-age
pensions and in 1893 a Royal Commission was established to
consider the problem of the aged. While its report did little to solve
the confusion on pensions, it did urge improvements in the
provision of Poor Relief to the aged. It suggested that outdoor relief
should be the normal provision and it should be adequate in amount
and where resort had to be taken to indoor relief it felt there should
be improvements in accommodation. Thus by the mid-1890s there
was an increasing belief that the aged should be regarded as a more
deserving category of pauper.[69]

The Local Government Board were mindful of the changing
climate of public opinion. Thus they supported allowances of
tobacco and snuff to aged inmates and later allowances of tea to
female aged in order that they could make brews as they felt

157

convenient. However, the permissive nature of the regulations meant that in many workhouses the only concession to recreation remained the backless bench and depersonalization was strengthened by the failure to provide even the minimum storage space for individual possessions.[70]

The confidence which had marked the early years of this period had diminished considerably by its close. In part this was influenced by the wider doubts on the nature of the economy and society which were more noticeable at this time. Yet many of the most respected features of the New Poor Law appear to have originated in this period, although in no case were the improvements universally adopted. In the larger urban unions, particularly in the metropolitan area, there were undoubted improvements in the care of the sick, notably in the provision of separate and better staffed infirmaries. Yet the majority of sick inmates remained within workhouses and in many provincial unions, especially in rural areas, there appears to have been little progress. Moreover, increasing population and popular demands for improved standards meant that even the more progressive unions had little time to rest on their laurels. Staffing continued to pose problems as low pay and low esteem made it difficult to attract medical staff of suitable quality. Resident medical officers were often recruited from the young and inexperienced. Nurses, particularly in rural areas, continued to be recruited from the inmates and, since the able-bodied were in short supply in such institutions, many continued to be regarded as incompetent on physical or mental grounds. For children the need for separation from the workhouse was now widely recognized and a number of interesting experiments were being undertaken. However, as with the sick, progress depended on the locality and too often economy stifled initiative.

Although the central authority, and its ally the COS remained committed to the crusade against outdoor relief both were facing critics who viewed their analysis as irrelevant to the problem of poverty. The workhouse test was plainly both ineffective and expensive in the case of cyclical unemployment and in the case of vagrants was being suggested as insufficiently deterrent. Finally the growing sympathy with the more deserving was threatening to extend itself to the aged, promising further demands upon the ratepayer.

Although the unions had been strengthened at the start of this period by financial reform, long-term increase in expenditure had never been intended as the result. Supporters of economy now stressed variations in value between rich and poor unions, a point advanced by Charles Booth in support of old-age pensions. At the close of the second thirty-year period lack of uniformity continued to be a strong feature of the New Poor Law, indeed, the extent of progress in the more enlightened unions may well have widened the range of service provided. To some extent this reflected the continuing limitations of the central authority, although it is also significant that they did not seek an extension of their powers. Thus the New Poor Law was to enter a period of more sustained and better organized criticism, with many of its problems apparently unresolved.

NOTES

1. M.E. Rose, 'The Crisis of Poor Relief in England, 1860–1898', in W.J. Mommsen (ed.), *The Emergence of the Welfare State in Britain and Germany,* (1981), 62.

2. Calculations are based on the returns of expenditure in the Annual Reports for the years stated.

3. Poor Law Board, Twenty-Second Annual Report, (1869–70), xiii–xiv, xxxv.

4. See P. Wood, 'Finance and the urban Poor Law', in M.E. Rose (ed.), *The Poor and the City. The English Poor Law in its urban context 1834–1914,* (1985), App, 3, 49.

5. 24&25 Vic c55. See Poor Law Board, Fourteenth Annual Report (1861–2), 356. 25&26 Vic c103. *Ibid.,* Fifteenth Annual Report, (1862–3), 30–4. 28&29 Vic c70. *Ibid.,* Eighteenth Annual Report, (1865–6), 26–8. See also M. Caplan, 'The New Poor Law and the struggle for union chargability', *International Review of Social History,* xxiii, (1978).

6. P.L. Cotterell and B.L. Anderson, *Money and Banking in England 1694–1914,* (1974), 247–8.

7. Public Works (Manufacturing Districts) Act 1863, 26&27 Vic c70. Poor Law Loans Act 1869, 32&33 Vic c45.

8. M.A. Crowther, *The Workhouse System 1834–1929,* (1983), 80–2.

9. Lord George Hamilton, 'A Statistical Survey of the Problems of Pauperism', *Journal of the Royal Statistical Society,* lxxiv, (December, 1910).

10. The overall result was a continued lack of uniformity.

11. M. Flinn, in D. Fraser (ed.), *The New Poor Law in the Nineteenth Century,* (1976), 63.

12. Report of *The Lancet* Sanitary Commission for Investigating the State of the Infirmaries of Workhouses, (1866).

13. E.g. Dr E. Smith, *Report on the Metropolitan Workhouses and Sickwards*, lxi, 1866 can be quoted as showing need for reform as in R.G. Hodgkinson, *The Origins of the National Health Service,* (1967), 498 and F.B. Smith, *The People's Health,* (1979) 388. However, he can also be quoted suggesting the considerable progress which had been made as in B. Abel-Smith, *The Hospitals 1800–1948,* (1964), 64.

14. *Hansard,* 8 February 1867, clxxxv, 163. J.E. O'Neill, 'Finding a Policy for the Sick Poor', *Victorian Studies,* vii, (1964), introduces the background to the Act.

15. B. Abel-Smith, *op. cit.,* (1964), 79.

16. R.G. Hodgkinson, *op. cit.,* (1967), 511.

17. Local Government Board, Twelfth Annual Report, (1882–3), xxxv.

18. R.G. Hodgkinson, *op. cit.,* 521.

19. Given in *ibid.,* 523.

20. Marland is described in F.B. Smith, *op. cit.,* 392.

21. The circular is quoted in full in M.E. Rose, *The English Poor Law 1780–1930,* (1971), 175–8.

22. A. Digby, *Pauper Palaces,* (1978), 168.

23. R. Pinker, *English Hospital Statistics, 1861–1938,* (1966), 50.

24. F.B. Smith, *op. cit.,* 389.

25. R. Pinker, *Social Theory and Social Policy,* (1971), 79.

26. On rural medical officers see M.A. Crowther, *op. cit.,* 170–1. On the Local Government Board and pauper nurses see F.B. Smith, *op. cit.,* 388. On Norfolk see A. Digby, *op. cit.,* (1978), 171–2.

27. Local Government Board, Fourth Annual Report, (1874–5), 59–60. R.G. Hodgkinson, *op. cit.,* 542. R. Pinker, *op. cit.,* (1971), 76.

28. R. Pinker, *op. cit.,* (1966), 75.

29. G.M. Ayres, *England's First State Hospitals 1867–1930,* (1971), 41–2.

30. K. Jones, *Mental Health and Social Policy,* (1961), 16–18.

31. F. Hill, *The Children of the State,* (1894), 74.

32. Poor Law Board, Twenty-Third Annual Report, (1870–71), 414–30.

33. Local Government Board, Third Annual Report, (1873–4), 341–3.

34. A.F. Young and E.T. Ashton, *British Social Work in the Nineteenth Century,* (1956), 134.

35. For a description of a model provision at Sidcup by the Greenwich Union see M.E. Rose, *op. cit.,* (1971), 357.

36. Local Government Board, First Annual Report, (1871–2), xxviii.

37. For a good example see *ibid.,* Twenty-First Annual Report, (1891–2), xxxviii.

38. F. Duke in D. Fraser (ed.), *op. cit.,* (1976), 81–3. For a general discussion of developments in this period see P.F. Ashchrott, *The English Poor Law System,* (1902), 253–65 and S. and B. Webb, *English Poor Law History, The Last Hundred Years,* (1929), 246–306.

39. M. Mackinnon, 'English Poor Law Policy and the Crusade Against Outrelief', *Journal of Economic History,* xlvii, 3, (1987), 605.

40. Young and Ashton, *op. cit.,* 51–2.

41. Local Government Board, First Annual Report, (1871–2), App. A, No. 20.

42. G. Stedman Jones, *Outcast London,* (1984 edn.), 241– 54.

43. Poor Law Board, Twenty-Second Annual Report, (1869–70), App. A, No. 4.

44. As n. 41 above.

45. For London see P. Ryan, 'Politics and relief: East London unions in the late nineteenth and early twentieth centuries', in M.E. Rose (ed.), *op. cit.,* (1985), 142–5. For examples of model provincial unions see Local Government Board, Fifth Annual Report (1875–6), App. B. No. 18, (on Manchester) quoted in M.E. Rose, *op. cit.,* (1971), 230. Also Local Government Board, Eighteenth Annual Report, (1888–9), 134, (Sunderland).

46. See P. Ryan, *ibid.,* 146–9 and in the same collection K. Gregson, 'Poor Law and organised charity: the relief of exceptional distress in north-east England, 1870–1910', 100–105.

47. P. Thane, *The Foundations of the Welfare State,* (1982), 35.

48. Local Government Board, Eighteenth Annual Report, (1888–9), 135.

49. Charity Organization Society, Second Annual Report, (1872), quoted in Young and Ashton, *op. cit.,* 59.

50. M. Mackinnon, op. cit., 613.

51. S. and B. Webb, *op. cit.,* 378–81.

52. As n. 46 above.

53. K. Williams, *From Pauperism to Poverty,* (1981), 170–1.

54. Statistics are taken from the appropriate Annual Reports.

55. Second Report of the Select Committee on Distress from Want of Employment, (1895) provides useful evidence on attitudes to test labour. K. Gregson, *op. cit.,* gives several examples taken from unions in north-east England.

56. *Pauperism and distress: Circular letter to Boards of Guardians,* P.P. (1886), vol. xxxvi, 179–81.

57. B.B. Gilbert, *The Evolution of National Insurance in Great Britain,* (1966); D. Winch, *Economics and Policy,* (1969).

58. Local Government Board, Sixteenth Annual Report, (1886–7), 76.

59. P.A. Wood, 'The Sunderland Poor Law Union', M. Litt thesis, University of Newcastle, 1976, 274–8.

60. M.A. Crowther, *op. cit.,* 253–4. R. Vorspan, 'Vagrancy and the New Poor Law in late-Victorian and Edwardian England', *English Historical Review,* xcii, (1977).

61. On the role of the police see: T. Mackay, *A History of the English Poor Law,* vol. 3, (1904), 382; and C. Steedman, *Policing the Victorian Community,* (1984), 56–9. Local Government Board, Second Annual Report, (1872–3), 36; G.M. Ayres, *op. cit.,* 224–6 on 1864 legislation.

62. J. Greenwood, 'A Night in a Workhouse', reprinted in P. Keating (ed.), *Into Unknown England,* (1976), 33–64. Greenwood returned to this theme in *The Seven Curses of London,* (1869, reprinted 1981), 276–82.

63. General orders on these matters in 1882 and 1887. See W.C. Glen, *The Poor Law Orders,* (1898).

64. Local Government Board, Twenty-Third Annual Report, (1893–4), 14–15.

65. General Booth, *In Darkest England and the Way Out,* (1890), 68–72. But

see also J. London, *The People of the Abyss,* (1903), ch. 9, 'The Spike' which describes the casual ward at Whitechapel Workhouse.

66. R. Vorspar, *op. cit.,* 76–80.
67. F.B. Smith, *op. cit.,* 385.
68. C. Booth, *The Aged Poor In England and Wales,* (1894), 330–1.
69. See D. Collins, 'The introduction of Old-Age Pensions in Great Britain', *Historical Journal,* (1965); and P. Thane, 'Non-Contributory versus Insurance Pensions, 1878–1908' in P. Thane (ed.), *The Origins of British Social Policy,* (1978).

CHAPTER FIVE

EPILOGUE – THE DOUBTS OF MIDDLE AGE c. 1895–1914

The individualist society of the mid-Victorian period was based on an exceptional degree of confidence in important features of its economy and society. Economically, the nation was the world's leading manufacturing and trading nation and this position was protected by the world's largest navy. In society the values of organized religion claimed widespread respect among the middle and upper classes and male supremacy was virtually unquestioned. Both economic interests and social values were founded on a common belief in the inevitability of future progress based on the acceptance of the principles of the free market economy. However, there were always those who doubted and by the close of the Victorian period these certainties had become a matter for increasing debate.

Economic supremacy was recognized as being under challenge from the rise in the manufacturing strength of both Germany and the United States. The fact that these rivals appeared to prosper at a time when many members of the British business community were complaining of a depression in prices and profits gave additional cause for alarm. Although the term 'Great Depression' is now largely discounted when applied to the years 1873–96, contemporary doubts can be observed in the reports of the Royal Commissions on the Depression in Trade and Industry (1886) and Agricultural Depression (1897). Economic growth was an uneven process and the fluctuations of the trade cycle added to contemporary gloom. On the military aspect, the rise of foreign navies and the advance of new technology threatened our traditional mastery of the seas, while our performance in the Boer War cast considerable doubt on the capabilities of our land forces. Diplomatically, the change was recognized in the replacement of 'splendid isolation' with a search for friends.[1]

Social changes are more difficult to assess. Organized religion, particularly Anglicanism, was weakened by increasing urbanization. The urban working class was certainly more secular, or, where religious, tended to favour the chapel. The entry of the State into education also appeared to threaten an area of traditional religious authority. At an intellectual level science, as popularized by Darwin and Huxley, and socialism, for some a substitute religion, provided new threats. One response was for churchmen to take a more active role in social affairs. This was not new, churchmen of all denominations had long played an active role in the relief of poverty. However, signs of increased interest in the 1880s included the founding of the Settlement Movement, with the opening of Toynbee Hall in 1884, the establishment of the Christian Social Union in 1889; and in the same year the Roman Catholic Cardinal Manning acted as mediator in the dock strike.[2]

The threat to male supremacy, while of enormous potential significance, was in its infancy in the years before the First World War. For those who left the shelter of the 'Doll's House' progress was never easy and in this matter it was not the limited achievements but the example offered which was to prove significant.

For some, a more serious threat appeared to come from the working-class male. Greater urbanization and the increasing size of companies made organization easier and there was a notable, if uneven, advance in trade-union activity from the late 1880s. The fact that unions were strongest in the heavy industries where cyclical fluctuations had the greatest impact appeared to heighten the significance of their activities as they strove to defend their living standards in times of depression and to make gains in times of economic advance.

It is now generally accepted that despite the reverence in which the principles of *laissez-faire* and the free market were held by many mid-Victorians, a considerable expansion in the role of government was taking place at that time. In terms of extent, however, this 'revolution' was merely providing the foundation for what was to occur later. Expenditure by both central and local authorities showed a five-fold increase between 1870 and 1914, with the rate of growth accelerating over the period. Even the most sacred tenet, free trade, was being questioned, initially in the interests of 'fair trade' and later in the unity of the Empire.[3]

Increasing intervention was aided by the fact that governments were able to accomplish more. The improvement in party organization enabled the planning of legislative programmes with a fair measure of certainty that they would be completed. The development of a professional bureaucratic machine, which has been seen as providing the final impetus to the evolution of the Victorian administrative state, had grown both in size and quality by the close of the century, and was assisted by a much improved local administration.

The relationship between government and people was also changing. Both central and local government were elected on a more democratic franchise. Greater urbanization not only made problems more obvious, but such communities were often to be in the vanguard of those organizing demands for solutions. However, strong pressure on many subjects was countered by defensive organizations making it difficult to assess the impact of demands for reform on government.[4]

Historians have found it difficult to arrive at definite conclusions concerning this questioning of traditional attitudes and the emergence of new views on social policy. In the mid-Victorian period, the role allocated to the voluntary sector had virtually confined debate on State intervention in the field of poverty to discussion over matters of Poor Law administration. Concern was expressed over the powers to be given to the central authority and to reforming the system of finance rather than debating the nature of relief. By the close of the century discussion was more concerned with the welfare of the poor, although finance remained of central importance.

Greater concern was in part the result of an increased awareness of the problem. Some publicity came from the extension of the explorations into the lifestyle of the poor by investigative journalists and writers, which had commenced in the early and mid-Victorian period. This evidence was now strengthened by the statistics provided by the social surveys. By measuring the extent of poverty such enquiries appear to have carried more weight and their impact can be observed in the reaction of the contemporary press and the comments of the politicians. The analysis of poverty provided by the social surveys occasioned less surprise. The main causes revealed had long been recognized as characteristics of poverty by both the voluntary agencies and the Poor Law. In this respect their main impact was in gaining recognition of the existence of poverty among a larger group of deserving citizens. This was an indirect criticism of the adequacy of existing voluntary action and, for some, an argument in favour of increased State intervention. However, the evidence provided of self-inflicted poverty was a source of support for the individualist. The result was that State intervention continued to be conditioned by a desire to separate the deserving from the undeserving. Thus the provision of public works schemes were always intended to assist the respectable unemployed. Old-age pensions, probably the area where the early social surveys may have had the greatest impact, were paid below subsistence level to encourage the savings habit, and the legislation contained clauses aimed at excluding the undeserving. There was moreover, a recognition among a wide range of social reformers of the continued need for strict institutional supervision of those regarded as 'scroungers'. However, the limitations of the social surveys as a force for legislative change is best illustrated by the fact that the prime causes of poverty which they exposed, low wages and family size, received such limited political attention. Minimum wage legislation was restricted to the special cases of the sweated trades and the miners. The Trades Boards Act of 1909 was the result of at least two decades of intermittent discussion and was in the tradition of intervention to assist those unable to protect themselves. The minimum wage for miners was achieved in 1912 only after the threat of strike action by one of the most organized sections of the labour force. Family allowances remained a fringe issue with very limited support and the best that was achieved for child poverty was intervention in the areas of school meals and school medical inspection, which were to a considerable extent a logical extension of the tradition of state protection for children.[5]

Politicians and civil servants were responsible for many aspects of enquiry into areas of poverty. The decade before the Liberals came to power in 1906 was a period of considerable discussion, preparing the way for State intervention in the case of old age, sickness and unemployment, and a Royal Commission to consider the future of the Poor Law. It has been held that political interest was enhanced by the expansion of democracy, but the relationship between electoral reform and social reform was never a simple matter of cause and effect. Historians have debated the popularity of social reform among the working class and the extent to which the working class influenced the politician. Social reform competed with other issues for the attention of both politician and worker. Working-class attitudes are difficult to ascertain and, even among the more politically active and more vocal, views differed markedly. While the friendly society member suspected any State incursion likely to undermine the practice of self-help, others suspected the State of offering palliatives aimed at preventing demands for a more radical redistribution of wealth. Between these extremes a wide range of views was possible showing a varying and often conflicting order of priorities.[6]

The politician and the administrator also had their differing views on the values of social reform on the priorities to be given to different aspects of reform; and of the agencies of administration and methods of finance to be adopted. Underlying and conditioning these issues were a confusing mixture of motives for taking action. Left-wing groups provided the strongest critics of mid-Victorian attitudes to poverty. However, as with the working class, the range of organizations, motives and preferred methods placed severe limitations upon their influence. They ranged in method from the revolutionary Social Democratic Federation to the gradual accretions of the Fabians and this suggested that any long-term concerted action was unlikely. Yet, for the Liberals in particular, socialism was always a factor to be considered. Both Conservative and Liberal parties contained factions which were prepared to support some measure of social reform. For some this was the product of humanitarian concern, while others gave pride of place to economic and military efficiency in the face of emerging rivals. Naturally many saw the situation in political terms; attracting votes, holding back socialism, gaining tactical political advantage over the main opposing party, and individual political ambition. This tangle of motives can be difficult to unravel but often the overall effect was to advance the cause of State intervention in the area of social reform.[7]

The civil servant and local official were as wide-ranging in their motives as their political masters. Government departments differed in their attitudes to reform. The Board of Trade, with its greater statistical expertise and more dynamic officials was more likely to produce plans for reform than the defensive and tradition-bound Local Government Board, although it was this department which had the greatest vested interest in the relief of poverty. The respective roles of central and local authorities were also debated and here the crucial issue was often the question of finance. Rateable values, while rising in the urban areas were unevenly matched to the demands placed upon them. Expansion of social services at local level required either a new system of local finance or increased assistance from central government. Since both of these alternatives posed serious problems it appeared to many reformers that the future lay with central government. A subordinate, but important, issue at both national and local level was the extent of overlap developing between both government departments and between the unions and other local authorities.[8]

The divisions among reformers gave greater opportunities to those who remained convinced of the need for individualist solutions. Although greater public interest has been seen to cause some moderation of opinion, even in the ranks of the Charity Organization Society, the general conclusion is that the range of differing approaches was to result in rendering the progress of social reform both slow moving and unpredictable. Issues were most likely to succeed where they could capture widespread interest, such as proposals claiming to promote national efficiency. In consequence most schemes for reform claimed to be in the interest of the nation. Proposals involving limited expenditure remained more attractive and this tended to favour proposals using existing institutions. Finally, such a situation leant itself to political compromise. Hence, the more flexible the supporters of a proposal the more likely they were to succeed.

The increased discussion of poverty brought the Poor Law under closer scrutiny. Most criticism had as its foundation the desire for a more humane treatment of the deserving. Such attacks were partly in the tradition of the earlier complaints of Dickens and Louisa Twining. However, the frontier of those thought to be deserving expanded considerably in this period and, at both national and local level, a variety of political and religious groups provided more organized opposition. The critics received widespread press publicity. Inspector J.S. Davy reported in the mid-1890s that, 'The newspaper press has teemed with criticism both of the law and of its administration, and in fact the whole fabric of the poor law has been subjected to a keen and in many cases a hostile scrutiny.'[9]

Discussion was to increase in the decade which followed but it was to display a wide range of opinion. For the doctrinaire supporter of nineteenth-century values the existing Poor Law was showing a dangerous tendency to depart from its fundamental principles. Alongside the spokesmen for reaction there were ranged reformers who varied both in the method and extent of change they wished to see introduced. This debate was to culminate in the establishment of a Royal Commission in 1905 to investigate Poor Relief.[10]

The members of the Royal Commission were remarkably expert and were selected as representing a variety of opinions. At the extremes were the believers in doctrinaire solutions who ranged from the supporters of nineteenth-century orthodoxy, as represented by the officials of the Poor Law Division of the Local Government Board, to the experimental Fabian analysis advanced by Beatrice Webb. The majority of members had been appointed on the grounds of their practical experience in the administration of relief, but even here the range of opinion was formidable. Favouring orthodox solutions were those such as C.S. Loch of the Charity Organization Society and F.H. Bentham, Chairman of the Bradford Union, who remained a firm supporter of the specialist test workhouse for the relief of the unemployed. At the other extreme were George Lansbury, the prominent left-wing Chairman of the Poplar Union and Francis Chandler, Secretary of the Amalgamated Society of Carpenters and Joiners. Thus after four years of gathering evidence and discussing its implications the Commission was to produce two reports. The Majority Report broadly reflected the view of the moderate reformer who retained Charity Organization Society leanings, while the Minority Report represented the Fabian reasoning of the Webbs. In this the Reports represented contemporary divisions.[11]

Reform could be sought by change in the existing administration of relief. Canon Barnett, a founder member of the Charity Organization Society who had resigned in protest at its opposition to the extension of State intervention, was a stern critic of Poor Law defects. However, he consistently argued that the defects were the result of inadequate administration and that a suitably reformed Poor Law could be the basis of any programme for social reform. Such a view was broadly compatible with that advanced by the Majority Report of the Royal Commission of 1905–9.[12]

Socialist organizations, despite their internal differences, had followed a broadly similar path during the 1880s and 1890s. Attacks were generally aimed at greater democratization of the boards of guardians and an amelioration of the provision of relief. Thus while the near Marxist Social Democratic Federation wished to abolish workhouses, they saw election to boards of guardians as a valuable training for working-class activists and believed that the Poor Law could offer popular local control of relief. The pauper stigma was merely another capitalist device for controlling the working class. Thus they informed the Royal Commission of 1905–9 that so long as the land and wealth of the nation were privately owned poverty would continue and the Poor Law or its equivalent would remain a necessary aspect of administration.

Other socialist organizations had always recognized that the taint of the Poor Law made it an unsatisfactory agent for dealing with the relief of poverty. However, during the 1890s both the Labour Representation Committee and the ILP did discuss how the administration of the Poor Law could be ameliorated and the Fabians gave Poor Law reform considerable attention. By the time of the Royal Commission most held the Fabian view advanced by the Webbs in the Minority Report that the Poor Law should be abolished.

The parties of government were more cautious. The abolition of the Poor Law involved the complexities of local government reform. Both Conservative and Liberal parties appear to have preferred to approach the problem of deserving groups by providing for their limited withdrawal from the Poor Law in accordance with the political priorities of their party. The major difference lay in the question of finance. Here the Conservative solution of tariff reform was less popular and probably more limiting than the 'New Liberal' support for progressive taxation. Not all Liberals were in favour of such a solution, although as a contribution to national efficiency, social reform was a means of holding the diverging streams of

'Liberal Imperialism' and the 'New Liberalism' together.[14] However, any measure for change had to be concerned with the need for economy thus improving the prospects for some degree of continuity of the existing system.

The Poor Law which survived the period of increased discussion was changed in the process. In addition to attack from outside bodies it was also subject to internal criticism. The reduction of the property qualification for guardians in 1892 had made it easier for women and working men to be elected to boards of guardians. The Local Government Act of 1894 greatly extended the franchise for women and working men and abolished the property qualification. By 1909 there were almost 1,300 women guardians. Women elected were not a uniform group, varying from ardent feminists to strict defenders of the status quo, including the protection of the lesser ratepayer. In general female guardians tended to be used in matters concerning women and children a restriction which undoubtedly limited their overall contribution.[15]

The image presented by the working men elected has been coloured by the early successes of activists such as George Lansbury and Will Crooks in Poplar. The autobiography of Lansbury and the biography of Crooks show both men as determined to alter the pattern of relief and well aware of the advantage of gaining publicity for their actions. As a guardian Lansbury stated his prime aim:

> From the first moment I determined to fight for one policy only, and that was decent treatment for the poor outside the workhouse, and hang the rates . . . . I know people drink, gamble and are often lazy. I also know that taken in the mass the poor are as decent as any other class, and so when I stood as a guardian I took as my policy that no widow or orphan, no sick, infirm or aged person should lack proper provision of the needs of life, and able-bodied people should get work or maintenance . . . . I also determined to humanize Poor Law administration; I never could see the difference between outdoor relief and a state pension.[16]

Lansbury's objection to indoor relief was emphasized by his description of his initial visit to the Poplar Workhouse. his account has become the classic description of an inadequate institution in the late nineteenth century:

> . . . these prison or bastille sort of surroundings were organised for the purpose of making self-respecting decent people endure any sufferings rather than enter . . . Officials, receiving ward, hard forms, white-

171

washed walls, keys dangling at the waist of those who spoke to you, huge books for name, history, etc., searching and then being stripped and bathed in a communal tub, and the final crowning indignity of being dressed in clothes which had been worn by lots of other people, hideous to look at, ill-fitting and coarse – everything possible was done to inflict mental and moral degredation.[17]

Thus, although the workhouse was clean it was the loss of personal identity which was to be feared and detested. All groups of inmates were 'herded together in one huge range of buildings' and generally regarded as 'a nuisance and treated accordingly'. Diet was as inadequate as clothing. Lansbury described a serious disturbance he had had to create to change the supper provided, porridge seasoned with 'rat and mice manure'.

For Crooks' biographer it was the dietary improvements that were introduced at Poplar which were to provide the model for the general improvements eventually adopted by the Local Government Board. Thus: 'The man who fed the poor in Poplar saw the workhouse poor of the kingdom better fed in consequence.'[18]

In general working-class guardians do not appear to have been as influential as either their supporters or their opponents claimed. They seem to have rarely dominated boards of guardians and in many cases represented the lesser ratepayer rather then the socialist reformer. Even when convinced of the need for reform they were often reluctant to see increased expenditure on the salaries of major officials and were ill-disposed to spending on improved workhouse facilities.[19]

Although the Royal Commission made every effort to gather improved statistics the evidence leaves much to be desired. The percentage of paupers in the total population had declined markedly during the years of the New Poor Law. The quickening of the decline during the campaign against outdoor relief provided the central authority and its supporters with a vindication of their insistence on the use of the workhouse test. Although it is widely accepted that the campaign was losing its impetus from the 1880s the fall was to continue from the 2.7 per cent in 1890 to around 2.5 per cent by the close of Victoria's reign. The contrast between this low figure and the statistics of primary poverty presented by the social surveys is such that it would appear to confirm that the New Poor Law had not lost its deterrent image. In spite of this continued decrease in pauperism the Local Government Board was dissatisfied.

The fall in the percentage of paupers was not being matched by a reduction in expenditure. Indeed, in the two decades preceeding the First World War the rate of expenditure on Poor Relief showed a sustained annual rate of increase of 3.5 per cent. For the senior officials of the Local Government Board's Poor Law Division, a group still largely promoted from within the department, such a departure from previous experience suggested serious inefficiency. For such officials and for leading spokesmen of the Charity Organization Society reform meant a return to the principles of 1834. To the supporters of traditional values, new and inexperienced guardians were being-misled by contemporary concern for the poor into dangerous and unjustified excess. By the early twentieth century the central authority, while urging that outdoor relief should be adequate in amount, were also urging boards of guardians to make fuller use of relieving officers and to adopt the case-paper system used by the Charity Organization Society as a check on unjustified claims.[20]

Although some boards of guardians had adopted more generous relief scales, particularly for the aged, the major cause of increased expenditure does not appear to have been generosity to those on outdoor relief, but the treatment of larger numbers of indoor paupers. The number of recipients of outdoor relief, although fluctuating, was declining as a percentage of the total population. In 1870 outdoor paupers had formed 39.1 per 1,000 of the total population. By 1885, largely as a result of the campaign against outdoor relief, this figure had fallen to 22 per 1,000. Progress was then slower, but by 1895 the number had fallen to 20 and by 1914 to 10 per 1,000. Even allowing for the dubious accuracy of the official figures and for the fact that individual years could be abnormal, the trend was plainly downwards. In contrast, the indoor paupers remained a surprisingly constant proportion of the population. In 1870 the indoor paupers had made up 7.1 per 1,000 of the total population, 6.8 in 1885, 6.9 in 1895 and 6.9 in 1914. In the context of a growing population the number of indoor paupers had shown a considerable increase. Thus even after the campaign against outdoor relief had lost its vigour the trend continued. The cost of maintaining an indoor pauper was now between three and four times that of an outdoor pauper and expanding numbers meant increased expenditure on staffing and a rising cost of borrowing to provide new buildings. Much of this increase in the number of indoor paupers was the result of improvements in the care of specialist groups, such as the children and the sick, and the growing proportion of infirm aged. Here the Poor Law could be seen as a victim of its own success. In practice the level of advance was far from uniform and left both the supporters of traditional principles and those desirous of reform unhappy.[21]

The Majority Report of the Royal Commission reflected what was a widespread concern:

> It is very unpleasant to record that notwithstanding our assumed moral and material progress, and notwithstanding the enormous annual expenditure, amounting to nearly sixty millions a year, upon poor relief, education, and public health, we still have a vast army of persons quartered upon us unable to support themselves, and an army which in numbers has recently shown signs of increase rather than decrease. To what is this retrogression due? It cannot be attributed to lack of expenditure. Is this costly and elaborate machinery we have established defective, and if so where does it fail to accomplish its end? Is the material upon which this machinery operates becoming less amenable to the methods applied?[22]

Later reflecting the growing concern with the efficiency of the race it stated:

> No country however rich, can permanently hold its own in the race of international competition, if hampered by an increasing load of this dead weight; or can successfully perform the role of sovereignty beyond the seas, if a portion of its own folk at home are sinking below the civilisation and aspirations of its subject races abroad.[23]

Both the Majority and Minority Reports condemned the lack of uniformity of treatment. In respect of outdoor relief the Minority Report pointed out that:

> So far as the orphans and deserted children, the aged and infirm, the sick and the mentally afflicted, and the widows with legitimate offspring are concerned – and these make up nine-tenths of the pauper host – the Boards of Guardians . . . exercise unchecked their powers of awarding doles and allowances under such conditions as seem fit.[24]

The most frequent reasons supplied by local regulations for the refusal of outdoor relief were found to be related to the character of the applicant. They quoted the vague terms used to define such groups including; 'immoral habits', 'habitual drunkards and bad characters', 'known to be in the habit of frequenting public houses', 'persons known to be addicted to begging'. Others disqualified anyone whose previous conduct was such that the applicant 'has wasted his substance in drinking and gambling, or has led an idle or disorderly life'. In addition most unions were found to prohibit outdoor relief to 'any person who may have given birth to an illegitimate child'. Widows with only a 'small family', sometimes defined as 'not more than two children', were also often ineligible, while in some unions no relief of any kind was offered to a widow with one young child. Some boards refused relief to those 'residing with relatives of immoral, intemperate or improvident character, or of uncleanly habits' and others continued to refuse outdoor relief to wives and families of men serving a prison sentence. Most confusing were the references to the state of an applicant's home. In some unions outdoor relief was refused to those whose abode was 'kept in a dirty or slovenly condition', whereas in others 'too good a home is as fatal a disqualification'. This could apply to those who 'live in cottages rented above the average rent of the neighbourhood'. Finally many unions required evidence of 'having shown some sign of thrift', although possessions and savings could provide a reason for refusal. Although the central authority continued to urge that outdoor relief should be adequate there was a considerable variation in scales of relief. For an adult scales could be as high as 5s. per person per week or as low as 1s. plus 5 lb of flour or its bread equivalent. Rates for children varied from 2s. to 6d. and a supply of flour. The Minority Report quoted a clerk's description, 'starvation out-relief'.[25]

Both Reports were also united in their condemnation of the General Mixed Workhouse, which was home for around 250,000 paupers. Although there was a recognition that most workhouses were clean and provided adequate food and heating they again found considerable variation in standard. The Minority Report compared the sumptuous and palatial conditions in newer workhouses of London with the remaining old workhouses, 'hideous in their bareness and squalor'. However, they found both objectionable in that they were unable to practice effective segregation of classes of inmate: 'The dominant note of these institutions of today, as it was those of 1834, is their promiscuity . . . . It has not surprised us to be informed that female inmates of the great establishments have

175

been known to bear offspring to male inmates, and thus increase the burden on the Poor Rate.' Equally distressing was the failure to separate 'young and old, innocent and hardened'. Thus in the female day-rooms and sleeping quarters a most varied group were in constant contact:

> The servant out of place, the prostitute recovering from disease, the feeble-minded women of any age, the girl with her first baby, the unmarried mother coming in to be confined with her third or fourth bastard, the senile, the paralytic, the respectable deserted wife, the widow to whom Outdoor Relief has been refused, are all herded indiscriminately together.

In the smaller rural workhouses, where segregation was least practicable, they found that even the sick were mixed with others without any regard for classification: 'We have more than once seen young children in bed with minor ailments, next to women of bad character under treatment for contagious disease, while other women in the same ward were in advanced stages of cancer and senile decay.'[26]

Under the pressure of continued attacks on its efficiency and its inhumanity the Local Government Board had continued the trend described in the previous chapter of seeking to remove the deserving classes from the workhouse, the children and the sick now joined by the aged in this category. In seeking alternatives to the workhouse the Poor Law of this period has been aptly described as 'a social laboratory with a bad name'.[27] The concern for national efficiency supported by the findings of the poverty surveys meant that the plight of children continued to receive much attention.

The trend of removing children from institutional environments can be illustrated by the fact that between 1895 and 1907 the number of children in large district schools was halved.[28] This change was accompanied by an expansion in the use of boarding-out, the development of the scattered homes experiment, and a wider use of other institutions. Nevertheless, while the number of children under sixteen dependent on Poor Relief had shown a considerable decline in the period 1871–91, their numbers showed little reduction in the period 1891–1905. Thus a considerable number of children, approaching 250,000, remained paupers, although only around 5,000 remained in the workhouse proper. In 1900 the Local Government Board issued a circular to all boards of guardians, recommending the removal of children from the workhouse environment and coupled this with the suggestion that where additional space was required for other groups such as the sick, the opportunity should be taken to create additional accommodation by the removal of the children. In effect the central authority was recognizing that, although economy remained of paramount concern, the children should receive prior consideration.[29]

Children could be retained in the workhouse by the more parsimonious unions whose overall standards were usually low, although even larger, and otherwise progressive, unions often held the children of the 'ins and outs' in the workhouse. Such children now had the benefit of attending the local elementary school, but life in the workhouse left much to be desired. The supervision of the schoolteachers was now replaced by cheaper industrial trainers, or, in some rural unions, aged and feeble-minded inmates. A similar situation appeared to apply to the nursery. Here, allowed only limited access to the natural mother, frequently supervision was by constantly changing and unsatisfactory, pauper inmates. In one union babies were the overall responsibility of the laundress, who was also responsible for female tramps and young women. In the worst cases the Reports found the children in bleak surroundings, often dirty and badly clothed and inadequately segregated from other inmates. In consequence both Majority and Minority Reports were convinced that children should be removed from the workhouse. However, despite this unanimity the central authority was not to issue an order compelling the removal of children from the workhouse until 1913.[30]

Despite the growth of voluntary and other public sector hospital provision, the number of beds provided for the sick by the Poor Law increased by almost 70 per cent in the period 1891–1911, and in the same period the percentage housed in separate Poor Law infirmaries had risen from 20 to almost 48 per cent. Such was the improvement in standard in the best hospitals that the Royal Commission found some boards of guardians able to operate pay-bed schemes for those desiring a higher standard of privacy and attention. However, there remained considerable variation for those remaining in workhouse sick wards. The least improved appear to have been the rural workhouses with medical officers being criticized for their inadequate attendance, and nursing remaining largely dependent on the untrained. The limitations of the Poor Law in respect of the sick can be illustrated by two examples. In the face of overwhelming medical evidence on the significance of tuberculosis and of the need to isolate consumptives, by 1905 only 32 of the 695 unions were making such provision. This suggests the slowness of a deterrent system of Poor Relief to react to a changing situation. The second example shows the strength of traditional practices. The Report recorded over 60,000 mentally defective inmates housed in the workhouses. Where there was no segregation this was to the disadvantage of both the feeble-minded and the other inmates. The Minority Report found overwhelming evidence that in the smaller workhouses such inmates were regarded as an indispensible source of manual labour.[31]

Both Reports accepted that the sick pauper was unsuited to less eligible treatment. However, for the Majority, the Public Assistance Committee, a committee of a borough or county council which was to take over the functions of the boards of guardians, would coordinate public and voluntary provision and they would be backed up by Provident Dispensaries paid for by contribution. In effect this represented making the best use of existing provision. From the Minority came the recommendation that all medical services should be unified and placed under the control of the Health Committee of the local council. The same service would then apply to all classes, with a registrar recovering the cost of treatment where a patient was able to pay. By destroying the distinction between pauper and the general citizen the Minority have been seen as anticipating the National Health Service. However, such an approach is also seen as impractical in view of the limitations on existing administrations and has also been criticized for its extension of the means test into the provision of essential relief.[32]

The Local Government Board had continued to support the giving of adequate outdoor relief to the aged poor and where use was made of indoor relief, the easing of conditions. In 1900 a circular to boards of guardians indicated the main direction of central authority thinking:

> With regard to the treatment of the aged deserving poor, it has been felt that persons who have habitually led decent and deserving lives should, if they require relief in their old age, receive different treatment from those whose previous habits and character have been unsatisfactory, and who have failed to exercise thrift in the bringing up of their families or otherwise. The Board consider that aged deserving persons should not be

urged to enter the workhouse at all unless there is some cause which renders such a course necessary but that they should be relieved by having adequate outdoor relief granted to them. Such relief when granted should be always adequate.[33]

Where indoor relief was necessary they felt that the deserving aged should be granted privileges, many of which were related to limiting their contact with the undeserving. These included separate day-rooms in which they could have some of their meals, separate cubicles for sleeping and a relaxation of the hours for going to bed and rising. Such inmates were to be granted greater freedom to leave the workhouse and to receive visitors, to have their own lockers, and it was felt that previous recommendations on the supply of tobacco, tea and sugar to such inmates should be compulsory. Although this circular showed the extent to which the central authority was prepared to move on this issue, it was unfortunately merely advisory. Moreover, the terms 'deserving' and 'adequate' were capable of a variety of definitions. Finally, it has been pointed out that the limited nature of these concessions only serve to illustrate the severity of the former regime.[34]

It is diffcult to estimate the extent to which the condition of the aged pauper improved as a result of greater public sympathy and central authority directives. In a handful of progressive unions outdoor allowances to this group exceeded old-age pensions when they were introduced. However, the social surveys show many in receipt of Poor Relief below the level of primary poverty, illustrating the continued inadequacy of relief payments. The idea of separate buildings for the aged inmate had been experimented with in the 1890s but appears to have made very limited progress. The dread of the workhouse remained and this accounts for the welcome given to the not very generous pension scheme in 1908.[35]

The Liberal Government had proceeded to introduce old-age pensions without waiting for the recommendations of the Royal Commission. The Majority while accepting that in general the aged were unsuited to a deterrent policy, would have preferred a contributory scheme, whereas the Minority desired a more generous non-contributory scheme. Where poverty meant that the aged found it necessary to seek relief the Majority supported what was regarded as the best current practice; outdoor relief where possible and small specialized homes for those needing indoor treatment. However, in the allocation of indoor relief it believed that account should be taken of both physical condition and previous character. The Minority believed that its more generous pension policy would take care of the majority of cases and where additional assistance was required it merely suggested the matter should be referred to a local pensions committee.[36]

Despite their differences both Reports were agreed that the workhouse was no place for the deserving classes of applicant for Poor Relief. However, the issue of dealing with the unemployed was much more contentious. It is widely accepted that the problem of the unemployed became a major matter of public concern in the latter years of Victoria's reign. Although left-wing critics were prepared to countenance varying degrees of intervention in the economy, orthodox beliefs continued to hold such policies as certain to produce more harm than good. Thus, although by the 1890s the problem was seen as increasingly complex in origin, the solutions remained administrative rather than economic.[37]

Interest was strongest at times of depression. On these occasions local public and private schemes of work creation, on the lines of those suggested by the Chamberlain circular, with the assistance of more traditional forms of charity continued to be the preferred method of relieving the deserving. The long-term under-employment of the casual worker had been highlighted by such as Charles Booth, and, particularly in London where the problem appeared greatest, there was the establishment of a variety of farm colonies to provide training and assistance. Experiments which commenced in London in 1903 to coordinate relief work were applied nationally by the Unemployed Workmen Act of 1905. The Act authorized the establishment of Distress Committees in urban communities with a population in excess of 50,000. Consisting of representatives of councils, boards of guardians and local charities, the committees were to seek to provide local relief works, farm colonies, labour exchanges and to assist in the emigration or migration of the deserving unemployed.[38]

The distress committees were set the almost impossible task of distinguishing the deserving unemployed from those more suited to relief under the Poor Law. To be favourably regarded the applicant for relief was required to be genuinely desirous of work being prevented by temporary factors over which he could have no control. For such cases the distress committees could attempt to obtain work but they were not allowed to contribute any financial help towards such provision. Although intended to assist the worker who would normally be in employment negotiate a period of crisis, the work provided remained of a type more likely to prove attractive to the casual worker.

For the opposition parties this Act was significant in marking the first recognition of unemployment as a matter requiring the intervention of central government, although the minister made it clear that this was certainly not its intention. While the Act did recognize the problem, its failure has been seen as paving the way for the Beveridge solutions of Labour Exchanges and National Insurance.

The Royal Commission of 1905–9 was to show itself very divided upon the treatment of the problem of unemployment, although there were also important areas of agreement.[39] Both Reports supported Labour Exchanges and both sought a more limited form of insurance, worked via the trade union schemes, than was to be provided in 1911. There was also a considerable measure of agreement on the provision of better educational facilities for the young and the acceptance of the need for training and retraining of workers. Finally, both Reports were prepared to be very tough in the handling of any thought to be scroungers. Here compulsory detention at training centres was urged. Such a policy was similar to that advanced by Charles Booth for the treatment of his class B and was also akin to proposals being suggested for habitual vagrants.

The recommendations of the Majority Report concerning the bulk of the unemployed were very much in line with current practice. Thus the Public Assistance Committee in effect was to adopt existing Poor Law practices. 'Home Assistance', either in money or in kind, could be given to applicants with 'a decent home and a good industrial record' on the performance of the equivalent of the outdoor labour test. 'Partial Home Assistance' could be provided for the dependents of an applicant who was himself prepared to enter an institution, in effect the existing partial workhouse test. Finally, there could be longer-term assistance given where an applicant agreed in writing to remain in an institution or training centre for a longer period. For all three of these groups work could be undertaken in the same institution, which could be a former workhouse. Thus for the able-bodied pauper conditions would have been little changed.

181

For the Minority Report the bulk of the unemployed were the victims of the prevailing economic system. They pointed out that; 'Distress from want of employment, though periodically aggravated by depression of trade, is a constant feature of industry and commerce as at present administered.' The problem of unemployment was regarded as too serious to be handled by local authorities. Responsibility was to be given to a new department of central government, termed the Ministry of Labour. Not only was the new ministry to supervise Labour Exchanges and National Insurance but it was also to be given extensive powers to intervene in the labour market to minimize unemployment. This was to include supervision of many areas of government spending in a complex arrangement designed to operate as a contra-cyclical public works programme. Since this was a new departure in governmental practice the Minority Report saw the new ministry learning by experience, as it felt had been the case in the fields of public health and education.

It is sometimes held that the uncompromising attitude taken by the Webbs may have diminished the chances of government action even where the Reports had much in common. However, theoretical solutions involving widespread administrative changes were unlikely to have had any great appeal. For the Majority there was to be the installation of a new tier of administration in the Voluntary Aid Committees, whereby organized charity selected the deserving from those who would receive the attention of the Public Assistance Committees. While the Minority Report largely avoided the trap of seeking to distinguish the deserving from the undeserving in so far as the impotent poor were concerned, their proposals required widespread alterations in local authority committee structure with the only coordination resting on the ill-defined registrar of public assistance. Their proposals for central government were widely regarded as totally impractical. Hence the central government proceeded on the established path of removing those thought deserving from the Poor Law. Although neither Report wished to retain the boards of guardians and both wished to see an end to the general mixed workhouse, both were to be retained for another twenty years.

Although few would see the foundations of the welfare state having been established by 1914, the wider acceptance of state responsibility in such fields as old-age pensions and national insurance did mark a significant change from the limited and deterrent role envisaged in 1834. By improved provision for the deserving groups the State was continually moving towards the concept of a national minimum for a widening range of citizens, which has been termed 'the introduction of the "social service state".'[40] The term 'welfare state' is often held to represent the provision of an optimum standard for all. This was not, however, the proposal in 1942. The position in 1914 was at variance with the Beveridge proposals because of the concept of selectivity rather than its belief in minimum standards.

The limited growth of state provision left a considerable role for the voluntary sector. The acceptance of friendly societies and commercial insurance companies as 'Approved Societies' to administer Health Insurance appeared to have stengthened their position. In practice State insurance has weakened the role of the friendly society and allowed trade unions to place their emphasis on other priorities. However, commercial insurance may well have gained from the connection. Philanthropy remained important to both fill in the gaps of State provision and to pioneer new areas of activity. The early nineteenth-century dependence on the support of the rich was, by 1914, being increasingly augmented by the contributions of the working class, making the doctrinaire assumptions of the COS enthusiast much less acceptable and leaving the future to organizations such as the Guilds of Help.[41]

NOTES

1. For a modern introduction to the general background to this period see either: D. Read, *England 1868–1914*, (1979); or K. Robbins, *The Eclipse of a Great Power. Modern Britain 1870–1975*, (1983).
2. To these could be added General Booth's Darkest England programme in the 1890s.
3. On expenditure see A.T. Peacock and J. Wiseman, *The Growth of Public Expenditure in the United Kingdom*, (1961), ch. 3. On tariffs see W.H.B. Court, *British Economic History 1870–1914*, (1965), ch. 9, and D. Winch, *Economics and Policy*, (1969), 64–70.
4. See H. Ausubel, *The Late Victorians*, (1955), 37–46.
5. For a useful introduction to many of the above issues and a guide to further reading see J.R. Hay, *The Origins of the Liberal Welfare Reforms*, (1975), 33–4, 52–3. On family allowances see H. Land in P. Hall *et al.*, *Change, Choice and Conflict in Social Policy*, (1975), 158–60. On school

meals and medical inspection see B.B. Gilbert, *The Evolution of National Insurance* (1966), ch. 3.

6. J.R. Hay, *ibid.*, 25–9 introduces the main literature and the same author provides documents in *The Development of the British Welfare State 1880–1975*, (1978), documents 1–12. See also P. Thane, 'The Working Class and State "Welfare" in Britain', *Historical Journal*, (1984), vol. 27.

7. Supplement the references in J.R. Hay (1975), 29–38 with K. Laybourn, *The Rise of Labour*, (1988), ch. 2.

8. On the Board of Trade see R. Davidson, 'Llewellen Smith, the Labour Department and Government Growth', in G. Sutherland (ed.), *Studies in the Growth of Nineteenth Century Government*, (1972). The Royal Commission on Local Taxation, (1901), cd 638 is summarized in C.P. Sanger, 'Report of Local Taxation Commission', *Economic Journal, xi*, (1901), 321ff. Both Majority and Minority Reports of the Royal Commission on the Poor Laws and Relief of Distress, (1909), cd 4499 condemned the degree of overlap. See Majority Report, 228 and Minority Report, 1007–8. (Henceforth cited as Majority Report and Minority Report.)

9. Local Government Board, Twenty-Fifth Annual Report, (1895–6), App. B, report of Mr J.S. Davy.

10. J. Brown, 'The Appointment of the 1905 Poor Law Commission', *Bulletin of the Institute of Historical Research*, 42, (1969).

11. K. Woodroffe, 'The Royal Commission on the Poor Law, 1905–9', *International Review of Social History, xxii*, (1977); U. Cormack, 'The Royal Commission on the Poor Laws and the Welfare State', reprinted in A.V.S. Lochhead, *A Reader in Social Administration*, (1968). On Bentham see T.G. Wright, 'Poor Law Administration in Bradford 1900–1914', MA thesis, Huddersfield Polytechnic, 1981, 7, 51–2.

12. On Barnett see D. Read, *op. cit.*, (1979), 298–9 and M.E. Rose, *The English Poor Law 1780–1930*, (1971), 248–50.

13. See P. Ryan, in M.E. Rose (ed.), *The poor and the city: the English poor law in its urban context, 1834–1914*, (1985), 153–4.

14. H.V. Emy, 'The Impact of Financial Policy on English Party Politics before 1914', *Historical Journal*, 15, (1972).

15. M.A. Crowther, *The Workhouse System 1834–1929*, (1981), 77–8. P. Thane, 'Women and the Poor Law in late-Victorian and Edwardian England', *History Workshop*, (1978), vol. 6. *op. cit.*, 206.

16. G. Lansbury, *My Life*, (1931), 133.

17. *Ibid.*, 135–7 for quotation and following paragraph.

18. G. Haw, *From Workhouse to Westminster. The Life Story of Will Crooks M.P.*, (1917), 116.

19. M.A. Crowther, *op. cit.*, 78–80. N. McCord, 'Ratepayers and Social Policy' in P. Thane (ed.), *The Origins of British Social Policy*, (1978), 23–5.

20. For statistics see C.S. Loch, 'Statistics of Population and Pauperism in England and Wales 1861–1901', *Journal of the Royal Statistical Society, lxix*, (1906) and the Annual Reports for the years stated. For view of officials see n. 9 above.

21. C.S. Loch, *ibid.*, 291–2. Also M.E. Rose, *The Relief of Poverty*, (1972), App. A, 53.

22. Majority Report, 78.
23. *Ibid.*, 644.
24. Minority Report, 739.
25. *Ibid.*, 739–44.
26. *Ibid.*, 727–9.
27. J. Brown, 'Poverty and Social Policy in Britain 1850–1919', in Open University Press, *Poverty and Social Policy 1850–1950,* (1974), 8.
28. M.A. Crowther, *op. cit.,* 206.
29. Local Government Board, Thirtieth Annual Report, (1900–1), 18.
30. E.g. Majority Report, 186–7. The Local Government Board order was supposed to take effect in 1918 but the impact of the war appears to have delayed matters in some unions until the early 1920s.
31. See R. Pinker, *Social Theory and Social Policy,* (1971), 78. On rural workhouses see M.A. Crowther, *op. cit.,* 176–81. On tuberculosis see F.B. Smith, *The Peoples' Health,* (1979), 387–9; Minority Report, 894–5.
32. Minority Report, 1019, 1031–2. For criticism see G.R. Searle, *The Quest for National Efficiency,* (1970), 239.
33. Local Government Board, Thirtieth Annual Report, (1900–1), App. A, No. 11.
34. P. Thane, *The Foundations of the Welfare State,* (1982), 37.
35. See F. Thompson, *Lark Rise,* (1939), 100.
36. On old-age pensions see B.B. Gilbert, *op. cit.,* ch. 4 and P. Thane, 'Non-contributory versus Insurance Pensions 1878–1908', in P. Thane,(ed.), *op. cit.,* 84–106. Majority Report, 164–7.
37. The standard authority on unemployment in this period is J. Harris, *Unemployment and Politics,* (1972). However, see also J. Tomlinson, *Problems of British Economic Policy, 1870–1945,* (1982).
38. Public General Acts, 5 Ed V11, c 18, (1903–5). For comment see: B.B. Gilbert, *op. cit.,* 237–46 and J. Harris, *ibid.,* ch. IV.
39. Majority Report, 427; Minority Report, 1175–1215. For comment see J. Harris, *ibid.,* 245–64.
40. D. Read, *Edwardian England 1901–15,* (1972), ch. 6.
41. For regional examples see N. McCord, *North East England,* (1979), 175–8, 253–4 and M. Cahill and T. Jowitt, 'The New Philanthropy: The Emergence of the Bradford City Guild of Help', *Journal of Social Policy,* (1980), 9.

CONCLUSION

Poverty, however narrowly defined, was always a matter of considerable concern during the reign of Queen Victoria. Although the growing wealth of the first industrial power produced improvement in living standards particularly in the final quarter of the century, progress was less than many contemporaries had expected and the position of the poorest appears to have shown the most limited advance.

A significant feature of the nineteenth century was the belief that poverty was largely self-inflicted, producing the distinction between deserving and undeserving poor. Initially, this crucial distinction was simply that between poor and indigent and it was on this basis that reformers sought to draw a line between poverty and pauperism. This frontier was always more fluid in practice. Humanitarian concern and parsimony were both influenced by the need to preserve the existing society. At times of economic crisis the desire to maintain social control often adopted the guise of humanitarian concern weighting the balance in favour of a more generous approach. On other occasions hostility to expenditure preferred to masquerade as social control with economy being presented as in the national interest.

Over the century the inadequacy of the initial simple definition became increasingly apparent. As the awareness of the need to offer assistance to the deserving poor became apparent voluntary activities faced a formidable task and inevitably, as the residual service, the Poor Law was forced to handle problems which made nonsense of theoretical distinctions. The problem for both the Old and the New Poor Law was the burden of those thought to be deserving.

CONCLUSION

The Old Poor Law with its massive variations of practice contained the main features of the New Poor Law and most of its alternatives. The basic pressures of humanitarian concern and desire for economy found their working compromise in an administration whose imperfections ranged from corruption to serious financial limitations. The strength of the Old Poor Law was its ability to adapt to the local situation and its major weakness was its lack of any uniform sense of direction. It is, therefore, as easy to find abuses as blessings in its records. Modern research has to some extent improved its image. It was certainly not the principle cause of population increase and its less regimented approach to the problem of underemployment and unemployment contained much to be admired. However, in the long-run the larger ratepayers sought to manipulate the system to their advantage.

The diagnosis of the Royal Commission of 1834 was based on a mixture of popular prejudice and a limited and theoretical view of the problem. The Report represented a compromise between abolition and leaving things as they were. Its curtailed analysis was rendered even weaker during its political passage. The result was that the early years of the New Poor Law presented neither the best nor the worst features of the new regime. In many areas continuing local control meant considerable overlap with the personalities and practices of the former administration. To some extent it could not have been otherwise and this was rendered inevitable by the failure to reform either finance or settlement. Hence, in practice the New Poor Law often appears almost as flexible as its predecessor, or, to the dismay of the central authority, as lacking in uniformity.

The weakness of the central authority, the strength of localism and financial limitations all favoured variation. This trend was reinforced by the impracticality of the theory of the workhouse test. This was difficult enough to justify in some agricultural areas and was even less related to the needs of expanding urban communities. Indeed, in the context of rapid population increase institutional provision was always likely to prove too expensive a solution. There was, moreover, always a problem in drawing a line between deserving and undeserving when considering the role of the workhouse. This applied particularly to the growing recognition of the problems of the children and the sick, although there was always confusion on the role of the able-bodied during seasonal or economic slackness. Despite these difficulties the New Poor Law had estab-

187

lished sufficient bureaucratic common ground between central and local authorities to survive the crises of the early 1860s. Administrative inertia, the lack of a viable alternative and most of all financial reforms had produced a more confident Poor Law by the late 1860s.

Statistics suggest that the New Poor Law was at its most active, for both better and for worse, during the 1870s. At its best there were striking improvements in the care of the children and the sick, and at its worst was the harassment of many helpless paupers by the threat of the campaign against outdoor relief. There was also much where change was minimal. The stronger image coincided with the greater certainty in the individualist approach which provided the central authority with its greatest ally, the Charity Organization Society. However, recognition of the needs of the more deserving children and sick meant progress was expensive. Moreover, as the century advanced the concept of a more deserving pauper group tended to expand to cover the aged infirm and finally the aged as a group. Greater awareness of the problem of the unemployed produced a further blurring of distinctions and debate on solutions. Even the vagrant, always the least eligible of cases, began to be recognized as containing some worthy of more sympathetic treatment.

By the close of Victoria's reign institutional relief could no longer be seen as a guide to destitution and had become a most expensive solution. However, while the workhouse test was to figure little in the future treatment of the able-bodied poor the desire for less eligible treatment continued to be a feature of relief. The 'genuinely seeking work clause', the Anomolies Act, harsher means tests, and training camps in the inter-war period and the 'Wages Stop' in the period since the Second World War all showed a desire for cheaper and more effective administrative solutions. The workhouse survived in the variety of institutions providing relief for the impotent, alongside a growing use of social security benefits that were topped up by a continued dependence on the voluntary sector to provide a more acceptable standard. Thus poverty remains a problem of definition and the area of public concern retains its confused frontiers. The Victorians sought to adapt the values of our agrarian past to the newly-emerging industrial world of the nineteenth century and our continued debate is the legacy of their achievement.

BIBLIOGRAPHY

References to appropriate books and articles have been included in the Notes. Only works which provide useful introductions or are of more general significance are included below. Unless otherwise stated the place of publication is London.

Introductory

Of the many textbooks on social policy the following are recommended as providing both useful introductions and guidance with further reading.
D. Fraser, *The Evolution of the British Welfare State*, (2nd edn., 1984).
U. Henriques, *Before the Welfare State*, (1979).
P. Thane, *The Foundations of the Welfare State*, (1982). Two documentary collections of special value are: M.E. Rose (ed.), *The English Poor Law, 1780–1930,* Newton Abbot, (1971) which provides an introduction not only to the Poor Law records but also its critics. E.J. Evans, *Social Policy 1830–1914,* (1974) which introduces the wider development of state intervention and the role of the voluntary sector.

Poverty

For an introduction to changing views on poverty see: S. Woolf, *The Poor in Western Europe in the Eighteenth and Nineteenth Centuries,* (1986).
This should be supplemented by: G. Himmelfarb, *The Idea of*

189

Poverty. England in the Early Industrial Age, (1984) which is also useful on the reform of the Old Poor Law.

Rural poverty is introduced by A. Digby, 'Rural Poverty', in G.E. Mingay (ed.), *The Victorian Countryside,* vol. 2, (1981) and P. Horn, *The Rural World 1780–1850,* (1980). However, for the problem in the early nineteenth century see K.D.M. Snell, *Annals of the Labouring Poor. Social Change and Agrarian England, 1660–1900,* (Cambridge, 1985).

Urban poverty receives good coverage from J.H. Treble, *Urban Poverty in Britain, 1830–1914,* (1979). G. Stedman Jones, *Outcast London. A Study in the Relationship between Classes in Victorian Society,* (1976) and S. Meacham, *A Life Apart. The English Working Class 1890–1914,* (1977) provide valuable additional reading in their respective fields. H.J. Dyos and M. Woolf (eds.), *The Victorian City: Images and Realities,* 2 vols., (1973), introduces many aspects of value to the study of poverty. Useful introductions to contemporary material are provided by: B.I. Coleman (ed.), *The Idea of the City in Nineteenth-Century Britian,* (1973) and P. Keating (ed.), *Into Unknown England 1866–1913,* Glasgow, (1976).

The analysis of living standards can commence with P. Mathias, *The First Industrial Nation,* (2nd edn. 1983).

For a clear and interesting description see the appropriate section of J. Burnett, *A History of the Cost of Living,* (1969).

Supportive issues are introduced by: R.Lawton (ed.), *The Census and Social Structure. An Interpretative Guide to the 19th Century Censuses for England and Wales,* (1978).

A.S. Wohl, *Endangered Lives Public Health in Victorian Britain,* (1983). J. Burnett, *A Social History of Housing, 1815–70,* (Newton Abbot, 1978).

Useful contemporary works which cover the period before the social surveys and are readily available include: J.P. Kay, *The Moral and Physical Conditions of the Working Classes Employed in the Cotton Manufacture in Manchester,* (1832, reprinted, 1969).

E. Chadwick, *Report on the Sanitary Condition of the Labouring Population of Great Britain,* (1842, reprinted with a useful introduction by M.W. Flinn, Edinburgh, 1965). F. Engels, *The Condition of the Working Class in Britain,* (1845, translated by W.O. Henderson and W.H. Chaloner, Oxford, 1958). H. Mayhew, *London Labour and the London Poor,* 4 vols., (1861–2, reprinted New York, 1968).

E.P. Thompson and E. Yeo (eds.), *The Unknown Mayhew. Selections from the Morning Chronicle, 1849–50,* (1973).

P.E. Razell and R.W. Wainwright (eds.), *The Victorian Working Class,* (1973). Selections from the *Morning Chronicle* by Mayhew and others givings a wider national picture of life in mid-century.

J. Greenwood, *The Seven Curses of London,* (1869 reprinted 1981).

A. Mearns, *The Bitter Cry of Outcast London,* (1883, ed. by A.S. Wohl, Leicester, 1970).

For additional reading on the social surveys see:

T.S. and M.B. Simey, *Charles Booth: Social Scientist,* (1960).

A. Fried and R. Elman (eds.), *Charles Booth's London,* (1969). Selections from *Life and Labour of the People in London.*

A. Briggs, *Social Thought and Social Action: A Study of the Work of Seebohm Rowntree,* (1961).

A good documentary introduction to the social surveys is provided by W.H.B. Court, *British Economic History 1870–1914 Commentary and Documents,* (Cambridge, 1965). The most readable of the social surveys has been reprinted, Lady F. Bell, *At the Works,* (1907 reprinted 1969). See also Mrs Pember Reeves, *Round About A Pound A Week,* (1913 reprinted 1979).

The Relief of Poverty. The Voluntary Sector

P.H.J.H Gosden, *Self-Help. Voluntary Associations in Nineteenth-Century Britain,* (1973).

On friendly societies a useful introduction is provided in G. Crossick, *An Artisan Elite in Victorian Society. Kentish London 1840–1880.* For the later period see B.B. Gilbert, *The Evolution of National Insurance in Great Britain,* (1966). Charity has a greater coverage. To the works cited in the text should be added: B. Harrison, 'Philanthropy and the Victorians' in *Peaceable Kingdom. Stability and Change in Modern Britain,* (Oxford, 1982).

D. Owen, *English Philanthropy, 1660–1960,* (Cambridge, Mass., 1965).

F.K. Prochaska, *Women and Philanthropy in Nineteenth-century England,* (Oxford, 1980). K. Heasman, *Evangelicals in Action. An Appraisal of their Social Work in the Victorian Era,* (1962).

On the COS see C.L. Mowat, *The Charity Organization Society 1869–1913: Its Ideas and Work,* (1961). *The Relief of Poverty. (b) The Role of the State.*

Good introductions to the poor law are provided by: A. Digby, *The Poor Law in Nineteenth-Century England and Wales* (1982). M.E. Rose, *The Relief of Poverty 1834–1914*, (1972). The fullest coverage remains S. and B. Webb, *English Poor Law History* (1929 reprinted 1963), 3 vols. This work should be read in the light of modern research. The best single volume guides are: M.A. Crowther, *The Workhouse System 1834–1929* (1981) and K. Williams, *From Pauperism to Poverty* (1981).

On the Old Poor Law see: J.D. Marshall, *The Old Poor Law, 1795–1834*, (1968). On the rural problems see: P. Dunkley, *The Crisis of the Old Poor Law in England 1795–1834* , M. Neumann, *The Speenhamland County* (1982) and G.R. Boyer, *An Economic History of the English Poor Law, 1750–1850*, Cambridge, (1990).

G.W. Oxley, *Poor Relief in England 1601–1834*, (1974), is a good guide to the sources. J.R. Poynter, *Society and Pauperism*, (1969) is the outstanding guide to the contemporary debate.

On the Report of 1834 and the subsequent administration see: S.G. and O. Checkland (eds.), *The Poor Law Report of 1834*, (1974), A. Brundage, *The Making of the New Poor Law 1832–39* and S.E. Finer, *The Life and Times of Sir Edwin Chadwick*, (1952).

Useful Introductions to other aspects and local reactions can be found in: D. Fraser (ed.), *The New Poor Law in the Nineteenth Century* (1976), A. Digby, *Pauper Palaces* (1978), N. Longmate, *The Workhouse*, (1974), E. Midwinter, *Social Administration in Lancashire*, (1979) and M.E. Rose (ed.), *The poor and the city: the English Poor Law in its urban context, 1834–1914*, (Leicester, 1985).

On the rise of alternatives to poor relief see: P.A. Kohler and M. Zacher (ed.), *The Evolution of Social Insurances 1881–1981. Studies of France, Great Britain, Austria and Switzerland*, (1982), B.B. Gilbert, *The Evolution of National Insurances in Great Britain*, (1966), P. Thane (ed.), *The Origins of British Social Policy*, (1978) and J. Harris, *Unemployment and Politics: A Study in English Social Policy 1886–1914*, (Oxford, 1972).

INDEX